The Big Book of Animal Devotions

WILLIAM COLEMAN

◊ BETHANYHOUSE
Minneapolis, Minnesota

Published by Bethany House Publishers
11400 Hampshire Avenue South
Bloomington, Minnesota 55438

Bethany House Publishers is a division of
Baker Publishing Group, Grand Rapids, Michigan.

Printed in the United States of America by Bethany Press International, Bloomington, MN.
March 2010, 3rd printing

Library of Congress Cataloging-in-Publication Data

Coleman, William L.
    The big book of animal devotions : 250 daily readings about God's amazing creation / William L. Coleman.
        p.   cm.
    Summary: "Teaches children about God's creation while also using each animal to illustrate a character-development lesson from the Bible. Each reading includes a Scripture verse, discussion questions, and a concise nugget of take-away wisdom"—Provided by publisher.
    Includes index.
    ISBN 978-0-7642-0669-6 (pbk. : alk. paper) 1. Animals—Religious aspects—Christianity—Juvenile literature. I. Title.
    BT746.C65   2009
    231.7—dc22

                                                                                    2009014977

Dedicated to
Ian and Evan

Acknowledgment

Jim Coleman played a big part in putting this book together.
His help in research and reading copy are greatly appreciated.

God Made an Amazing World

od made an octopus that can eat its own arm and grow another one. Some insects sleep for seventeen years and know just when to wake up. A cheetah cat can run seventy miles an hour. These are just a small part of our Creator's great imagination.

When Jesus Christ taught, He used fish, lilies, sparrows, and foxes to help us remember. When Paul wrote about anger, he reminded us of the sun. Ezekiel called the pharaoh a bubbling crocodile.

In this book, we use the Bible and nature to teach about God, ourselves, our feelings, and our friends.

Enjoy it and grow.

WILLIAM L. COLEMAN

AURORA, NEBRASKA

1 Main Attraction

Where is the biggest crowd at the zoo? On most Saturday afternoons, people are probably packed around the monkey cage. These cute animals often put on the best fun in any town.

Some of the most popular monkeys in the zoo are rhesus (REE-sus) monkeys. They come from the jungles of India and are in almost no danger of becoming extinct. They are like noisy bees in the wild.

Noisy is the right word to describe them. Rhesus monkeys will jump, fight, argue, chatter, and swing. That is why there's usually a crowd watching them.

They have large families and evidently love to argue with each other. But they don't stay angry. After a string of harsh chatter and some fast action, they calm down and become friends again. In a few minutes they are picking bugs off each other like good buddies.

Most monkeys are afraid of water, but not the rhesus. Give one a small pond and it looks like a champion swimmer.

If you study monkeys closely, you can soon tell one type from another. The proboscis (pra-BOSS-iss) monkey is easy to pick out. Its nose sticks out like a large flat thumb and hangs down to its chin.

The only place proboscis monkeys live is in Borneo, an island in southeast Asia. They don't seem to do well in zoos, so most people won't get to see them.

We are more likely to see spider monkeys. They get their name from their long, thin arms and full tail. The fur makes them look well rounded, but don't be fooled. Underneath they are skinny creatures.

If spider monkeys had their way, they would always stay in the trees. Swinging from limb to limb is their idea of living. Swinging from their tails and picking fruit with their hands and feet keeps them happy all day.

If you are lonely, you might think about buying a howler monkey. Not only do they like to talk, but they do it so loudly you might wonder if the house is falling in. Their sound is something like a car horn. Imagine yourself in a room with this thing going off continuously! Just listening, you might think the howler monkey is being attacked, but he is actually just making a great deal of unnecessary noise.

Sometimes people talk the same way a howler monkey does. We often talk too much. Even worse, we say things that get others upset for nothing. If we say good things about people, talking is helpful, like medicine. But when we merely chatter and don't think, we might really hurt someone's feelings.

You are supposed to be a wise man, and yet you give us all this foolish talk. You are nothing but a windbag. It isn't right to speak so foolishly. What good do such words do?

JOB 15:2–3 (TLB)

Do You Remember?

1. Which monkey likes to swim?

2. Where do spider monkeys like to stay?

3. How can we stop from saying cruel things about others?

Guard our lips.

2 The Pincushion

The porcupine is not a large animal, but it is feared by some of the biggest. Even a tiger will think twice before tangling with this two-foot-long terror.

Most of the time this prickly pincushion merely minds its own business. But if something wants to start trouble, "Pokey" will give it a fight.

From its neck to its tail is a heavy coat of quills that look like knitting needles. Each quill is sharp and painful if it sticks you.

Porcupines seem to be slow and helpless. Yet if you attack one, it will turn quickly and try to back into you. It is so fast that it will probably get its attacker by surprise. Sometimes dogs will run at a porcupine, expecting an easy dinner. Pokey will turn, lift its tail, and push its back at the rushing dog. The quills stick into the dog's face and come loose from the porcupine. The dog limps away with a painful howl. Some quills are fifteen inches long and sink deep into the skin. Porcupines can't really shoot their quills like arrows, but they can push their body fast enough to cause serious injury.

A porcupine has thirty thousand quills on its back and sides. Don't try to count them, or Pokey might give a few to you. But that would be no problem since he would quickly grow them back.

A quill is not merely a sharp stick. Each quill has tiny blades all over it. After it goes inside an animal, the quill will push itself deeper and deeper, even after it has left the porcupine. The result is often a nasty wound.

Mountain lions can successfully hunt porcupines, but even they have to be careful to attack only the head or belly.

A coyote that attacks a porcupine may get killed. When a coyote gets a face full of quills, the quills begin to work their way into the coyote's throat and head. It won't be long before the wounded coyote dies.

Usually an animal that gets hurt by a porcupine doesn't realize or care what the porcupine can do. It just rushes in and comes away the loser.

We often do the same thing, but if we don't stop to think, we might end up in more trouble than we ever imagined.

The wise see danger ahead and avoid it, but fools keep going and get into trouble.

Proverbs 22:3 (NCV)

Do You Remember?

1. What does a quill do after it enters a body?

2. How does a porcupine attack?

3. Have you ever gotten into more trouble than you expected?

Help us think before we do something we might be sorry for.

3 Chocolate Cake or White?

That pretty much depends on you. One person enjoys carrot cake, but his sister can't stand it. A third person doesn't eat dessert at all. People are different. And so are animals.

The same is true of dolphins. One type has learned to survive well in salt water. However, another kind, the Amazon dolphin, loves swimming, playing, and raising children in fresh water. As a river dolphin, its lifestyle fits exactly into the surroundings.

In fact, by living there long enough, the river dolphin will begin to change its appearance. Often a river dolphin will take on a pinkish color and might even be called "pinky" to easily identify it. Dolphins get around and can be found many places in rivers. However, the larger pink dolphin hangs out almost exclusively near Iquitos, Peru.

When the river dolphin goes fishing (and it does love fish), it needs neither a hook nor a worm. It simply sends out a series of clicks and listens for the return sound. When it hears the returning clicks, it knows how many fish are around and where they are located.

The round, melon-shaped area in the dolphin's head as well as the sensitive nasal parts read out material to the animal very similar to a computer. While receiving no printout, the dolphin does receive a distinct message telling it exactly where it can pick up lunch, plus a meal or two for the weekend.

River dolphins probably never think of their lives as dull or monotonous. As with the rest of nature, they have enemies who might hide away and later attack.

Sometime each of us will change. We probably won't turn pink, and so far I have not been able to catch fish by making clicking sounds. But someday God will cause me to change. My body will be different. My appearance might become considerably better. My grandchildren hope my singing might improve.

Frankly, though, I am content to stay the way I am. I am quite pleased that the Lord made me a person.

Instead of changing, we might do well to keep doing the good things we already do.

If you really change your ways and your actions and deal with each other justly, if you do not oppress the alien, the fatherless or the widow . . .

JEREMIAH 7:5–6 (NIV)

Do You Remember?

1. Who is better? Those who eat chocolate cake or the ones who eat white cake?

2. Name one thing you do particularly well.

3. Name one thing you might improve.

My God is a God of change.

4 Hiding in China

Travelers used to talk about a giant bear with black-and-white fur. Few people believed them. More than a hundred years ago a missionary sent a black-and-white fur to Paris, but people still didn't believe.

Finally, in 1937, a beautiful giant panda was captured, and by now everyone has heard of them.

It is easy to understand why most people had never seen them. Giant pandas live in only one part of the world. They are found high in the mountains of China. But even in China, few people have seen giant pandas in the wild. They live such hidden lives that, for a long time, little was known about them.

The giant panda is an endangered species. They are generally picky eaters and eat mostly bamboo shoots. Their favorite type of bamboo is found only in one part of China. If people move too far into their territory,

13

pandas will be pushed onto poor land. The lack of food there could cut the number of giant pandas way down.

Giant pandas look loving and playful, but don't be fooled. Pandas don't like to be handled. One quick swipe of their sharp claws could do a lot of damage.

The panda is often called a bear, but it really isn't one. For one thing, pandas eat only vegetables—unlike bears, who eat a lot of meat. The panda is an animal like none other. A woman named Ruth Harkness was the first person to capture the rare animal for an American zoo.

A great many things are scarce in life. Expensive jewels, gold, and some animals are hard to find. The Bible tells us about something else that's rare. Sometimes a person will give his or her life for a friend or a relative. But almost never will a person die to save a bad person.

Jesus Christ did a rare thing. He knew you and I would be sinners, but still He died to pay for our sins. Christ is more rare than a panda or anything else. There can be only one Son of God. He did a most unusual thing in dying for us.

Very few people will die to save the life of someone else.
Although perhaps for a good man someone might possibly die.
But Christ died for us while we were still sinners. In this way
God shows us his great love for us.

ROMANS 5:7–8 (ICB)

Do You Remember?

1. Where do pandas live?

2. Are there lots of giant pandas left in the world?

3. Why did Christ die?

Thanks for loving sinners like me.

5 The Long Nap

There is an odd little insect that if you want to see, you have to be in just the right place at the right time.

The cicada (sih-KAY-da) comes out of the ground once every seventeen years. If you miss it, move farther south. The cicadas there appear every thirteen years. But even if you get the correct year, you can't sit around. Cicadas live for only six weeks above the ground. If you miss them, you have a long wait coming.

During the few weeks above ground, cicadas have much to get done. When they come out, they are wrapped in a tight shell, like a jacket. Immediately, they start climbing something, such as a tree or a plant. They have an urge to go up.

The young cicada is looking for something to hold on to. When it settles down, the insect begins shedding its wrap. Usually it takes an hour of hard struggle. Now the cicada is a strong adult that needs to make the most of its time.

The female starts laying eggs in the first week. She uses a special blade on her tail to saw holes in tiny twigs. In each hole she'll put dozens of eggs. Each twig will have several holes or nests. One female will lay up to six hundred eggs.

In six weeks the eggs hatch, and the tiny cicadas crawl out. They fall directly to the ground and start digging in. Their home will be nearly two feet below the surface. They are looking for juicy roots to live on. For the next seventeen years, the cicada will suck on these roots. They don't seem to do any damage to trees.

Birds eat many of the adult cicadas. Mites and other insects feed on the eggs. This helps to keep the cicada population in balance. Each group has forty thousand eggs, and they could easily get out of control.

The cicadas know when their seventeen-year nap is done. A few weeks before, they dig their way up toward the top. They sit there only

15

one inch below the surface. Then some signal comes, and they dig their way out.

Cicadas have some sort of unknown clock inside them. They don't come out during the wrong year. They don't complain and start up after two weeks. There is a safe time for everything, and they seem willing to wait.

Often our timing gets off. Adults try to act like children, and children want to be adults and drive cars too soon. Young people try to tell their parents what to do.

Life takes patience. When we are adults, we can make decisions we can't make now. Matches, machines, money, and marriage are usually better handled with experience and time.

There is a right time for everything.

ECCLESIASTES 3:1 (TLB)

Do You Remember?

1. Where do cicadas live?

2. How long do the adults live?

3. What would you like to do as an adult?

Time is a beautiful gift.

6 The Beautiful Jaguar

Don't ever get a jaguar mad at you. This huge cat has a terrible temper. It has been known to hunt armed men for days and then try to kill them.

Jaguars are the largest cats in Mexico. They are almost as big as tigers, weighing four hundred pounds. Their coats are a beautiful yellow with black spots. But don't let their beauty fool you. Jaguars are among the strongest hunters in nature.

There is one story told of a jaguar who killed a horse. He then dragged the dead animal for more than a mile.

16

The people of South and Central America aren't too happy with this talented cat. Every year it kills thousands of cattle and some people. If an area floods, a jaguar may roam into a village looking for dry land and food.

These cats aren't picky eaters. They like crocodiles, turtle eggs, and deer. They are also excellent fishermen. According to some stories, they will stand over a river and look into the water. Fish will come near to see what it is, then become a jaguar's dinner.

Jaguars are so dangerous in parts of Brazil that men used to be paid to hunt them. One man used dogs to corner a four-hundred-pound jaguar. When the cat charged the hunter, the hunter killed it with a simple spear.

In the world of nature, the jaguar has no enemies. There is no animal that can defeat this big cat. Only humans can effectively master it, and not always.

Jaguars are one of the few cats that like to swim. They are so good at it that they can push a dead cow into a river and then jump in themselves. Guiding it with its mouth, the jaguar can push its catch for miles.

Jaguars are just as much at home in a tree as they are on land or sea. They prefer to roam at dusk or at night but do make some trips during the day.

The jaguar takes such good care of itself that it may live to be twenty years old. Each year the female gives birth to two to four cubs.

It is hard for people to enjoy the jaguar. Though it is beautiful, it doesn't mix well with people. Yet if kept far from humans, jaguars play an important part in nature. They keep it balanced so there are not too many crocodiles, turtles, or even fish.

Every creature has its place in nature. Each person has his or her important role in life. Everything God has made is good if it is used correctly.

For everything God created is good, and nothing is to be rejected if it is received with thanksgiving.

1 TIMOTHY 4:4 (NIV)

Do You Remember?

1. How much does a jaguar weigh?

2. How did one hunter kill a jaguar?

3. Name two good reasons God has for using you.

Thanks for calling me good.

7 How Deep Is the Ocean?

Would you like to get into a specially built ship and travel to the deepest part of the ocean? Don't say yes too quickly. It is possible to make this trip, but it is terribly dangerous.

The deepest part of the ocean is believed to be near the Philippine Islands. The bottom of the sea at that point is about seven miles, or 35,800 feet, beneath the surface.

In 1960, two men were courageous enough to take a submarine to the bottom. A normal submarine would have been crushed like a smashed soda can because the pressure at that depth is so great. The men had to build a special craft called a bathyscaphe (BATH-ih-skafe).

The men's names were Jacques Piccard and Don Walsh. They saw things that no man had ever seen before—and lived to tell about it. Their total stay was around fifteen minutes. The bathyscaphe started to squeak under the pressure, and they had to come up.

Now, many years later, no one else has gone to that depth again. So far, it is entirely too risky.

Will man ever walk on the ocean bottom at its deepest point? Almost anything is possible, but a protective suit strong enough for the job hasn't been made yet. Today, oceanographers (ocean scientists) rely on machines and cameras to stop just a few feet from the ocean floor and take pictures of fascinating creatures.

The sea is so dark at this depth that even the fish have to carry flashlights. It's true! Some fish have tiny lights on their foreheads like coal-miner hats. It allows them to be seen by each other.

Fish adjust to the heavy pressure at seven miles beneath the surface. Their bodies are made of thin material. Some are so clear we can see through them.

More than just an interesting place to study, the ocean is where God began His creation. Peter tells us that our great God made the world out of the waters around us. Our faith in God can grow stronger when we look at the ocean floor He made. That amazing Creator is our personal heavenly Father.

But they deliberately forget that long ago by God's word the heavens existed and the earth was formed out of water and by water.

2 Peter 3:5 (niv)

Do You Remember?

1. How deep is the ocean at its deepest point?

2. Why don't people visit the ocean bottom more often?

3. What can the ocean floor remind us of?

The small fish living seven miles deep are proof of the good hand of God.

8 Little Night Creatures

Would you like to go on a bat hunt? Would you like to see them hanging upside down in a cave? It isn't difficult to do. There are over two thousand types of bats, and they live almost all over the world.

Before you start your search, there are a few facts to keep in mind. The best places to find bats are in dark attics, abandoned mines, the roofs of barns, rotted trees, and of course, caves. If you find one, you will probably see a half dozen or more; they love to hang around in groups.

For those bold enough to look for bats at night, there is added help. Listen for a whistling sound like boiling water in a teakettle. A bat sends out these sounds to tell itself where it is. A bat depends on its ears to get around in the dark. Called a *sonar system*, the sound waves bounce off walls and rocks and guide the flying mammal. Bats are quick and can go great distances. Some travel eight hundred miles and return home again safely.

Bats are likely to eat anything. The little brown bats live on insects. The flying fox bats make a meal of fruit. Often they take only small bites from each fruit and ruin large crops. There is also the fish-eating bat. It snatches its food right out of the water. Long-nosed bats drink nectar from plants.

The most famous bat is the vampire bat—and it really does exist. They don't turn into people, but they do drink human blood.

Vampire bats are found from Mexico to Brazil. They have teeth as sharp as razors. Their food choice is animal blood, but they also attack people. The bat looks for a place on the body where it can get plenty of blood. It may select the earlobe or tip of the nose.

The top layer of skin is opened painlessly. If sleeping, the victim often won't even wake up. The vampire doesn't suck the blood but laps it up like a kitten drinking milk from a saucer. These bats drink blood until they feel stuffed. Some can barely fly when they are done.

The real danger of the vampire bat is not the amount of blood they take. Some people wake up completely unaware, except for the cut on their nose. The more serious problem is the diseases they carry. Bats may have the dreadful Chagas disease or rabies. A number of people in Central and South America have died as a result of the diseases spread by the vampire bat bite.

Most bats are harmless. They live on fruit and bugs. There is probably nothing to fear from the bat you may find in your attic. But we certainly don't want to be bitten by one, and especially by the vampire bat. People camping in Central and South America should be warned. A good warning can save a person's life.

Paul said that everywhere he went he warned people—not about bats but about evil and sin. They could do more damage than any bat. He invited everyone to find safety in Jesus Christ.

So everywhere we go we talk about Christ to all who will listen, warning them and teaching them as well as we know how.

Colossians 1:28 (TLB)

Do You Remember?

1. How do bats get around in the dark?

2. What do bats eat?

3. Why did Paul want to warn people?

The sooner we come to Jesus Christ, the less we will be hurt by sin.

9 Nature's Clowns

The otter doesn't take life too seriously. If it had its way, everything would be fun and games. The otter's idea of a good afternoon is getting together with a bunch of friends. They will take turns sliding down a wet hill on their bellies. A few minutes later, otters might play follow-the-leader. If these games get boring, they'll start a wrestling match with their brothers and sisters.

King James I of England enjoyed watching otters play. He kept a collection of otters and used them to catch fish.

The otter is an intelligent animal and would make a good pet. As wild animals, they have a terrific bite, but when tamed, they can be good friends.

Sometimes they especially enjoy people. The sea otter has been known to swim alongside a boat and check it out. If the people are sleeping, the otter may climb in. At the slightest noise, he takes off for the sea again.

Otters are fun-loving clowns, but they are more than that. When necessary, they are excellent hunters. Their favorite meals are bass, crab, crayfish,and sometimes an unsuspecting bird. Their hunting habits can be terribly messy. Too often an otter will take one bite out of a fish and then throw it away.

Otters have beautiful fur. This is one of the reasons they are hunted in many areas of the world. It is also the reason why sea otters are afraid to come to land. Their slick fur coat does a great job of keeping them warm in cold waters.

They seem to prefer water, but otters can get along on land. In Europe, they make long trips from one lake, across the mountains, to another lake.

Otters take time to train their young. Each one can hunt and swim before it leaves its parents. The mother may spend a full year before she releases her young. Otters often grow up to three feet in length.

The otter can take life seriously, but it also enjoys itself. Good times are a healthy part of their lives. Sometimes Christians take life too seriously. If we aren't careful, we will forget how to laugh, play, and enjoy ourselves. Not everything should be quiet and dull. A good laugh or a funny game will help most of us stay healthy.

A cheerful heart does good like medicine, but a broken spirit makes one sick.

PROVERBS 17:22 (TLB)

Do You Remember?

1. What do otters do for fun?

2. Why are otters hunted?

3. When was the last time you laughed out loud?

Laughter can be a gift from God.

10 The Fearless Rodent

It doesn't scare easily. The short, chubby badger will take on almost any enemy. Even the poisonous rattlesnake isn't safe around this fighter.

Most of us would stay away from a rattlesnake. They are extremely fast and definitely deadly. But the badger, a three-foot-long rodent, thinks it is just a little quicker. After dancing around a snake, the badger will make a fast dash for the back of its head, and the snake is finished.

Their odd appearance shouldn't fool us. Badgers are speedy. They can run almost as fast backward as they can forward. They can also dig faster than most machines. If a badger sees a human or another foe, it will start burrowing into the ground. In two minutes it will have a big enough hole to completely disappear.

Badgers' ability to dig helps them tremendously when searching for food. A badger will find a hole and smell a rat, mouse, or snake. In a second, it starts tearing the hole apart in search of its dinner. Once the badger begins, its victim often has little chance of escape.

Badgers enjoy the ground so much that they dig long, fancy homes. Their tunnels may stretch for thirty feet. Inside, they will have a special area just to hide from enemies. In another section, they will dig a nursery to place the five young they bear every year. Even when they catch food aboveground, badgers still prefer to take it into their tunnel for meals.

23

Badgers have become a problem to some farmers because their natural food is becoming harder to find, and badgers now have developed an appetite for farm animals, vegetables, and grain.

The badger has a strange relative and sometimes acts just like it. This cousin is the skunk. Mr. Badger can't give off the same odor as this stinker, but he does have a strong and noticeable odor of his own.

Anything that decides to fight a badger is in for a real battle. A badger can defeat a dog twice its size and give a grown man a terrific struggle. With all this strength, you might think they wouldn't have to be sneaky, but they are.

If a badger is afraid, it can pretend it is dead. Its body will stiffen, and it will stop breathing. A person can turn it over, thinking the badger is lifeless. Then, suddenly, the badger will strike and tear a piece of flesh with its long claws.

Many people are pretenders just like badgers. We act nice in front of our parents. We try to give the right answers. But when we are away from home, we often act differently. We might get into trouble in school or go places we are told not to go. Then we come home, looking like little angels with sweet smiles. We act one way when, in fact, we are something entirely different.

God is concerned about pretenders. In the long run they will hurt themselves. We need to be kind and thoughtful around our parents and away from them.

You try to look like saintly men, but underneath those pious robes of yours are hearts besmirched with every sort of hypocrisy and sin.

MATTHEW 23:28 (TLB)

Do You Remember?

1. How long a tunnel can a badger dig?

2. How long does it take a badger to dig a hole large enough to disappear into?

3. Why are people "sneaky" instead of honest?

Help us to do what is right all of the time.

11 Lost and Confused

The lemming is a small field animal that is related to mice and rats. It enjoys the northlands and multiplies rapidly.

The amazing thing about these small animals is the trip that kills many of them.

Lemmings depend on grass, moss, and small plants to live. Though they are small rodents, they are big eaters. Scandinavian lemmings move in large circles as they eat everything in sight. Soon they are spreading in large numbers across highways, farms, and ditches.

Some lemmings go all the way to the ocean looking for food. They soon leave the shore and start swimming. When they get tired, they can't turn around, so hundreds merely drown.

People used to think lemmings were killing themselves intentionally. There certainly was no way to get across the huge ocean. Now we have a better answer. In their search for food, lemmings cross many rivers and lakes. They can be excellent swimmers. When they come to the ocean, the lemmings probably think it is just another river, so they jump in. They swim until they are exhausted, then die at sea.

This doesn't happen every year to lemmings. Their numbers increase and decline. After several years of healthy growth, there are so many they have to keep moving. Only a small group of lemmings throw themselves into the sea.

They have a fancy name, but lemmings are really field mice. Some are fat, some are brown, and some are white. They are busy little creatures, constantly looking for food and having babies.

Like other small animals, the lemming has to be on the watch for enemies. None is a worse enemy of this little rascal than the snowy owl. When the lemming population is high, this owl also has more little ones. Owls move across the countryside, and their breeding depends on how many of these tiny mice are running around.

The lemming leads a short, busy, dangerous life. Those that reach the ocean have finally become lost and confused. It looks like a river, but there is no way to swim it. Because they can't think it through, they perish.

Jesus Christ described *us* as something like this. Apart from God, we would be lost. We wouldn't know good from bad. We wouldn't know about heaven, where we can live with God.

Christ invites us to believe in Him and become His followers. Each of us can be safe by becoming Christians.

For the Son of man came to seek and to save what was lost.

LUKE 19:10 (NIV)

Do You Remember?

1. Why do lemmings jump into the sea?

2. Where do they live?

3. Do you believe in Jesus Christ, the Son of God?

Thanks for being our guide in a confusing world.

12 Where Did the Buffalo Go?

Pretend you are riding a train across the plains of Kansas in 1870. You stick your head out the window and see large buffalo walking along the tracks. Then you look at the countryside, and as far as you see there are thousands of buffalo.

They aren't really buffalo. Their actual name is bison, but we have called them buffalo for hundreds of years.

When the white man arrived in America, the buffalo roamed from the East Coast to the West Coast. By 1819 they had been entirely killed off in the East.

The killing of the buffalo was especially hard on Native Americans. Many of them depended on the buffalo for life. They ate buffalo meat. They used hides for shirts, dresses, and shoes. Buffalo fur became blankets and robes. Tepees were made of buffalo hide. The hooves were boiled to make glue. Buffalo bones were carved into sleds, their horns were used for spoons, and muscles were made into bowstrings.

Native Americans didn't waste any part of the buffalo. They knew their survival depended on keeping these animals around. The Native Americans were excellent hunters. One way of hunting buffalo was to chase them toward a steep cliff. The buffalo would run over the edge and be killed by the fall. The Native Americans then had plenty of food and clothing for the winter.

Whites had little or no respect for buffalo. They had rifles that made hunting easy. Rather than use the entire buffalo, they shot them for silly reasons. Some collected just buffalo tongues, which were worth only twenty-five cents. They would hunt all day, kill one hundred buffalo, and make twenty-five dollars. Others took the hides at $1.25 each. Hunters destroyed thousands of buffalo, thinking the large animals would always be there.

From 1865 to 1885, almost all the buffalo in North America were killed. That quickly, sixty million buffalo were destroyed.

Today they are being raised on ranches, and the number has grown greatly.

God has been generous in supplying animals for humans. Some are for fun, while others are good workers. Many make excellent food. None of them are to be wasted.

Too many people want to kill merely to kill. Others will even torture animals. God is not pleased when humans are cruel. Animals are created to be used but never wasted.

A good man is concerned for the welfare of his animals.

PROVERBS 12:10 (TLB)

Do You Remember?

1. How many buffalo lived in North America at one time?

2. How much did bison tongue sell for?

3. Why did God create animals?

It never makes sense to waste God's gifts.

13 The Target-Shooting Fish

It's hard to believe. For years scientists laughed and said it couldn't be done. How can a fish spit water at a tree branch and hit a small bug? But today we know that archerfish can shoot water as far as fifteen feet away, aiming for their victim. They are highly accurate at hitting a ladybug six feet away.

Most of us have never seen archerfish because they live off the coasts of Asia and northern Australia. They enjoy tropical waters. Some archerfish spend most of their lives far out at sea. They are unable to use their special "gun." But the ones that do come to shore are excellent marksmen.

Archerfish are now kept in captivity in the United States. They are popular attractions. In some places, hamburger is sprinkled in fine pieces along the wall of the tank, and the archerfish will shoot the meat off the side.

In order for a fish to do this, it has to overcome a couple of problems. One of these difficulties is sight. Since the archerfish stays in the water, how can it see clearly enough to aim straight? Somehow its eyes overcome the distortion.

The second problem is spitting with that much force. Somehow it traps water in its gills and with great power forces it through the mouth. Its tongue both pushes the water and forms a tunnel to help aim. In some ways it is much like a person spitting.

Archerfish may be especially intelligent. One reason for believing this is their ability to learn. Archerfish are not born with the ability to shoot water at insects. Their aim is terrible, and they can't shoot far enough. That is why they have to practice. If they stay at the job long enough, they develop strength and accuracy. Even as adults they are not always good shots. When an archerfish shoots too quickly and without good aim, it might miss its dinner by far.

Archerfish face the same problem people do. If we don't practice, we won't do well. Whether it is reading, baseball, or Ping-Pong, we do better if we stay at it.

A smart parent will help a child practice being good. Sometimes it doesn't come easily. But the more we choose to be kind, sharing, and careful, the easier it becomes.

Train up a child in the way he should go: and when he is old, he will not depart from it.

PROVERBS 22:6 (KJV)

Do You Remember?

1. How far can archerfish shoot?

2. How does an archerfish learn to shoot?

3. Is it easier to practice being good or bad?

Thanks for parents who expect us to practice being good.

14 Animals That Hide

Have you ever broken your mother's favorite dish? Right away you probably wished there were someplace to hide. It would help if you could become the color of the wall and no one could see you.

If you were an animal, it might be easy to escape. Some creatures match the forest or desert so well you could practically step on them without knowing it.

The white-tailed jackrabbit does this extremely well. It lives in the cold northern and mountainous areas. When the snows come, this rabbit turns white. It can flatten itself so even the sharpest eye will miss it. In the spring the same rabbit turns brown-gray and is just as difficult to find.

Coyotes blend into their background, and this makes them excellent hunters. They can sneak up on their dinner because the coyote is the same color as the field.

If you had to choose the animal that is the easiest to find, you might say the zebra. Some states used to dress prisoners in black-and-white stripes to make them easy to see. But don't be fooled. The zebra can be terribly hard to find.

The zebra lives in central Africa and likes to stay in crowds. Their herds may number twenty or sometimes grow to one thousand. If it had its way, the zebra would merely stay with its own kind and munch on grass all day. Sometimes they are captured and used as horses. The result is usually a disaster. They have mean tempers and can't be trusted. A zebra isn't afraid to kick, and it can do a tremendous amount of damage.

If not for man, the lion could be the zebra's only natural enemy. It would seem the zebra is an easy victim for the lion. Actually, zebras can put up a terrific fight. They have sharp teeth and can kick a lion dizzy. When three or four zebras start smashing a lion, it may wish to be home.

Usually lions go hunting just before dark. This is when the zebra stripes start working. In the half-dark twilight, zebras are extremely difficult to see. What seems like a strange color combination really helps the zebra disappear.

Even in the gray evening, God would have no trouble seeing the zebra. No one can hide from Him or get lost in the crowd. Wherever we are and whatever we are doing, we are still under the careful eye of God.

Each of us is special to our heavenly Father. When no one else knows what we are doing, He does. He knows about the good things we do even when no one else thanks us.

If I try to hide in the darkness, the night becomes light around me. For even darkness cannot hide from God; to you the night shines as bright as day. Darkness and light are both alike to you.

PSALM 139:11–12 (TLB)

Do You Remember?

1. How does the white-tailed jackrabbit hide?

2. How does a zebra fight a lion?

3. Who carefully watches us day and night?

God loves me and stays around me all the time.

15 The Zoo on Your Skin

If you want to see exciting wildlife, there is no need to head for the thick jungle. There are strange and crawling creatures living on your arms, legs, and face. A strong microscope would show us great surprises.

A few of these creepy-crawlies come from harmful fungus, such as athlete's foot. The fungus is alive and growing like little mushrooms between our toes.

Other living things on our bodies look like tiny bugs. They are called mites. Everyone has small, dry flakes of skin. The mites love it. They eat the skin flakes for regular meals.

No amount of baths will get rid of these small visitors. Warm water seems to make them grow and multiply. But don't be too concerned. Most of these microscopic creatures are good for us. One type of creature is often eating another kind. It is happening right now as you sit there. If they didn't eat each other, we would get too many of one kind, and that wouldn't be healthy.

Dead skin falls off all day long. In twenty-four hours we probably drop ten thousand flakes. Most of the dust we see around the house is actually particles of dead skin.

Adults are continuously concerned with dandruff. Actually, there is no need to worry. Dandruff is not alive. It is harmless dead skin.

While we are looking at our heads, we might as well check into the follicle mite. A follicle is the hole from which a hair grows. There are probably 120,000 of them on your head. Each is like a small factory, and its full-time job is to manufacture hair.

The follicle mite loves making a home in these tiny holes. A lazy creature, it merely rests and eats delicious bacteria. If it gets thirsty, a tall glass of hair oil will do the trick.

These mites sound unpleasant, but they really are friends. Most people have them. They actually help keep the head clean.

A few people are born without this little jungle on their body, and then they are in trouble. Their skin can't fight the bacteria that will attack them.

Sometimes we think everything important has to be big. But we need all these little things on our bodies, and we can't even see them. Little people are very important. A little bit of kindness goes a long way. Just a little "thank you" can brighten someone's day. God loves the little things we do because we belong to Him.

> *"Fine!" the king exclaimed. "You are a good man. You have been faithful with the little I entrusted to you."*
>
> **LUKE 19:17** (TLB)

Do You Remember?

32

1. What is a follicle mite?

2. What is usually dropping from our skin?

3. How many little things can you name that God uses?

The important things in life aren't measured by their size.

16 The Animal in Armor

Animals have the most interesting ways to protect themselves. One kind of lizard can change colors, skunks send odors, and porcupines stick little spears into their enemy. But none of these ways is more amazing than that of the armadillo.

This chubby creature is able to grow a real armored suit on its back. In some ways it is just like the old suits worn by knights hundreds of years ago. When the armadillo is finished growing, it looks something like a tank.

A special overcoat spreads across its back, neck, and sides. It is made of bones. A small piece of skin is between each round bone to hold them together.

If someone attacks an armadillo, it could try to run away, or it might turn around and fight with sharp claws. But if neither of these defenses work, the armadillo will wrap up into a ball with the armor blanket to protect it. The armor suit will hold off most enemies.

33

Armadillos have a real enemy in people. Armadillos' flesh is considered excellent eating by many, and their armor is sometimes used as a basket.

Not only do armadillos make good tanks, but they can become fairly tough battleships.

When they come to a large creek, they are able to inhale great amounts of air. Their body parts fill up like small balloons; then the armadillo crawls into the water and starts to swim.

Some armadillos are found in the southern United States, but they are found more often in Central and South America.

In some areas the number of armadillos is decreasing, but the number seems to be growing in Louisiana, Florida, and Mississippi. They are hunted often, but they do not disappear. Armadillos would come farther north, but they can't stand frost.

An average armadillo's dinner would be a handful of maggots, ants, or termites. On special days they eat fresh snake.

The armadillo found in the United States is called the nine-banded armadillo. They almost always have four young born at one time. New babies begin to develop their stonelike shell at once.

In some ways we are like the armadillo. We need protection against the evil and sin around us. It is easy to give in and do things that are wrong. After all, everybody else disobeys, steals, and lies.

God says there is a way to keep from doing these things. We need to depend on God and follow Him. When we do, He wraps His arms around us and gives protection.

So use every piece of God's armor to resist the enemy whenever [Satan] attacks, and when it is all over, you will still be standing up.

EPHESIANS 6:13 (TLB)

Do You Remember?

1. What is the armadillo's armor made of?

2. How do armadillos cross large creeks?

3. Name one way God protects us from sin.

God wraps us in armor to keep us safe.

17 Which Is the "Right" Whale?

The captain brought the boat to a stop and cut off the engines. Rocking quietly on the water, we watched and listened for any sign that whales might be close at hand. My wife, Pat, and I had traveled many miles to Nova Scotia, Canada, in search of this magnificent sight.

Suddenly a huge body rose to the water's surface. We had trouble containing our excitement. This tremendous forty-five-foot-long, fifty-ton creature had risen from the deep and parked itself close by.

The sea monster we met was called a right whale. Reportedly, whale hunters of old gave them this name because it was the "right" whale for hunting. This particular mammal was fairly easy to catch, produced a great deal of oil, and seldom sank after being harpooned.

Our watery friend remained visible for ten to fifteen minutes. The right whale needs air to breathe, so it surfaces to fill its lungs before diving back deep into the Bay of Fundy. Right whales look like they are wearing hats but actually have white skin patches on their heads.

Suddenly the whale next to us began to move and arch its back, preparing to dive. And then it did. Going headfirst, the whale tossed its gigantic tail straight up into the air on its way down.

Their tails are called flukes. It's an awesome experience to watch them hoist straight up and then slide into the massive sea.

We remained in the area for two or three hours while the whale parade came and went. We saw as many as twenty whales that afternoon. Many shot water eight feet high out of the hole on top of their heads.

Right whales never get a toothache, but that's because they have no teeth. Some whales do have teeth and enjoy fish or squid for dinner. But the right whales are baleen whales. They're not exactly picky eaters—they filter their food from the water and munch on whatever files in.

There are "right" whales and "wrong" whales, depending on what you are looking for. For many reasons this was the "right" whale for whale hunters because it supplied their needs. If they kept chasing the "wrong" whales, they might not have earned enough money to support their families.

Smart people learn early that life is filled with right and wrong decisions. If we make the right choices, we can live at peace with God. The wrong choices could leave us sad and disappointed.

The Bible encourages us to go after the right choices.

Learn to do right! Seek justice, encourage the oppressed.
Defend the cause of the fatherless, plead the case of the widow.

Isaiah 1:17 (niv)

Do You Remember?

1. Describe the right whale's hat.

2. Why don't they get toothaches?

3. How can we learn what is the right thing to do?

Help me know the difference between right and wrong.

18 Bugs With Flashlights

We used to catch them in glass jars. When we had a half dozen or more, it looked like a lantern. The light given off by fireflies in the jar was enough to read by. In the late spring and summer they filled our backyards. When we held them against our finger, we felt a little heat each time they flashed.

At the time the flashes didn't mean anything to us. But each one meant a great deal to the flies. (Actually, they are beetles.) They are sending out messages to flies of the opposite sex. The male might hold his light on for half a second, and the female sends back a flash. If the flashes are not timed correctly, the fireflies stay away.

Sometimes a firefly might hold a flash for too long or wait too long to send it; the result may send it to the wrong insect. Because its signals were off, it might be eaten by a stranger. It is possible that some types send out the wrong signals on purpose. They aren't looking for a mate—just dinner. Many of us call the firefly a glowworm. They are easy to confuse, since there are two thousand types of bugs with lanterns on their tails.

The firefly can control its light. A substance that can burn fills the firefly's tail section. When air gets to this section, it starts a small fire. The firefly can hold the substance back or push it forward. That is why fireflies are sometimes hard to catch. They simply turn off their lights. The air is breathed in so the firefly can stop the signal whenever it wants to.

In the winter fireflies become coal miners. They dig in to the top of the soil to escape the cold. If we were to dig them up, we might find their lamps still lit. They could be getting heat from their lanterns.

Fireflies are used for beauty and light. In other countries some women wear them on their dresses or as jewelry. Men who have had to travel in the dark often make lanterns from them or put them on their boots to light their paths. The fireflies will become excited and light more often.

In some ways you are like a firefly. Jesus told us to let our light shine before men. When people see our good behavior, we are like a light shining in darkness. When they see this light, they can then see the God we serve. Like fireflies, we control our light. We can make it shine as much as we want to.

In the same way, let your light shine before men, that they may see your good deeds and praise your Father in heaven.

MATTHEW 5:16 (NIV)

Do You Remember?

1. What is another name for the firefly?

2. How many types of bugs have lanterns on their tails?

3. What are some ways you let your light shine?

A dark world needs more light.

19 The Mighty Gorilla

The tall man couldn't believe his eyes. He had come a long way from Europe to study the gorilla, but he didn't expect this. There in the branches of a tree was a bed. It was made by tying the limbs together, and the tying was finished with real knots. Gorillas are intelligent enough to tie a double over-and-under twist knot. The largest ape in the world is an amazing animal to study.

We may want to study gorillas, but they don't want to study us. This huge African creature would rather be left alone. He is a quiet banana eater who isn't looking for an argument or a fight with anyone.

Gorillas live in thick forests, whether in the mountains or the lowlands. Those living in the higher regions grow thicker coats to fight the cold.

Some people think gorillas are nearly as intelligent as people. Others who work with them deny this. One thing is for sure—if you get a chance to fight a gorilla, DON'T! With one swing of its powerful arm, a gorilla can tear your entire shoulder off. Gorillas probably don't realize just how strong they are.

Gorillas are family-oriented. They have the cutest, quietest little babies. Their families often travel together. In some areas they are members of large groups. Nigeria has an entire nation of gorillas living together.

We often see pictures of gorillas walking on their two legs. Many of them do. But they can also move on all four limbs. Older gorillas rely almost entirely on all fours.

A gorilla has a strong body but is still weak. It is weak because it can't think well enough to stay out of trouble. Gorillas will charge at men carrying rifles and get themselves killed.

Strong people are often weak in the same way. We don't stop to think. Later we are sorry because we did something stupid.

The Bible can be a big help. It holds excellent advice. We can learn how to avoid trouble. We can get strong guidance from God. The fool says,

"I don't need advice." The really strong people are the ones who look to God for direction.

A wise man is mightier than a strong man. Wisdom is mightier than strength.

PROVERBS 24:5 (TLB)

Do You Remember?

1. Should you make friends with a gorilla?

2. Do gorillas travel alone?

3. How can the Ten Commandments keep us out of trouble?

Thanks for making us strong by giving us direction.

20 Bird Buffet

There is a popular eating place about twenty miles from where I live in Nebraska. The food is so good at this dining area that half a million sandhill cranes stop there every year to sample the salad bar. And they enjoy it enough to tell their friends, and they all come back again each March.

Cranes travel from their winter homes in Texas and Mexico to their summer homes in far-off Alaska and Siberia.

Plenty of birds migrate, flying great distances between seasons. But this trip is definitely different. During this journey, the half million birds squeeze into a small area like the middle of an hourglass. If it's easier, picture a belt pulled very tight on a tiny waistline. These cranes come from many areas to land at this same restaurant.

What's so great about this bird buffet on the plains? Mostly it's the food. Cranes enjoy the corn special left sprinkled over the farmers' fields. Corn adds a bit of fat to a crane's diet. But no self-respecting crane will leave without snacking on the other treats. They may munch an earthworm here or slurp an insect there. Dessert might be a slimy snail or a piece of small plant.

Not only are the meals delicious, but they're also plentiful. Thousands of the cranes stay around for three or four weeks, happily trying to put on weight.

With so many visiting birds, one would think the fields would be packed with temporary nests. But don't worry, there is more than enough motel space. Cranes sleep standing up in the shallow riverbed of the Platte River. They seem to feel safe there in case some animals try to attack them.

Cranes are fortunate. They can't farm, but there is usually plenty of food. Not every field is as nutritious as these few square miles in Nebraska, but birds normally do well.

If God treats cranes like they are valuable, think how much more valuable people are. That's why we help feed other people. They are valuable to God too.

God provides for us, and we help God provide for others. That's one way we see how good our heavenly Father is.

Look at the birds of the air; they do not sow or reap or store away in barns, and yet your heavenly Father feeds them.

MATTHEW 6:26 (NIV)

Do You Remember?

1. Where do the cranes spend their summers?

2. What do cranes eat at this bird buffet?

3. What is one way we can help God feed other people?

Help us to become thankful for the way God meets our needs.

21 Crybaby Crocodiles

When someone cries to put on a show, sometimes we say that person is shedding crocodile tears. The saying is not so silly, because crocodiles are big criers. They aren't pushing big tears because they are sad; their bodies can't handle all the salt they get, so they cry to keep their bodies clean.

Don't let the tears fool you. Crocodiles aren't softhearted. They will eat anything, from a tiny beetle to a baby hippopotamus. If they fail to find one of these, another crocodile or a human will do just as well.

These long, funny-looking creatures get their prey two ways: Their powerful tails can take a victim down in a second, and their crushing jowls can finish it off. Their speed demands a great deal of respect. Only man or another crocodile attacks one.

41

Crocodiles move so smoothly and quietly that they can pluck a bird off the water. They can be excellent fishermen. One crocodile was opened up in South Africa, and twenty-two dog licenses were found inside.

Crocodiles' brownish-green color and lumpy skin make them hard to see. They merely lie still and look like a log or clump of weeds.

The crocodile's nearest relative is the alligator. For most of us, the two would be difficult to tell apart, especially if they were chasing us. The easiest difference can be seen in the mouth. When a crocodile closes its mouth, some of its teeth stick out. Alligator teeth all fit inside.

After a crocodile attacks, it will drag its victim to a hideaway and let the dinner rot. This is probably because of the crocodile's teeth. They are excellent for attacking but poor for chewing. They don't line up straight.

Crocodiles carry rocks in their stomachs. They even gobble down soft drink cans and bracelets. Scientists think the rocks help digest food.

At one time the Nile River in Egypt was crowded with crocodiles. Today they are gone, except for an occasional lost one that may wander in.

Some pharaohs (kings) of Egypt became proud and thought they were special. They didn't think they needed God or anything He had to say.

God sent one of the kings a message. He told him not to be so proud. Next to God he was nothing. The pharaoh saw himself as a mighty lion. God looked at him as simply a crocodile blowing bubbles in the river.

Often we get too proud of ourselves. We think we are the smartest, the fastest, the trickiest. Why do we need God? Look at all we can do. God tells every bragger to calm down—you are just blowing bubbles in the river. If you really have good sense, trust and follow our living God.

Son of dust, mourn for Pharaoh, king of Egypt, and say to him: "You think of yourself as a strong young lion among the nations, but you are merely a crocodile along the banks of the Nile, making bubbles and muddying the stream."

Ezekiel 32:2 (tlb)

Do You Remember?

1. How do you tell an alligator from a crocodile?

2. What color are crocodiles?

3. To what did God compare a proud king?

Teach us to do good but not to talk about it.

22 The Bad-Tempered Rhino

One of the loneliest creatures in all the outdoors is the grumpy rhinoceros. Not only is it short of friends, but even its enemies stay away.

Rhinos have a great deal going against them. Part of their problem is their lack of intelligence. Frankly, they do some dumb things. Another source of trouble is their nearsightedness. They don't see well and therefore don't trust anything or anyone.

For instance, most animals know when people are around, and they get out of the way. Not the rhino. It doesn't know humans are close until they get next to it. Frightened, the rhino will suddenly attack rather than hide. Pity the poor jeep or truck parked nearby. The rhino will ram it into a junk heap.

The female rhino even has trouble getting along with boyfriends. If the female sees a male she likes, she backs up and charges him. She knocks him down and steps on him just to say she likes the boy. Kindness doesn't come easily to her.

In spite of its size, the rhino isn't slow. It can turn quickly and gain a speed of thirty miles an hour. Not bad for two to four tons.

The rhino begins as a bulky baby. The kangaroo is only the size of a quarter at birth, but the rhinoceros weighs sixty pounds on the first day.

Humans have hunted the rhino into near extinction; today only thousands of these African "tanks" exist. There are laws to protect the rhino, but the laws are often broken. Rhinos are sometimes killed just for their horns. There is a story in Asia that says, "Anyone drinking from a rhino horn cannot be poisoned." Those who believe this pay a large amount to buy the useless cup.

Others think dried rhino blood is good medicine.

There are few happy moments in the life of a rhino. They don't seem to get along with anything or anyone. The brightest spot in a rhino's life is

43

a little tickbird. These birds land on the huge monster's back and help out by eating the ticks and other dangerous insects off the rhino's skin.

If the rhino takes a nap (often standing up), the tickbird will be a watch bird. Should danger come, the bird picks itself up and starts screaming. The rhino wakes up immediately, ready for whatever is coming.

All rhinos know is how to attack and fight. On more than one occasion, they have charged full speed into moving trains. With all of this bad temper, a little bird has become the rhino's only friend.

Our neighborhoods, schools, and churches have people who are lonely. They need a good friend who will spend time with them and won't tease them or treat them badly. They are lonely for a friend just like you.

I have called you friends.

JOHN 15:15 (NIV)

Do You Remember?

1. How does a female rhino treat a male rhino?

2. Why are rhinos hunted?

3. Name one person you think might need a friend.

Somebody needs my friendship.

23 Birds That Swim

Penguins have wings, but they can't fly. Their beaks and eyes look like they belong to a creature in the sky, and scientists insist it is a member of the bird family, but so far the penguin isn't convinced. It merely waddles along on the ice and swims in the cold ocean.

These aren't the only things that make the penguin different. If it can't be a bird, it has decided to be a helicopter. Penguins' wings flap like propellers. It might swim to the side of an ice bank, then shoot straight up out of the water with such force that it lands feetfirst on the ice.

A penguin's heavy body and short legs make it look funny when it walks. But despite their clumsy appearance, penguins aren't so easy to catch. Not that their enemies don't try. A sea bird, the skua, enjoys penguin eggs and baby chicks. Skuas can't fight healthy penguins, so they try to steal eggs. If the nest is guarded well, the skua birds act as a team. One will distract the penguin while the other grabs the egg.

Adult penguins are usually safe from the leopard seal. These enemies swim in the sea and wait for penguins, but most healthy, careful penguins can avoid their tough hunters. A penguin will peck its opponent and hit it with its flippers if necessary.

Generally, penguins don't grow tall. A foot and a half is probably average for the Adélie variety.

Penguins build their nests in areas called rookeries. Thousands of them get together but keep their homes a safe distance from each other. They love to be with a crowd. These neat-looking creatures chatter constantly.

When they build their nests, the mother and father play different parts. Dad is in charge of finding materials, while Mom takes care of construction. One by one, Dad collects pebbles from the shoreline. Work isn't their favorite sport, so if a nest is left unguarded, a neighbor will probably steal a couple of pebbles.

God has sprinkled His earth with fascinating characters and sights. They are each a reminder of the imagination and wonder of our Creator. It is amazing what God can do.

45

He quiets the raging oceans and all the world's clamor. In the farthest corners of the earth the glorious acts of God shall startle everyone. The dawn and sunset shout for joy!

PSALM 65:7–8 (TLB)

1. Why are penguins called birds?

2. When are they "helicopters"?

3. Can you see God's work in nature? How?

With God's imagination, He didn't settle for a dull world.

24 The Twelve-Inch Tongue

A friend offered me a delicious-looking piece of chocolate candy. Naturally, I ate it. When it was safely in my stomach, my pal revealed that he had given me a chocolate-covered ant! Ants aren't part of my diet if I can help it, but anteaters love them. They spend most of their waking hours looking for a delicious meal of live ants.

It would be hard to call the anteater cute. The largest one in Central America can grow to eight feet in length. It has a long nose, though not all anteaters do. The tongue is often one foot long, so it can lick up many ants at one time.

The anteater walks on its knuckles instead of flat on its feet, so it appears to be tiptoing. Under the best conditions, this creature isn't fast. When it has a baby, it moves even slower. For the first year of the baby's life, the mother carries the infant on her back.

Not all anteaters roam the fields. Some, such as the three-toed anteater, live in trees. Its diet is made up of termites and insects.

Anteaters look friendly, but don't be fooled. The silky anteater can be mean. It sleeps in tree branches, and if a strong wind blows, it simply sleeps on. But let a person or animal shake a branch, and Silky wakes up with a violent temper and takes a swing with its claws straight out.

Most anteaters prefer to travel through life alone. When two are seen together, they are most often mother and child.

Anteaters have their share of persistent enemies. The small anteaters are hunted by eagles, hawks, and owls. The larger ones are attacked by jaguars and other large cats. In a battle between the two, an anteater will hold its own with its long, sharp claws. These claws also come in handy when looking for food. An anteater will smash a decayed log with its claws. The bewildered ants try to run in any direction to get away. This is when the remarkable tongue comes to work.

Not only is the tongue extremely long, but it also has a sticky glue. The anteater's saliva is like flypaper, and ants are gobbled up by the scores.

Tongues are fast and helpful to both animals and humans. They are important not only for eating but also in controlling our talking.

The psalm writer was glad he had a tongue. It gave him a chance to praise God. In song, testimony, and teaching, our tongues explain how we feel about our heavenly Father.

My lips shall greatly rejoice when I sing unto thee; and my soul, which thou hast redeemed. My tongue also shall talk of thy righteousness all the day long.

PSALM 71:23–24 (KJV)

Do You Remember?

1. Why do anteaters walk strangely?

2. What hunts anteaters?

3. Name two ways our tongues can praise God.

The wise person's tongue speaks well of God.

25 Pearl Divers

Instead of becoming a lawyer, policeman, or doctor, have you ever considered a job as a pearl diver? If you enjoy swimming and exciting work, this may be just the work for you. But you may have to move, since the best pearl diving is done on the Persian Gulf, off of southwest Asia.

When divers first started hunting for pearls, two men went out in a boat together. One stayed in the small boat while the other dove for pearl oysters. By merely holding his breath, the diver dropped one hundred feet to the bottom of the Gulf. For one minute, he filled a basket full of shells and then took off for the top. The man in the boat pulled the basket up with a rope. This was terribly dangerous. Newer methods have made pearl diving safer.

Pearls are the only valuable gem presently taken from living creatures. Normally we think of pearls as white or pink. But actually they come in a large selection of colors like bronze, brown, green, and even blue. One of the most expensive pearls is black.

Most of the pearls we think of come from oysters. But they can grow in a number of shellfish of the mollusk family.

Pearls begin when a tiny speck of sand or other material gets inside the shell. The oyster is bothered by it in the same way that dust hurts our eyes.

The oyster starts to cover the piece of sand so it won't be painful. Layer after layer of covering finally turns the speck into a pearl. Some of the pearls end up lovely and round, while others are odd-shaped.

Fake pearls are made of plastic. They aren't worth much but are fun to wear and play with.

Not all the great pearls are found in Persia. One highly valued pearl was discovered in New Jersey about 140 years ago. It weighed 1.64 ounces.

If diving isn't for you, don't let that stop you. There are plenty of people catching gorgeous pearls who never dive. They have opened pearl farms.

The job still isn't easy. The "farmer" keeps a large bed of shells. He places a tiny piece of sand in each shell. Twice a year the owner cleans each one of seaweed and sticks. After seven years it's ready to open. One out of twenty shells holds a usable pearl.

People have loved pearls since long before the birth of Christ. Job knew how valuable they were during his lifetime. One day Job was thinking about all the foolish things people do. They pick bad friends and get into trouble. Sometimes they do the exact opposite of what their parents tell them. A few break the law.

Job thought how much better it would be if people took time to think of the right things to do. Doing what is good would be more valuable than the black pearls of the Persian Gulf.

The price of wisdom is above pearls.

JOB 28:18 (RSV)

Do You Remember?

1. Describe how divers collect pearls.

2. How are pearls farmed?

3. Give two reasons why people get into trouble.

Thanks for showing us what is important in life.

26 Monkeys in a Hot Tub

Often it is hard to change the way we live and act, but we can do it. Animals can too when they really have to.

Some of the macaque (ma-KACK) monkeys in the mountains of Japan discovered that they could change when they really wanted to. This type of monkey prefers the warmth of India or Malaysia, and normally when it gets cold in northern Japan, they head for the lower regions. That was true until one day a few of the monkeys decided to make a change.

They looked over the hot tub (or volcanic springs) high in the freezing mountains. Soon they began to enjoy those warm swims and thought this felt pretty comfortable.

Despite the snow that covered the rocks all around them, the macaques liked hanging out and taking baths. Even when the snow stuck to their heads, they could simply duck beneath the surface of the springs and wash it off.

49

Some of the monkeys changed their behavior and spent the winter in the cold. Other monkeys thought it was a terrible idea and headed down to a milder climate. They decided to come back in the spring.

This kind of change in nature isn't as unusual as it might sound. A few types of birds that may have flown at one time don't fly anymore, like the ostrich and the penguin. Rhinoceroses used to live in Nebraska, but they don't anymore. Elephants roamed the middle of America at one time, but now they're all gone. Jaguars living in Central America might be moving farther north toward the United States.

Nature does not always stay the same. Animals give up old habits and start new ones. Change is sometimes an excellent idea whether we are talking about macaque monkeys in Japan or kids who go to school.

Human beings often do bad things. We might be rude or even lie or cheat. Too many of us have stolen something or been terribly unkind to another person. Most of us have done some really nasty things.

The good news is that we can change. We may not be able to change everything about us, but we could begin to obey better, become kinder, and not take anything that doesn't belong to us.

Monkeys can change the way they behave, and so can human beings.

Keep your tongue from evil and your lips from speaking lies.
Turn from evil and do good; seek peace and pursue it.

PSALM 34:13–14 (NIV)

Do You Remember?

1. Where do macaque monkeys enjoy a "hot tub"?

2. Which birds probably used to fly and don't fly anymore?

3. Is there something you should change in your life?

Help us get rid of the bad habits we need to get rid of.

27 The Big Eater

The next time you carry the groceries in from the car, be thankful. If you owned an elephant, you would need to bring in a half ton of food every day. On top of that, the elephant would drink a small tank of water.

Elephants aren't very practical pets, but they are fascinating animals. They are the largest beasts to walk on earth.

Besides their size, elephants are best known for their two large tusks. Both males and females have them. Elephants have been hunted just for their tusks, which are made of beautiful ivory. Each tusk can weigh up to three hundred pounds.

Elephants' teeth stay hidden in their mouths. Their teeth crush the fruit, grass, or leaves that elephants' trunks pull up for lunch.

The trunk is one of the handiest tools of any animal. It may look odd, but it does a long list of jobs. The trunk works as a fork, shovel, and picker. All day long it collects food and pushes it into the huge mouth. It also doubles as a hose. The trunk isn't really a straw. An elephant doesn't drink through it; it fills its trunk with water and then squirts the water into its mouth.

If the elephant gets an itch, the trunk becomes a back scratcher. When the elephant's owner wants a ride, the trunk turns into an elevator. On a hot day, trunks make great showers.

Elephants prefer to live in the wild, but in India they have been trained. Sometimes they are used to plow farms. Others are used as freight trucks to carry heavy loads. Wealthy people ride elephants to go tiger hunting. During war, elephants are put to work as tanks to smash through the enemy.

Human babies take nine months to develop before they are born. Elephants need twenty-two months. They live a long time, and some are probably sixty years old.

In areas where elephants roam free, the farmers aren't too happy to see them. Elephants often move in herds of ten to one hundred. If they become hungry and move onto a farm, they could eat the place bare in a few hours.

Elephants are animals of habit. They may move for hundreds of miles, and each year they follow the same trail. Some countries have built highways on old elephant paths.

Elephants do the same thing over and over again, but the stories of their good memories are untrue. Elephants appear to forget as easily as any other animal.

When it comes to forgetting, human beings are especially good at it. We forget our lunch money, our homework, and even our phone number. If we were elephants, some days we might forget about our trunk.

One thing that we should keep repeating to ourselves is how kind God has been to us. It would be easy to forget His goodness and just think about what we *don't* have. God gave us better memories than elephants so that we could remember our Creator.

Bless the Lord, O my soul, and forget not all his benefits.

PSALM 103:2 (KJV)

Do You Remember?

1. How much does an elephant eat?

2. How do elephants drink water?

3. Name three good things God has given you.

We complain often when we forget how good God has been to us.

28 Nature in the City

While it's fun to hike mountain trails or spend the afternoon in the forest, they aren't the only places we can enjoy nature. Many of us who grew up in the city enjoyed watching the wildlife that lived among the buildings.

One of the most interesting of the downtown birds is the beautiful pigeon. Their relatives like to live among the rocks and are often called rock doves. But many animals, just like people, have moved to towns and cities.

Pigeons build nests on high ledges, where they lay eggs and raise their families. The baby pigeon is born blind but soon gains its sight after feeding on pigeon milk. In about ten weeks, the young bird is able to fly around the neighborhood all by itself.

Pigeons prefer some form of grain, but they are not picky eaters. Often they are happy to hop and walk around a city park and eat the food humans share with them. Living with people has allowed them to feel comfortable with children, and sometimes they get close if the child is quiet and gentle.

Not everyone likes to have pigeons living on their block. One of the biggest problems with pigeons is that they go to the bathroom wherever they want. Benches, sidewalks, cars, and strollers might get droppings on them.

Some people eat pigeons. Other people like to raise them. Homing pigeons can be taken hundreds of miles from home, and they will return to their owners by using special skills that we don't fully understand.

When Jesus Christ was a little over six months old, His parents, Joseph and Mary, went to Jerusalem to dedicate the baby to God. Obeying the Old Testament practice, they brought two pigeons along. These were a sacrifice to give to the Lord.

As He grew up, Jesus probably saw many pigeons where He lived and might have enjoyed feeding them. When we see a pigeon, we can remember how important it is for every child to belong to God and grow up to love Him.

And to offer a sacrifice in keeping with what is said in the Law of the Lord: "a pair of doves or two young pigeons."

LUKE 2:24 (NIV)

Do You Remember?

1. What is a rock dove?

2. Where do pigeons live in the city?

3. Why do parents dedicate their babies to God?

Everyone should dedicate his/her life to God.

29 Can Dolphins Talk?

Jill Baker will never forget the amazing dolphin rides she used to take. When she was only thirteen, a dolphin started visiting the beach near her home in New Zealand. People would come for miles to see the beautiful creature.

Normally, untamed dolphins stay away from humans. But this one was special. Almost every day he would swim close to shore and entertain the people. Those who watched named him Opo.

At first the dolphin was cautious, but as time went on, he became more playful. Opo started to play ball with the crowds. Sometimes he would balance a bottle on his nose.

The year 1956 was an exciting one for everyone who got to see Opo. But it was a very special time for young Jill. The dolphin developed an extra fondness for this teenager. If Opo was playing with others when Jill came, he left them immediately. He would dash to her side like a pup for its dinner.

Soon a law was passed that made it a crime to harm any dolphin in Hokianga Harbor. The people wanted to protect Opo, their new friend with the large black fin across his back.

This is a true story. Though Opo has since died, the people who visited the beach remember him well.

Some of this isn't too hard to imagine. After all, a dolphin is one of nature's smartest creatures.

Usually dolphins travel as families. The parents and children swim side by side. When one is injured, its family will come to its aid. They will push their kin to the top of the water so it can breathe. If possible, they will keep it up until the dolphin can swim for itself.

Dolphins are smart enough to have their own way of talking—though they can't say words. They make clicking sounds, whistles, and even barks, and their dolphin friends understand the sounds and answer in the same way.

Some scientists believe we will someday "talk" to dolphins and listen to them. By understanding their clicking sounds, we might be able to know what they are saying.

We can talk because we have vocal cords in our throats. But dolphins don't. They make sounds by blowing through the blowhole, whistling, or even smacking their mouths. The sound travels well through water, and a dolphin's child can hear it far away.

Being able to talk is a good gift from God. It's too bad some people use it to hurt others. Life would be hard if we couldn't say anything. We need to use our voices to say things that are kind and caring. Even dolphins care about one another.

Therefore each of you must put off falsehood and speak truth-fully to his neighbor, for we are all members of one body.

EPHESIANS 4:25 (NIV)

Do You Remember?

1. What was unusual about Opo?

2. How do dolphins "talk"?

3. How should we use our voices?

Help me watch the words I use. Show me how to make some-one feel better by what I say.

30 Cannibal Insects

The praying mantis is one of the big eaters in nature. It will even eat other praying mantises.

This bad habit often begins at birth. The first insects to hatch may start eating the other mantis eggs. From then on they would just as soon eat another mantis as anything. If one happens to land near its brother, it just might be eaten.

Even the ones that seem to like each other don't really like each other. After the male and female get together to mate, the female will then eat the male. The male seems to realize this and accepts it. He could fly away. But he seems to know it is now his time to become her supper.

After she has finished the meal, the mother mantis will lay her eggs. These eggs are stuck together in cases. She might lay several cases at once.

This big appetite isn't all bad. Mantises are a great help to farmers and gardeners. Every day mantises eat insects that otherwise would destroy crops.

They don't care what they eat. Plant lice, spiders, butterflies, wasps, grasshoppers, flies, bees, and caterpillars are all part of their diet. In some cases, they have even attacked moths, hummingbirds, and garter snakes. The mantis is tame to human beings, though. We can hold them and never be bitten.

One of the reasons mantises are such successful hunters is their color. Most of them are green or brown and look just like a blade of grass. They can sit motionless for hours.

During most days the insect will eat enough food to equal its own weight. This would be like you eating about seventy-five pounds of food daily. Mantises will take their time and pick out every edible part of their prey. When the mantis is finished, it will lick its hands much like a kitten does.

There are over fifteen hundred types of mantises. The praying mantis folds its hands, but its victims aren't sure it is religious.

The mantis is such a successful eater that farmers will even buy them. Some dealers will sell cases of eggs. As they hatch, the young mantises begin to feed on the pests that destroy crops.

Eating this much is good for the praying mantis. Their bodies can handle all this food. But eating all the time is bad for humans. Our bodies can't take it and soon may become sick.

God cares enough for us to even discuss our eating. In the Bible, He tells us to eat no more than we really need. He wants us to be healthy.

The good man eats to live, while the evil man lives to eat.

PROVERBS 13:25 (TLB)

Do You Remember?

1. How many types of mantises are there?

2. What color is the mantis?

3. Why does God care how much we eat?

Thanks for a healthy body.

31 A Lazy Creature

Isn't it terrible when someone calls us lazy? Most of us aren't, really. There are things we don't like to do, but other times we can move quickly.

It hurts to be called lazy. We might not deserve it, but the hairy sloth does. It moves only when it has to.

If a sloth is left alone, it will sleep for eighteen hours a day. It can sleep upside down holding on to a branch. Sloths aren't intelligent animals and don't care to get much done. It takes them an entire minute to move just fourteen feet.

My wife and I were fortunate to see a sloth in the rain forests of Costa Rica. As expected, the creature was hardly moving at all, but we did detect an arm in slow motion reaching for a branch.

The sloth lives in Central and South America. There are two types. One has two toes on each foot, and the other has three. They look somewhat the same, but their bones and eating habits are different.

A sloth spends most of its life hanging upside down. Its hair grows away from its stomach instead of toward it.

As the sloth sits almost motionless in the hot jungle, tiny plants grow on its fur. This is called *algae*. It looks like green moss and gives good protection to the sloth. Sloths often look like they are part of the trees. Some people confuse them for a termite nest hanging from a branch.

Sloths are too lazy to be friendly. Most of the time they don't want anything to do with other sloths. Usually if two are seen together they are a mother and child.

The closest sloths get to being active is when they happen to get into the water. They are excellent and fearless swimmers.

Fortunately, they don't have to catch their food. They probably would never get around to it. Almost their entire diet consists of leaves from the Cecropia (suh-KRO-pee-uh) tree.

There aren't many enemies for the sloth to fight off. When they are young, eagles try to catch them, but otherwise they are left alone. Sloths might be too lazy to defend themselves.

Laziness is all right for some animals, but it is a terrible habit for people. God knows lazy people are in for a long road of trouble. The person who does her work immediately and does it well will be a happy individual. The person who puts everything off is asking for hard times.

A lazy fellow has trouble all through life; the good man's path is easy!

PROVERBS 15:19 (TLB)

Do You Remember?

58

1. Where do sloths live?

2. How long do sloths sleep?

3. What do we call a person who puts off doing her work?

Thanks for warning us against becoming lazy.

32 Underground Fountains

I f you ever get to Yellowstone National Park, you can see water explode out of the ground. The water jumps 120 feet into the air. The place is called Old Faithful. Almost every hour this beautiful geyser blows.

The earth holds a great amount of water. It gets there from melting snow and mountain streams. But some of the water can't stay there because it gets too hot. Just like a teakettle, it has to blow off steam.

It is no small job to jump out of the ground. Normally, the water in a pot on your stove will boil when it reaches 212 degrees. Underground it has to reach 291 degrees before boiling. But for the water to leap 120 feet into the air, it has to be much hotter. The earth must be extremely hot to cause a geyser to blow up.

The more people learn about underground hot water, the more they use it. The town of Reykjavik, Iceland, sits on top of hot water springs, and the people there use the underground boiling water to heat their homes and run their industries.

The largest geyser to ever blow was in Waimangu, New Zealand. One day the steamy water broke through the surface and rose fifteen hundred feet into the air. This new geyser had enough force to lift a one-hundred-pound boulder far into the sky.

Some of the hot groundwaters contain valuable minerals. People often travel to these areas to use the water to relieve the pain of certain illnesses. Hot Springs, Arkansas; Mount Clemens, Michigan; and Saratoga Springs, New York, are just a few of the areas that have health resorts built on hot water springs.

Despite the intense heat, some forms of life manage to survive inside geysers. In some areas algae have been found alive.

For thousands of years we have known there was water flowing under the ground. In some places we can drink the water that is running out of the side of a mountain.

When the psalm writer saw things like this, his mind turned to the One who had made him. Water under the ground merely reminded him of how God supplied everything. He knew it all came from a loving Father.

Praise him who planted the water within the earth, for his loving-kindness continues forever.

PSALM 136:6 (TLB)

Do You Remember?

1. What causes geysers?

2. How does Iceland use its underground water?

3. Why did groundwater remind the psalmist of God?

The earth is filled with signs of the goodness of God.

33 The Tallest Animal

If only you could teach a giraffe to dribble a basketball! From its front hoof to the top of its small horns, a giraffe can grow up to eighteen feet tall. This makes it the tallest animal in the world.

There are some myths about giraffes that still go around. Maybe you have heard that the giraffe makes no sound. This is false. A mother giraffe calls her babies with a whistling noise. Giraffes can also make a strange gurgling sound. The next time you go to a zoo, listen carefully.

Another myth many people believe is that giraffes are weak and defenseless. But anyone who gets into a fight with a giraffe soon finds out how wrong that thought is. A giraffe can use its head like a powerful club. When it fights another giraffe, both of them often end up with painful head wounds.

Even lions are careful around this tall creature. If a giraffe gives a good kick, it could kill the big cat.

When given a choice, giraffes would rather depend on their vision and speed. They have an excellent tower to see what is around them. Giraffes run over thirty miles an hour and give many enemies a fast race.

Giraffes have two ways of walking. When they aren't in a hurry, they merely pace. Their left legs move together, then both right ones. But when danger comes, they take off in a gallop like a horse. First their front legs move, then their rear legs.

Baby giraffes have no choice but to be tall. They are born almost six feet high and weigh over one hundred pounds.

Their long necks usually help them, but sometimes they get in the way. The neck gives them good food selection. Giraffes eat leaves from the tops of acacia trees. When they want to eat leaves near the ground, they are in trouble. Their necks will not reach that far. They have to spread their legs to get closer to the ground. Only then can they come close to the earth.

A giraffe's neck is amazing for its size, yet in some ways its neck is like that of any other mammal. Giraffes have seven vertebrae in their necks, like most other mammals. The only difference is that the giraffe's bones are larger.

Each human being also has a fascinating neck. It is short but can turn quickly to either side so we can see what is going on.

When we are mad or upset, we do an interesting thing. Many of us sit still and hold our necks tight. We seem to be saying, "Nobody is going to get me to change." We have become stiff-necked, or stubborn.

This practice is dangerous. If our parents correct us, we shouldn't stiffen our necks and refuse to change. Sometimes we are wrong, and the smart person learns to admit it. God can't help people who won't change.

A man who remains stiff-necked after many rebukes will suddenly be destroyed—without remedy.

PROVERBS 29:1 (NIV)

Do You Remember?

1. How many vertebrae do giraffes have in their necks?

2. How fast can giraffes run?

3. Name one way you would like to improve yourself.

God wants to keep changing me.

34 Neat Baboons

If you visit a farm in Africa, you might get a huge surprise. In some places you will see baboons out in the fields picking fruit. They aren't stealing it; these large monkeys are so intelligent they can be taught to do simple jobs. They have stacked wood, herded sheep, and driven tractors.

The baboon is an exciting animal. About four feet tall, they prefer to live on the ground, but some travel in trees. They might weigh as much as ninety pounds. Baboons are quick animals that move on all fours.

The male baboon is larger than the female, who is usually more shy and eats less. Because of the differences, the male protects the female. Like human children, the female baboon grows up faster than the male, but the male passes her in size later.

There are many stories of human children being raised by baboons. Most of them are merely made up, but at least one seems to be true. In 1903 a boy was captured and raised by a troop of baboons in South Africa. He was named Lucas.

Over time, Lucas developed the characteristics of a baboon. He showed his teeth, barked, and ran on all fours. After his rescue and a year in the hospital, he got a simple job, but Lucas never learned to talk, and he died after a few years.

Not everyone thinks baboons are cute. They have terrible reputations for raiding farms. When traveling in large numbers, they have been known to steal crops and other food.

Baboons are able to plan their attacks. Farmers believe they send out scouts to inspect an area before raiding it. If the scouts see men with weapons, they go back and tell the others. They also appear to place scouts to watch while the others sleep.

A great part of the baboon's day is spent looking for food. They eat vegetables and search for them for twelve to fourteen hours a day.

Many people consider the baboon ugly and dirty. The truth is they are among the cleanest of animals. Part of the reason is their love of grooming.

If you want to make a baboon happy, merely spend an hour combing its hair and picking ticks. This is the way baboons treat each other. Most baboons spend several hours a day grooming and being groomed. They seem to use it to impress one another. They take pride in their neatness. After an argument, they make up by grooming each other. If a male and female like each other, they may pick each other's ticks. The baboon being groomed often rests on its back like a kitten having its tummy rubbed.

We all live longer because we stay clean. Those who aren't clean often have germs and become sick. But washing the body can only do so much. We also need to cleanse our minds.

People of all ages think about doing unkind things. We may think about hurting someone or stealing or telling a lie. God will help us by cleaning our minds. Jesus Christ promised to help those who follow Him.

Now ye are clean through the word which I have spoken unto you.
JOHN 15:3 (KJV)

Do You Remember?

1. How intelligent are baboons?

2. Why do they like grooming?

3. What can I do when I think about hurting someone?

63

Help me keep my mind clean.

35 Explorers of the Ocean

Would you like to visit the bottom of the ocean and see things no one has ever seen? Would you enjoy living in an underwater city?

Whatever we do in the future, we will be building on the knowledge, experience, and courage of people who first explored the sea. They did what others had only dreamed about. Some of the children of today might become the courageous sea explorers of tomorrow.

The most famous ocean pioneer of our time is Jacques-Yves Cousteau. His television specials have brought a knowledge of the ocean into millions of homes. However, Cousteau is far more than merely a television star.

In 1943 Cousteau joined Emile Gagnan to invent the famous aqualung. This allowed swimmers to carry air in a tank on their backs. As a result, they could travel freely to three hundred feet underwater and stay there for hours. With the aqualung, people have been given a new freedom under the sea.

Another amazing ocean explorer is Scott Carpenter. Before turning to the ocean, Carpenter was an astronaut. Today he is an aquanaut and the only person to have explored both outer space and the ocean depths. In 1962 Carpenter soared into space on the Aurora 7. Three years later, in 1965, he traveled into the mysterious world of the ocean.

Carpenter became the first person to spend thirty days underwater. He and other aquanauts lived in the thirty-eight-foot-long Sealab II. During this time, the explorers would leave the Sealab and investigate the underwater environment. They swam in water that was only fifty degrees.

Midway through their stay, Carpenter was stung by the dorsal spines of a red scorpion fish. The pain was so intense it looked at first as if Carpenter would have to be taken to land. Fortunately he was able to complete the mission.

Men are not the only explorers of the deep. Dr. Sylvia Earle, a marine biologist, is involved in some amazing underwater experiments. Sylvia has worked so much in the sea that she has made personal friends with dolphins.

Someday we might be able to travel under the ocean. We will look at magnificent creatures, see the majestic formations, and maybe pick up some fascinating seashells. If we travel into the sea, it will be because of courageous explorers who went before us.

When we go to heaven, it will be because Jesus Christ has gone there first. He is now willing to lead us to that same heaven if we believe in Him.

Even when walking through the dark valley of death I will not be afraid, for you are close beside me, guarding, guiding all the way.

PSALM 23:4 (TLB)

Do You Remember?

1. Who was the first astronaut and aquanaut?

2. Who invented the aqualung?

3. Who guides us to heaven? What do we need to do?

Thanks, Lord Jesus, for guiding us through life and death.

36 Robins Are Good Parents

The beautiful red-breasted robin is one of the most loved birds in the United States and Canada. They visit lawns and backyards all over the country.

Robins are probably most famous for their ability to pull worms out of the ground. They do a slick job of it. No other creature does it quite as well.

These friendly birds aren't limited to worm dinners, though. They also enjoy a fresh caterpillar, a wriggly spider, or a poky snail. Robins can destroy some crops, like cherries, but their help far outweighs the damage they may do.

Robins are strictly fair-weather fowl. When the autumn winds turn cool, robins head south. The spring daylight will call them to travel thousands of miles again to their homes.

The best place to see robins moving north is along the Mississippi River. They fly low over homes and farms. They push hard each day, as some have to get all the way to Alaska.

When a robin returns to my neighborhood, it is looking for my house on Ninth Street. The father robin can remember the area he left six or seven months ago. He arrives before the mother so he can reclaim his old grounds. Some fighting may go on as new birds try to find a nesting place.

During this time the male sings loudly. His song says this is his land and others should stay away. Father robin is getting ready to raise his family.

When the mother robin arrives, she has a busy job ahead. She needs to build a strong nest to hold her eggs and new chicks. The male will help collect materials, but the female will gather most of them.

The nest is built like a bowl. It is usually a three-stage operation. The outer part is made of sticks and twigs. An inner lining is made of mud. If no mud can be found, the mother will take dry earth in her beak and dunk it in water. The final step is making a soft cushion of tender grass.

She is a good mother, looking out for her young.

Two or three times she will lay eggs in this nest. It may take twenty hours for a baby robin to break open its shell. The mother sits tight. There are some things a chick must do for itself.

Both mother and father get busy feeding the helpless newcomers. They have to collect food quickly to avoid cats, which love to catch robins.

Often storms will throw baby robins from their nests. Usually the best way to help them is to leave them alone. They are difficult to feed, but the mother robin will try to find them and bring them food.

Robins are "only" birds, but they work hard at being excellent parents. Sometimes we forget how much our parents work for us. They not only earn money, but they also provide our food and clothing. We like to complain, but most of us have terrific parents.

Children, obey your parents in the Lord, for this is right. "Honor your father and mother"—which is the first commandment with a promise—"that it may go well with you and that you may enjoy long life on the earth."

EPHESIANS 6:1–3 (NIV)

1. What does a male robin do when he finds his home?

2. What is the mother's job?

3. Give three reasons why you are glad for your parents.

Those who have good parents are wealthy and sometimes don't realize it.

37 How Dumb Are Donkeys?

I f you would like a donkey for a pet, don't worry about not having enough space. There is one type of donkey that grows only thirty inches tall. It never gets as tall as a yardstick and can be fun to keep.

Donkeys are strong, tough-skinned animals that used to do a large share of people's work. They usually stand three to five feet at the shoulders and like to keep to themselves. People aren't their favorite friends, so they stay away if they can. Even during hot, dry seasons, when donkeys become terribly thirsty, they will still avoid humans.

The donkey is something of a family creature. Its family, called a *troop*, isn't like ours. Usually a troop consists of a father (called a stallion), several mothers, and a handful of youngsters. A troop will consist of ten to twelve donkeys.

The stallion takes his job seriously. He is the great protector of the troop. The father makes sure everyone in his "family" is safe from harm.

Generally speaking, the donkey has only two enemies. The first one is humans. People hunt donkeys, so their number has gone down greatly. The donkey's second problem is the wolf. Donkeys have nothing to fear if they stay together. But if one wanders off or gets lost, a wolf could catch it.

If most donkeys had their way, they would stay in the hot, dry land. They might enjoy the mountains but still prefer them to be dry.

Mules and donkeys aren't the same animal, but they are related.

67

A mule is an odd animal. It is the product of a father donkey and a mother horse. The result is a tough, strong, and somewhat intelligent animal.

Mules can carry two hundred to three hundred pounds. They get along better in hot weather and are less likely to overeat or drink. Mules aren't picky eaters and can gulp down almost anything. They will also put up with more from a careless owner.

In many areas mules have been more valuable than horses. George Washington thought mules were just the animal a young nation needed.

The biggest problem with a mule is that it can't have baby mules. There is only one way to have a mule: There must be a donkey parent and a horse parent. Mules cannot reproduce themselves.

In the southwestern United States and Mexico, there is a small donkey called the burro. Many of them live in the wild and roam the deserts.

Some people look at donkeys as pickup trucks. They are small and stocky and can carry heavy loads for long distances.

But dumb? That's another matter. In some ways they are smarter than people.

The prophet Isaiah put it clearly. He said the donkey knows who its master is. People aren't always as intelligent. Often we forget about our God and Creator. We begin to go our own way and ignore God. In this case, who is really dumb—the donkey or the person?

An ox knows its master, and a donkey knows where its owner feeds it, but the people of Israel do not know me; my people do not understand.

Isaiah 1:3 (ncv)

Do You Remember?

1. What is a mule?

2. What is a stallion?

3. How are donkeys sometimes smarter than people?

Thanks for reminding us that we have a Master in heaven.

38 The Bad-Name Lion

When the early pioneers crossed America, they found large numbers of lions. They weren't the huge cats from Africa, but they were their relatives.

The cougar, or mountain lion, was one of the most famous cats they found. It was an animal with a strange scream, which put fear into anyone who heard it.

Over the centuries, cougars have probably lived all across the nation. They like rocky areas with plenty of places to hide. Normally they are happy hunting small game. Often, their dinner consists of just a bird.

When small animals are hard to find, cougars attack deer and sometimes farm stock. They have killed sheep, cattle, and horses. Usually cougars drag a large victim to another spot and cover the body, and eat the animal over several days.

In spite of its rough reputation, the cougar is a thoughtful mother. She might give birth to five cubs every year, and she guards them carefully. For the first seven months she feeds them her own milk. When they get older, she brings them bones and meat.

It will often be two years before she lets them loose.

The cougar played a large part in the life of some Native American tribes. Apaches had great respect for the frightening scream of the mountain lion. They believed this sound meant someone was going to die. They used cougar paws to chase away evil spirits. Pictures of cougars were painted on the walls of caves in hopes of getting kind treatment.

White men did not have the same regard for the cougar; they hunted them. Today, few cougars exist, and most of them live in hard-to-reach sections of the country.

Cougars are dwindling in numbers because they have a bad reputation. Some of the stories about them are true. They have killed farm animals, and they probably have killed humans at some time. There are also a large number of false stories told about them. Most of us cannot separate the truth from the folklore. Cougars have such bad names that people continue to kill them even if they aren't sure why.

Sometimes people have a hard time separating the truth from lies too. If you get into trouble at school, you'll quickly get a bad name, and people won't know if they can trust you. Then you might get blamed for things you didn't do. But that can happen easily once you get a bad reputation.

Few things in life are as important as a good name. It has to be earned by good behavior.

A good reputation is more valuable than the most expensive perfume.

Ecclesiastes 7:1 (**tlb**)

Do You Remember?

1. How long does a cougar stay with its mother?

2. How long does a mother feed her young her own milk?

3. Describe someone you know who has a "good" name.

I want to live in such a way that I can be trusted.

39 The Bug That Eats Wood

We can only guess how much damage a termite does. Every day these busy little insects are eating wood from homes, sheds, barns, garages, and offices. They do hundreds of thousands of dollars' worth of destruction every day in the United States.

A man in Seattle was sitting in his kitchen, leaning on the table. Suddenly it collapsed, throwing him to one side. Termites had eaten their way through the floor.

Termites will attack some living trees, but mostly they enjoy a good snack on dead wood. A few prefer it wet, but most want it crunchy-dry.

This is a strange insect because it eats something that isn't healthy for it. There is something in wood called *cellulose*. A termite's stomach can't digest it. But there is a tiny creature, so small it can be seen only with a microscope, that lives in the termite. This one-celled organism eats the cellulose so the termite can get nourishment from it. Otherwise the termite would be eating wood and getting sick.

Termites are excellent at finding wood. It is possible that they can even smell it. Some types can dig under the ground and travel over one hundred feet. When they decide to come up, it will be directly under a tree.

One species of termite starts out in a quiet way. A female and male will dig into a piece of wood. They then make a glue and close up the hole. The queen starts immediately to lay eggs. Their family starts to grow and the children begin to eat the wood. Sometimes the family increases slowly. By the time the owner discovers the termites, his furniture will be practically wrecked by the little creatures.

The oddest termites live in Australia. The queen termite lays as many as three million eggs every year. She may live for twenty-five years. In her lifetime, this termite queen could lay 75 million eggs. To do this, her body has to swell to a gigantic size.

The biggest enemy to the termite is the ant. Termites are usually afraid of this pesky relative. Some termites fight off ants with a sticky glue that comes out of the top of their heads. Ants get stuck in it and are left helpless.

When termites get inside a piece of wood, it may look solid. But it is being destroyed without our knowing it. The Bible says a person who is proud is also hurting himself and doesn't know it.

Most of us like to brag. You might say you are the best, the fastest, the smartest. But someday you are going to get hurt. People will stop being your friends. Someone will outrun you or get a better grade. It is good to be honest about your ability. You'll get hurt by bragging.

Pride ends in destruction; humility ends in honor.
Proverbs 18:12 (TLB)

Do You Remember?

1. How do termites digest the cellulose they eat?

2. How many eggs can a queen termite lay?

3. How can we lose our friends?

Keep us from bragging.

40 The Huge Sun

The sun doesn't look too large hanging in the sky. If I put a quarter up to my eye, the entire sun is blocked out. This is merely the way it looks. The sun is so big that it is difficult for us to comprehend.

We know how large the earth is. It is so big we will never visit most of it. There are a few parts that haven't even been studied well.

The earth would be just a small speck against the sun. The sun is so large that the earth could be placed in it over 1,250,000 times.

This tells only part of the story. The sun is a star, and not even a big one! It is medium sized. Half of the stars around it are even bigger. Space is enormous, and we have only begun to study it. The sun is only one of the one hundred billion stars in the Milky Way.

The sun is a great help to the earth. It supplies heat and light. The sun is so powerful that in one second it can give off all the energy humans have used from the beginning of time. In one second!

We get most of our light from the gas surrounding the sun. It is about two hundred miles deep.

The sun is so hot that we couldn't even begin to get close to it. If a small dot were as hot as the middle of the sun, the heat from the dot would be strong enough to kill a horse standing one hundred miles from it. Naturally, this is impossible, but the illustration shows us the tremendous heat of the sun.

We are in no danger from the sun because it hangs 93 million miles away from us. In early July it is actually 94 million miles away.

There is some concern that the sun will burn out. If it does, the people on earth could be in serious trouble. But this isn't a problem that should keep you awake tonight. If the sun does burn out, it will take at least five billion years to turn to ashes.

One of the most colorful sights in nature is to watch a beautiful evening sunset. If you can see it in the country, it looks like melted butter and syrup. That sunset should be a good reminder to us. If you are angry about something, take care of the problem before the sun goes down.

Sometimes we can't help getting upset. A person may have cheated us or told a lie. But don't carry around a chip on your shoulder. If you stay angry, it might begin to make you a mean person. Drop your anger before the sun goes down.

If you are angry, don't sin by nursing your grudge. Don't let the sun go down with you still angry—get over it quickly.

EPHESIANS 4:26 (TLB)

Do You Remember?

1. How long would it take the sun to turn to ashes?

2. How much bigger is the sun than the earth?

3. What should we do with anger?

Help us control our anger before it hurts us.

41 Snake Stories

Has anyone ever told a story about you that wasn't true? That really hurt, didn't it? Sometimes the stories get passed around, and soon people think you actually did it.

For hundreds of years snakes have suffered from the same problem. They don't know it, but false stories are often spread about them.

Some of the stories we hear about snakes are true. Snakes can be poisonous, but nine out of ten snakes are harmless. Some snakes can swallow a victim larger than their mouth: An Asia python can gulp down an entire small deer.

Snakes can be amazing tree climbers. Black snakes can race through the top part of bushes as fast as they can move on the ground.

Do snakes lay eggs, or do they give birth to their young alive? Both are true. Most snakes hatch from eggs; about one-fourth are born straight from the mother.

Most false stories probably started because people are afraid of snakes. Because of fear, it is easy to stretch the truth and imagine things that we don't see.

Someone started a rumor about the coral king snake. It is often called the milk snake. The name started when a person reportedly saw a king snake climb a cow's leg and milk the creature. There is no truth to this, but people still tell it as fact.

Mud snakes have long had an odd story told about them. They sleep in a neat circle that looks like a wheel, so for years people have claimed the mud snake can put its tail in its mouth and chase people like a hoop or wheel.

That's not the only rumor about the mud snake. Some claim it has a poisonous sting in its tail, but this is far from the truth. If it is frightened, a mud snake might shake its tail in a menacing way, but it's only bluffing. The tail can do no more damage than a string.

There are plenty more myths about misunderstood reptiles. Snake charmers do not really control snakes by music; snakes are deaf and merely follow the movement of the charmer's head. If you kill a snake, its mate will *not* hunt you. A snake's tongue is harmless. If a snake is seriously wounded, it does not always wait until sundown to die. Most snakes will not attack a human if they can avoid it. A snake is just as afraid of us as most of us are of it.

74

Life is filled with rumors and half-truths. Often we aren't sure just what to believe. False stories hurt snakes, and some snakes are killed unnecessarily. Lies hurt people. Many lose friends and jobs because false stories are spread around. Jesus Christ had lies told about Him when He was on earth.

Before you talk about anyone, you should ask two questions: Is it true? Is it kind?

Lie not one to another.

COLOSSIANS 3:9 (KJV)

Do You Remember?

1. How did the milk snake get its name?

2. Name some false stories about snakes.

3. What two questions should you ask yourself before you talk about anyone?

Help us to say good things about people.

42 Apartments in the Forest

A rain forest isn't exactly an apartment building, but in many ways it seems like one. Filled with hundreds of monkeys, lizards, birds, jaguars, butterflies, sloths, snakes, and other creatures, it is packed with living species.

My wife, Pat, and I visited a rain forest in Costa Rica and were happily surprised. We were afraid it was going to be a place where animals lived but we wouldn't see them. But not only did we see a large assortment of wildlife, we heard their noises quite clearly!

We heard monkeys chattering at the top of their voices. There were birds singing and calling out to friends. We didn't hear the snakes, but we knew they were there.

Certain creatures live on the ground floor of the rain forest "apartment" and seldom go very high into the trees. Other animals roam around in the middle section without going up or down much. Still others have their living spaces in the tops of the trees. A few members of the top group might spend their entire lives up in the roof area.

A rain forest apartment building has all kinds of characters living there. Love birds coo away their time talking softly to each other. Butterflies dress beautifully as they flutter around. Howler monkeys talk loudly

75

and might keep some creatures awake. Earthworms crawl around on the ground eating leaves.

Of all the "apartment" dwellers, the Jesus lizard is one of the easiest to remember. This little guy's light weight and excellent speed allow it to run on top of the water a short distance.

Every once in a while I remember that Jesus really did walk on a lake. Not because He had flat feet or because He ran across the water. His disciples saw Him walking on the surface, and He didn't sink.

Jesus Christ is the Son of God and can do all kinds of miracles. If nature has a funny lizard and its actions remind me of how great Christ is, I'm glad I haven't forgotten.

During the fourth watch of the night Jesus went out to them, walking on the lake. When the disciples saw him walking on the lake, they were terrified. "It's a ghost," they said, and cried out in fear.

MATTHEW 14:25–26 (NIV)

Do You Remember?

1. Name one place you can find a rain forest.

2. How is a rain forest like an apartment building?

3. How was Jesus able to walk on water?

The Son of God is greater than nature.

43 The Masked Bandit

Be sure to lock your doors tonight. If you don't, you could get a visit from a sneaky raccoon. These small animals can work a doorknob, and once inside they take what they want.

A raccoon's hands are small and move easily. It can open your refrigerator and take out the jelly. Don't be too surprised if the raccoon robs the cookie jar and dunks sweets in milk. Raccoons aren't choosy; they will eat almost anything. If they are thirsty, they will turn on your faucet.

Expanding cities don't seem to bother the black-masked animal. Some have been found in downtown New York. Raccoons cross bridges at night to raid garbage cans.

Raccoons' ability to change has kept their numbers high. They would rather live in the forest but can get along in most places. Farmers aren't too happy with them because they steal corn and chickens.

If a raccoon could be given a test, it probably wouldn't prove to be very intelligent. But the raccoon is so clever that it can get away with almost anything. Some raccoons make beautiful pets.

When there is no danger close by, raccoons love to play. They are natural clowns trying to make life a game. It is almost as if they are trying to see how much they can get away with. Yet they have a healthy respect for their parents. When a baby raccoon gets out of line, the mother gives it a strong smack.

It would be a mistake to think of raccoons as just show-offs. They have a nasty bite and are terrific fighters. The masked bandit can triumph against a dog twice its size. If a raccoon traps a dog near water, it is strong enough to drown its attacker.

Raccoons' favorite foods are often found in water. They rest by a stream and watch for crayfish and minnows. Raccoons are also excellent swimmers.

With this type of personality, you can imagine how much raccoons enjoy a campsite. They will sneak in at night and steal practically any food left out. In the morning only open buckets and paper wrappers remain.

Raccoons can also be tender and loving. As with most animals, the mother takes good care of her young, which are called *kits*. If a mother raccoon dies, another mother will adopt the children.

Many people think of the raccoon as a favorite pet. Some even think it should be our national pet. The biggest problem with this furry creature is its constant stealing. It has no respect for the property of others.

In this way the raccoon is like too many people. It is easy to pick up something lying around. We think no one is going to miss it. We know it isn't ours, but we take it anyway.

Stealing is always wrong. We know how we feel when someone takes our things. God wants us to protect each other's property.

He who has been stealing must steal no longer.

EPHESIANS 4:28 (NIV)

Do You Remember?

1. What will a raccoon do in a house?

2. How do they treat orphan raccoons?

3. Have you ever had something stolen from you? How did you feel?

It is wrong to take what is not mine.

44 Getting Away From Winter

When the cold winds begin to blow, many animals have to find a place to hide. Their bodies aren't made to live in the deep freeze. They also run short of food. When the leaves and grass are buried under ice or snow, hunting becomes hard.

To get away, some animals will go to sleep. Bears, opossums, and skunks decide to take a nap. On a nice, warm day they might get up and go for a walk. This isn't hibernating, but merely taking a long sleep.

Other animals go into a deep sleep and their bodies change. This is called hibernating. Woodchucks, bats, and some rattlesnakes are among those that hibernate. An animal's heart may beat three hundred times every minute when it is busy looking for food or building a home. In hibernation, its heartbeat drops to about four per minute.

The woodchuck is a good example. When it hibernates, its heart beats only once every five minutes. Most people would think it is dead.

Children who want to investigate hibernation will want to visit bat caves. These are usually cool places. The hibernating bat hangs upside down and its body temperature drops. It is only a degree or two above freezing. But don't handle one or let too much light into the room. Bats that are disturbed can wake up and take off.

A few types of woodchucks get their hibernation backward. If the summer gets hot, the yellow marmot decides to find a comfortable bed. This is called *aestivation* and allows the animal to beat the heat.

Sooner or later all of us go into a deep sleep. It is something like hibernation, but we call it death.

When the Bible tries to explain death, it compares it to a heavy sleep. We close our eyes in death and open them to see Jesus Christ. It is much like going to sleep in your mother's bed and waking up in your own.

Like hibernation, there is much we don't know about dying. But we do know that death for the Christian means going to be with Jesus Christ.

For if we believe that Jesus died and rose again, even so them also which sleep in Jesus will God bring with him.

1 Thessalonians 4:14 (KJV)

Do You Remember?

1. Do bears hibernate?

2. How slowly may an animal's heart beat per minute in hibernation?

3. What are the hardest and the best parts about death?

Christ has made death a victory for the Christian.

45 Don't Drink the Water

Few people are as far from drinking water as the man in a lifeboat on the ocean. As one poet has said, "Water, water everywhere, but not a drop to drink."

What would happen if this lone human started drinking the salty seawater? He would soon find his thirst growing greater rather than less. If he continued to drink, he would become terribly sick. He might even become delirious. After a while his kidneys would stop working. Finally he would die.

Man is unable to drink seawater because it contains approximately 3.5 percent salt. While this may sound like only a small amount, it is enough to be very dangerous.

The ocean is a fascinating collection of minerals that we can't see. In one cubic mile of ocean water there are over 2 tons of nickel, 235 tons of iodine, and 38 pounds of gold. Before we start mining the seawater, however, one thing should be remembered. We would have to "mine" one million gallons before we removed one penny's worth of gold.

How did all these minerals become a part of the seawater? Water doesn't come out of the sky with salt in it. In fact, when man catches rainwater, he has a fairly pure liquid, although it may pick up some substance from the polluted air.

After it reaches earth, water picks up minerals from several sources. It runs down mountains, curves through riverbeds, and washes across plains. During its journey to the ocean, it collects many samples of different minerals. Then, when it has run its course to the ocean, the minerals have few places to go, so they settle to the ocean floor.

Already waiting for it are large salt deposits. They are resting on the floor, where they have flavored the sea for years. The Gulf of Mexico has a huge salt dome stretching its shoulders for five miles.

Researchers are spending large amounts of money in order to discover how to take salt out of the water. If they are successful, irrigation will be possible in many areas of the world that are now dry.

In some ways, people are like ocean water. We need to have our lives changed. Selfishness, anger, and every type of sin are as dangerous to us as drinking salt water. God wants to take these things out of us and put His goodness into us. This change can happen to anyone. People have given their lives to Jesus Christ and asked Him to change them. Only He can do this.

We are beginning to change salty water to fresh, but God has been making selfish people into kind people for a long time.

Can you pick olives from a fig tree, or figs from a grape vine? No, and you can't draw fresh water from a salty pool. If you are wise, live a life of steady goodness so that only good deeds will pour forth.

JAMES 3:12–13 (TLB)

80

1. Name some minerals that are in the ocean.

2. What would happen if you drank very much ocean water?

3. Do you know someone who has become a Christian? How was this person changed?

We thank you, God, for new life in Christ.

46 The Biggest Cat

The next time you are playing with a kitten, remember this: This cat has relatives that are fourteen feet long and weigh over five hundred pounds. Don't worry about them coming for a visit, though, since most tigers live in Asia.

Tigers would rather stay away from people. Their meetings have usually been sad for both man and animal. Over the years, tigers have killed thousands of people. Work on the Chinese Eastern Railway had to be stopped because tigers were killing too many workers.

Humans haven't been too kind to this beautiful cat. Tigers have been hunted for their furs and blood. Some believe tiger blood is a helpful medicine. Others have killed this cat simply out of fear.

Though it is a big animal, the tiger is as quiet as a cotton ball. When looking for food, it can move through thick brush without a sound. Tigers are looking for practically anything—from giant elephants to river fish.

Their hunt for food is no small order. A tiger needs fifteen pounds of meat every day. If one attacks a large animal, it could eat fifty pounds at one sitting. Tigers will stay by a fallen deer and eat for several days.

The tiger has a beautiful fur. Some have a rich orange color with dark black stripes crossing their bodies. Others are a light color coming close to white.

Tigers give birth to two to four babies at a time, and they stay at their mother's side for about a year. Tigers prefer to live alone but aren't unfriendly. When two meet, they might stop, lightly rub cheeks, and then move on.

The life of a tiger isn't easy. Even with its size, speed, and hunting ability, food is hard to catch. Because of its huge body, the tiger has to search for food most of the time. It hunts at night and hides by a water hole during the day. Sometimes tigers go a week without catching any food.

The Son of God is important to each of us. We need to know more about His life, death, and resurrection. He told us we can know Him better by searching the Bible. It's the best way to find out more about our friend and Savior, Jesus Christ.

You search the Scriptures, for you believe they give you eternal life. And the Scriptures point to me!

JOHN 5:39 (TLB)

Do You Remember?

82

1. Where do tigers live?

2. Why are their numbers going down?

3. Name three things you know about Jesus Christ.

When we learn more about Christ, we learn more about God.

47 Hidden in the Trees

Hiking through a park, my companion quietly told me, "Look over there."

"Where?" I whispered.

"Under those trees."

Then I could see it. Three sets of beautiful dark eyes were staring back at me. Silently, three deer sat motionless. They did not rise to run.

One of the things wildlife does best is hide. An animal can blend right in with a tree. A polar bear resting on the snow can barely be detected by the human eye.

Animals know that one of the safest things they can do is to not be seen. Zebras, for instance, can defend themselves, but they would rather let their black-and-white stripes blend into the evening dusk.

Chameleons are excellent at hiding. They can control their color by blending into the color of the material around them. If a chameleon is on a green leaf, its body chemistry goes right to work. A mixture of yellow and blue in its body comes together to create a green color just like the leaf it is standing on.

These changes are made automatically and quickly. In a matter of seconds, the chameleon turns from yellow to brown. Sometimes the chameleon will change color for no other reason than it wants to meet a boyfriend or girlfriend. If it believes the occasion calls for dashing green, *Presto!* it takes on a different look.

People aren't so different. We can't change into purple people, but we do a little adjusting. If we are frightened, some of us turn pale or white. When we get caught doing something wrong or we are embarrassed, our faces could turn red or pink. Our lips could tremble or our eyes get wide when we are frightened. That's why we might hide our faces so no one will know how we feel.

Hiding our faces works better with people than it does with God. If we do something wrong or something good, God can see it inside our hearts. Putting our hands over our faces or pulling a blanket over our heads won't keep God from seeing the truth.

That's good. We can enjoy life much better if we don't try to hide our feelings from the God who loves us.

You know my folly, O God; my guilt is not hidden from you.
PSALM 69:5 (NIV)

Do You Remember?

1. How do zebras hide?

2. How long does a chameleon take to change color?

3. Why can we be glad that God sees our hearts?

Thank you for knowing who I really am.

48 The Eight-Armed Swimmer

Did you ever try to shake hands with an octopus? If you did, you would have at least eight of them to shake. But stay away from the ones near the Antarctic. Some of them have forty arms.

There are many strange stories told about the funny-looking octopus, and most of them are true. For instance, there are large octopuses that measure thirty-two feet across the arms. They would stretch the length of some houses. Fortunately, they aren't often found. Twelve inches in diameter is the usual size.

Normally the octopus doesn't care to fight. Hiding is its first choice. But when cornered, the octopus can put up a terrific fight. One type, living near Australia, has enough poison to kill a human being. Should a person get tangled in octopus arms, he or she could easily be drowned.

Part of an octopus's ability is to change colors. When one hides in seaweed, it looks just like the seaweed. In a minute it can become the same color as a rock. Even an old machine will be an excellent hiding place. One octopus can turn the same color as rust.

It has often been said that the octopus is a cannibal. That means it eats other octopuses. This is only half the story. Some will even eat themselves. One might start munching on its own arm—and eat another one for dessert. Octopuses don't usually do this unless they are old and near death. But if given enough time, the arm will grow back. Even a wounded eye can mend itself.

A mother octopus has many babies. A female might lay fifty thousand eggs at one sitting. Few of these will ever become adults.

There are many sea creatures that enjoy octopuses and octopus eggs. The laying of eggs marks the end of the female's life. She dies soon afterward.

When in good health, the octopus can move quickly. It hurries backward through the water. It can suck water into its body and push the water out through a tube. The water leaving the body makes the octopus move backward rapidly.

One of the oddest features of the eight-armed monster is its ability to shoot ink. When in trouble, it gives off a dark liquid. This is all part of the octopus's disappearing act. The large cloud of ink hides the octopus while it finds a deep hole or underwater bush.

It would be fun if all of us could just disappear when we wanted to. We could shoot up a cloud and blot ourselves out. This would come in handy after we had broken a dish or come home late.

God has given us a better way. When we do something wrong and are sorry, He promises to blot it out. He won't remember it anymore. That is the kind of loving God He is.

Repent ye therefore, and be converted, that your sins may be blotted out.

ACTS 3:19 (KJV)

Do You Remember?

1. What does an octopus shoot out?

2. What are some colors an octopus can become?

3. What does God do with our sins?

Thanks for making my sins disappear.

49 Flying Animals

You can relax. There probably are no snakes flying over your house right now. But don't say it absolutely definitely could not happen somewhere.

There is a snake that flies. The paradise tree snake has no wings, and it actually does more gliding than flying. But it does leave a tree branch and sail through the air.

Moving quickly across a series of tree branches, the flying snake takes off in pursuit of its food. As it leaves the tree, the snake's body flattens out and goes into an S shape. By making its body wider, the snake is able to spread out like a kite and travel several feet through the air. Landing on an unsuspecting victim, this skydiving reptile is soon eating a lizard burger.

Most of us have heard of flying fish. The butterfly fish of Africa can dart out of the water and glide for six feet before landing again. But what about the flying squirrel?

A flying squirrel has two parts that aid its ability to sail through space from tree to tree. First, its arms and legs stretch out like a cape. This allows the squirrel to remain airborne. Second, its large tail is used to control direction. Turn this way to make it go right. Turn the other way to go left.

These aren't the only "airplanes" to be found in the wild. There are flying frogs in Central America, and a few lizards may be able to do the same thing.

Amazingly, there are animals that have not yet been discovered. Maybe a few more flying or gliding creatures will be seen in the jungles, the sea, or the mountains.

Like birds, these unlikely animals have two reasons to fly: Either they are trying to catch their food, or they need to escape.

Each of us is going to be tempted to do some terrible things. We might want to lie or steal. Maybe we feel like cheating or starting a fight. Those are the times when we need to spread our arms and legs like a frog or a squirrel and get out of there.

We can't exactly fly, but there is a time to get moving. Escaping from a bad or dangerous situation can be the really smart thing to do.

Flee the evil desires of youth, and pursue righteousness, faith, love and peace, along with those who call on the Lord out of a pure heart.

2 Timothy 2:22 (niv)

Do You Remember?

1. Name two animals that can fly.

2. How does the paradise tree snake fly?

3. Have you ever been in a bad situation and are glad you "flew" out of there?

Don't be too proud to get out of there if you need to.

50 The Seven-Hundred-Pound Racer

Be careful when walking on ice. Some of it is so thin that you'll crash right through it. Yet a half-ton polar bear can run across the same ice and not even break it. Its speed and balance allow this white monster to do things humans can't match.

Not only are they light on their feet, but polar bears are fast. Normally they don't chase people, but if they get hungry enough, no one is safe. They can sprint up to twenty-five miles an hour.

Polar bears are good on ice and snow, but they're even better in the freezing water. A polar bear might hitch a ride on a floating iceberg or swim through the sea. Some of them enjoy the water so much that they spend most of their life afloat.

The polar bear's color makes it difficult to see. It lies flat on the ice and crawls close to its victim. When the polar bear gets close enough, it makes a sudden lunge, and the seal is finished. The polar bear's favorite food is seal, which has little chance against the white ghost.

Part of the bears' quickness comes from the nonskid soles on their feet. Also, they have lived so long in the frozen Arctic that they don't have snow blindness. Therefore, very little gets away from them.

Mother bear has her cubs venture out of the den in March. They wander in search of food. By summer, the cute little things will weigh over two hundred pounds and be ready to face life alone.

Papa bear isn't a big sleeper. The night is one of his favorite times for hunting food. He can pick up a scent and follow it for miles to find food.

Most polar bears have beautiful fur, but if the polar bear were red or green, its life would change. Its victims would see it coming and most could get away.

The psalm writer was thinking about his own life and the things he had done wrong. His sins were like dark spots on his life. He asked God to forgive him and take the marks away. When God forgives our sins, we become whiter than the fresh snow—even whiter than a polar bear.

Sprinkle me with the cleansing blood and I shall be clean again. Wash me and I shall be whiter than snow.

PSALM 51:7 (TLB)

Do You Remember?

1. How fast can a polar bear run?

2. What is its favorite food?

3. What happens if we tell God about our sin and ask Him to forgive us?

Thanks for forgiving and forgetting my sins.

51 The Vampire Insect

It isn't easy to get away from mosquitoes. They live in every part of the world except the ice lands surrounding the North and South Poles. They live almost everywhere people do.

No one knows how many mosquitoes there are. So far, over twenty-five hundred different kinds have been identified and named.

We know about mosquitoes because they like to bite people and animals. But only the female will bite a living creature. Only one type goes after human blood, another bites only animals, and a third prefers blood from birds.

The male mosquito never sucks blood. He has the same mouth as the female but would rather get food from plants.

When a female mosquito bites a human, she sticks a tube into the skin, which shoots juice into the body. This stops the blood from getting sticky, and then the blood flows out quickly. The juice is what makes the mosquito bite itch so bad.

This same juice often carries diseases. In some countries, large numbers of people have died from malaria and yellow fever, which are carried by the mosquito. But don't fear—the diseases are under control in the United States and many other nations.

The female mosquito needs blood for her eggs. The blood helps the eggs grow and become stronger.

Mosquitoes multiply near water. Most of them lay their eggs in areas where there are many plants and weeds. Some will select a still body of water, like a pond or lake. Others enjoy the shore of a fast-moving stream. If there are no plants around, empty cans or old tires will do as well.

Mosquitoes go through four stages of growth: the egg, larva, pupa, and adult. The first three stages take place almost entirely in or near water. The adult stage is spent in the air.

Probably the most well-known feature of mosquitoes is their bite. Often they land on the back of the arm or leg, where it is hard to see them.

Sometimes people are like mosquitoes. We say unkind and cruel things behind someone's back. It is a mean habit, and many of us do it. The Bible calls this backbiting. When people aren't around, we talk about them. Often we do far more harm than a mosquito.

We don't like it when people gossip about us. The best example we can set is to refuse to say bad things about others.

I am afraid that I will not be what you want me to be. I am afraid that among you there may be arguing, jealousy, anger, selfish fighting, evil talk, gossip, pride, and confusion.

2 Corinthians 12:20 (icb)

Do You Remember?

1. How many different kinds of mosquitoes are there?

2. How many stages do they go through?

3. Do you gossip about people? How can you set a better example of a Christian?

There are so many kind things to say. Help us to say them.

52 The Lizard Family

Lizards have some of the strangest habits in all of nature. They come in different colors and sizes. Their lifestyle is often amazing.

One good example is the horned toad. Despite its name, the horned toad really is a lizard. These lizards are harmless, and children enjoy catching them. One type of horned toad has an ugly habit. When excited or angry, it can shoot blood out of its eye. A couple squirts of this and most people will put it down.

The horned toad has a relative called the collared lizard, which has four legs but doesn't always use all of them. When the collared lizard is in a big hurry, it raises up on its back two legs and runs at top speed. It looks like a bike popping a wheelie. Its name comes from the black marks on its neck that look like a collar.

The chuckwalla is the largest North American lizard. It measures up to fifteen inches long. Like most lizards, this one has its own means of defense. It normally hides among rocks. If an enemy attempts to pull it out, the chuckwalla enlarges its lungs. This "balloon" is then too big to pull out of its hole. In most cases the enemy gives up and leaves.

Usually lizards are quiet creatures. The colorful gecko lizard is the oddball. It earns its name by saying something that sounds like "gecko, gecko."

No lizard is more bewildering than the skink. Some types of skinks have a tail that looks like the head. A hawk will dive, thinking it is aiming at the lizard's head, but suddenly the skink will run in the opposite direction.

An anole (ah-KNOW-lee) has still another odd ability. If an enemy grabs the anole by the tail, this lizard can simply disconnect it. The unhappy villain is left disappointed.

Anoles are often mistakenly called chameleons, probably because both types of lizards are able to change colors. They can be green or brown, depending on their surroundings, the temperature, and their mood.

We aren't lizards, but someday Christians will change also. Our spirits will leave this earth and go into the presence of God. Then when Christ returns and raises the dead, our bodies will be changed—in a much greater way than the chameleon. We don't know what the change will be like, but it will be real.

In a moment, in the twinkling of an eye, at the last trump: for the trumpet shall sound, and the dead shall be raised incorruptible, and we shall be changed.

1 CORINTHIANS 15:52 (KJV)

Do You Remember?

1. How does the horned toad fight back?

2. How does a chuckwalla protect itself?

3. When will our bodies be changed?

Every part of our body will work well when we meet Jesus Christ in heaven.

53 Almost Like Us

Chimpanzees act a great deal like humans. When chimps grow old, they even get bald. They are easy to tame and have excellent memories. Like happy children, chimpanzees are extremely curious and excitable.

Even when it comes to colors, this animal seems to rise above the vision of other animals. Most creatures can see life in only a few shades of gray, but the chimp sees a large number of bright reds, greens, and yellows.

The female generally gives birth to one baby at a time. Her youngster will often stay at her side for as many as five years. Just like a human child, it loves to play games. Young chimps collect pieces of fruit and use them as toys.

When chimpanzees are old enough, they go out in search of food. This hunt may take them far from home. However, they enjoy their group, or large family, and return to it.

Most of the time chimps are looking for tasty leaves or fresh fruit. Once in a while they stop to eat a delicious bug.

If you want to see a chimpanzee outside of a zoo, you will probably have to travel to central or western Africa. There they live in the rain forests and spend most of their time in the trees.

Some people think chimps look a little like humans. They grow to five feet tall and weigh 180 pounds. Their faces are similar to humans. They show moods and emotions. When they get excited, chimps let out a loud hooting cry.

Chimps are hairy creatures; their bodies are almost entirely covered in hair.

A chimpanzee's arms and legs look like they are backward. It has long, powerful arms that seem to hang to the ground. Its legs are short and heavy. Most of the time a chimp walks on all four limbs, but sometimes it can stand up almost like a person.

This animal can't talk, but it can get its message across. Often they communicate by touching each other or by making signs with their hands.

If we were to make a list, we would see how much chimpanzees are like people. It is also interesting to see how different they are from us. A chimp can't do homework, cook a meal, or fix a bicycle.

The same thing happens when some people are "almost Christians." They are kind, helpful, and polite, but that doesn't make them Christians. Christians are people who trust Jesus Christ. They know Christ died for their sins. And they ask for forgiveness and cleansing.

For ye are all the children of God by faith in Christ Jesus.

GALATIANS 3:26 (KJV)

Do You Remember?

93

1. What do chimpanzees eat?

2. How are chimps like people?

3. How does someone become a Christian?

Thanks for inviting us to become the children of God.

54 Sunken Treasures

In 1692, nature shook the ground and dumped an entire city into the sea. On June 7, at 11:43 a.m., an earthquake hit Port Royal, Jamaica. A huge tidal wave brought tons of water on top of the town. Within thirty minutes the town was sitting on the bottom of the sea.

Sometimes nature gets out of control, and instead of helping humans, it hurts them. Two thousand people died in half an hour. It was one of the few cases in history where a city was thrown into the ocean all at once.

The city sunken under the sea has fascinated scientists. Divers have gone down and brought back gold, silver, bottles, cannons, and pipes.

One of the most interesting things recovered was an old watch. When they investigated it closely, scientists saw that the hands had stopped at 11:43, the time of the earthquake.

Finding sunken treasure is a dangerous and expensive operation. But still many people are looking for ships that went down years ago. Some places sell maps that show where ships probably are submerged.

Dr. Harold Edgerton, who grew up on the flat land of Aurora, Nebraska, helped greatly in underwater search. Dr. Edgerton invented a scanning sonar. When the sonar moved across the bottom of the ocean, it told the operator if there was something buried beneath the sand and mud.

Amazing wrecks are still being found. In 1960, Peter Throckmorton discovered a ship under eighty-five feet of water. The ship dated back to one thousand years before Christ. The date of the vessel was on the coins it was carrying.

Every once in a while sunken treasure is brought up in an unusual way. One group of busy treasure hunters are the fish that live there. They often swallow license plates, boots, watches, or silver cups.

More important treasures than these are in the ocean. Today a large number of submarines are moving beneath the surface. Once in a great while one gets stuck and can't come up. The navy is busy making ships that will go deep into the ocean to rescue submarine crews. This would be a dangerous job because of the pressure in the depths of the ocean, but such a ship would save many lives.

The ocean is so large and deep that it must hold many treasures long ago lost and forgotten.

One of the writers of the Bible wanted us to know God forgives our sins. He said it is just as if God threw our sins into the ocean. They are gone and forgotten. Speaking about God, he said:

You will tread our sins beneath your feet; you will throw them into the depths of the ocean!

MICAH 7:19 (TLB)

Do You Remember?

1. What happened to Port Royal?

2. What did Dr. Edgerton invent?

3. Why does the Bible compare our sins to the ocean?

Thanks for throwing away our sins and forgetting them.

55 The Underground Mole

Every person who has ever played in the dirt remembers how much fun it is to dig tunnels. Some of us made holes with our sticks and pretended they were homes. We made garages to park our small cars.

A chubby little creature called the mole does the same thing, but it isn't playing games. The mole spends almost all its life under the soft earth.

If a mole happens to come aboveground for a few minutes, it is practically lost. The mole has tiny eyes and can barely see at all. Most of its life, the mole doesn't have to see.

These diggers are especially built for earth moving. Their faces come to a point to help push through the ground. Their two front feet are extra large, for power. Completely covered, moles are actually swimming through the ground.

We don't often see moles, but it is easy to find their work. If a new lawn has a long, thin bump in it, it's likely a mole has been traveling through it.

Moles seem to enjoy snow. They can move rapidly through soft, cold flakes. The light and easy movement must feel particularly good to them.

While the mole digs through the ground, it is always looking for something to eat. Earthworms are especially tasty. Ants make an excellent dinner. Sometimes even a lizard is a tasty choice.

In March and April, baby moles are born. In America, moles usually build nests a foot or more underground. The babies are placed there until they are able to start digging for themselves.

The moles' relatives in Australia are just a little different. They have pouches for their babies. The young moles hold on inside and feed from their mothers.

If you are careful, you might be able to watch a mole work. When you see a lumpy tunnel on the ground, stand back a fair distance and look at it move. Don't get too close or the mole will feel your steps. When it does, it starts backing up as quickly as possible, using its tail as a guide.

During the days of the prophet Isaiah, some people owned little statues and pretended they were tiny gods. They would worship the statues, called idols, by bowing in front of them, praying to them, and offering burned grass or leaves. Isaiah said when we realize who the true God is, we can throw away the old statues. We can take them out and bury them and let the moles play with them.

Statues, or idols, cannot help us in any way. But our God is alive.

Then at last they will abandon their gold and silver idols to the moles and bats.

ISAIAH 2:20 (TLB)

Do You Remember?

1. Describe a mole's eyes.

2. What do moles eat?

3. Why is it useless to worship statues?

We have a great God who doesn't live in little statues or in the ground like a mole.

56 Wild Dogs

Dogs are some of the most popular animals in the world. They appear in a wide variety of breeds, from a gentle French poodle to the highly dangerous dhole (dole).

Some of the meanest dogs in the world are the Cape hunting dogs of South Africa. They even look cruel. A few times they have been tamed as pups, but as they grow older they usually get wild.

Cape dogs hunt in groups called packs. There might be as few as four, but there can be up to sixty in a pack. There is nothing they are afraid to attack. They can travel long distances just to capture an antelope and eat it.

They are greedy dogs and are continuously searching for food. The Cape dogs' hunting abilities are excellent. They can work in harmony to outsmart a victim. A few of the dogs might run ahead to cut off the path of an animal. Others will hurry alongside in case the victim tries to cut back. Then, as if well trained, the dogs will strike.

Cape hunters will have as many as twelve pups at a time. They build nests in the ground and live close to each other in colonies.

Dhole dogs are just as vicious. They live mostly in Russia, Korea, and the Indonesian island of Java. Like Cape hunters, they travel in packs. The stories of their fearlessness are often told. The dhole has attacked bears, and some believe this group has even killed tigers.

One of the strangest members of the dog family is the dingo, which lives in Australia. Dingoes look like dogs you might find in your neighborhood except for their pointed ears that refuse to lie down.

The natives who live in the bush may use dingoes as hunting dogs, but they aren't very good at it because many dingoes will run away the first chance they get.

The dingo is a dog without a bark. It can yelp or howl but cannot make a regular barking sound.

This dog is hated and hunted constantly. Farmers especially dislike dingoes because of the destruction they cause. Dingoes will attack sheep that they have no intention of eating. Their real problem is just greediness. The dingo wants more than it can use.

Most of us are like the dingo. Children and adults see so many things they would like to have. We spend a great deal of time getting things we can't really use. This is what greediness is. The person who learns to share has begun to fight greed.

And they are as greedy dogs, never satisfied.

Isaiah 56:11 (TLB)

Do You Remember?

1. How do Cape hunters work together?

2. What does the dhole dog attack?

3. Name one way in which we could share with others.

Thanks for sharing your only Son with us.

57 The Wasp Sting

Wipe the mud off your feet." Every child has heard this. Even adults sometimes forget and track mud into the house. Sometimes mud can only be called a mess, but other times it's great fun.

Children enjoy making mud pies or building little roads for toy cars. Older boys like to ride their dirt bikes and watch the mud spin off their wheels.

A certain type of wasp has enjoyed playing in the mud ever since it was an infant. In fact, the mud dauber wasp was born in dried mud. That is what its home was made of, and that is where the eggs were laid.

Mud daubers' homes can be seen on the roofs of old barns. Sometimes they are attached to the ceiling of an attic in a tall home.

The food of a mud dauber isn't anything special. It usually consists of fresh spider. The mother is the chief hunter. She swings down on the prey and stings it. The spider is paralyzed and easily carried back to the mud home. When the baby wasps break out of their eggs, they find a delicious supper stuck to their wall.

Mud daubers aren't the only wasps. Potter wasps don't make their homes out of dull mud. They carefully mix clay. The adult carries each tiny piece and attaches it to a tree branch. When the potter wasp is finished, it has a first-class home. Wind and rain have a tough time hurting this home.

Potter wasps would rather have fresh caterpillar for dinner than spiders. Young beetles also make a good meal.

This wasp looks dangerous to man but is really our friend. They eat insects that normally destroy fruit and vegetables.

The potter wasp also likes to pack its food on the walls of its home. When its egg and a caterpillar are placed neatly inside, the nest is sealed tightly. The new wasp develops inside its cell until it's strong enough to break out.

Don't look for every wasp nest on a ceiling or in a tree. The famous killer wasp makes its home in the ground. A full inch in length, it isn't afraid of its much larger enemies. In July and August, killer wasps attack the huge cicada.

This isn't the end of our search for wasp homes. One species of wasp lives inside a tree. The carpenter wasp can dig three or four inches into solid wood. Like its relatives, it also uses mud inside its home.

The stinger plays an important part in the wasp's life. Without it, wasps would be fairly harmless.

Almost everyone gets stung by a wasp or bee sooner or later. These stings can be terribly painful. Some people can even become sick from a wasp sting.

One of the hardest things we face is the death of a friend or relative. But the Bible says God sent Jesus Christ to help us. By giving us a place in heaven, He took the big sting out of death.

O death, where then your victory? Where then your sting?

1 Corinthians 15:55 (TLB)

Do You Remember?

1. How does a mud dauber wasp capture its food?

2. Where does a carpenter wasp live?

3. How does Jesus Christ change death?

Because Christ is alive, I can live with Him in heaven.

58 The Fastest Animal

The fastest animal on foot is the cheetah. It can run up to seventy miles an hour. After it runs a quarter of a mile, its speed cuts down considerably. But during that first sprint, nothing can outrun it.

To understand its speed, try this example: The next time you are in a car, ask the driver to tell you when the car gets to fifty-five miles per hour. When the automobile is going that fast, look out the window and imagine a cheetah passing the car. That is exactly what they can do.

Cheetahs can be terrible killers. They can also be tamed and kept as pets. The princes of India used to have them trained for hunting. Even as grown animals, cheetahs can be taught to obey commands.

Hoods are put on their heads until they arrive at the chosen fields. When the hood is removed, the cheetah will take off after its prey. It will then return to its trainer.

Cheetahs have beautiful black spots and are often confused with leopards. They have to be taught by their parents to hunt and kill. If taken as young cubs, cheetahs are not natural killers.

Despite its excellent speed, the cheetah prefers to use its head. A quiet hunter, it will sneak up on its victim. It glides slowly through the jungles until it is close to the animal. Then, without warning, it makes its move. Seldom does anything get away.

In some ways cheetahs are more like dogs than cats. They have long legs, a small head, and a call that sounds like a dog's. They are the only members of the cat family that can't draw in their claws.

Cheetahs prefer to eat antelope, gazelle, and other grazing animals. Usually they hunt in pairs or family groups.

There isn't much chance of a cheetah chasing most of us. (It wouldn't do any good to run; you might try hiding.) Cheetahs are found in Africa and India. Long ago they lived north of Israel, in Syria and Persia.

One of the happiest parts of being young is the ability to run. Those who are healthy enough can feel the breeze pushing through their hair. Your legs help you race, and you can imagine you are a cheetah.

Running is great for games. It comes in handy if you need to go for help. Some young people use running to get into trouble and try to get away.

One of the writers of the Bible thought about speed and about God. Wouldn't it be great if we were in a hurry to follow Jesus Christ, as if we could hardly wait to be like Him?

The Lord is a strong fortress. The godly run to him and are safe.

PROVERBS 18:10 (TLB)

Do You Remember?

1. How fast do cheetahs run?

2. What do they eat?

3. Who should we run after?

We are in a hurry for most things. Help us run to follow you.

59 Hatching Eggs

Every once in a while I see little blue-speckled eggs in my backyard. These are robin eggs that were blown out of their nests.

Do you ever wonder what a bird has to do to hatch a chick? It isn't easy, but the parent knows exactly how to handle the situation.

A bird controls the hatching by controlling the temperature of the eggs. Many eggs need a steady temperature of around ninety-nine degrees. Mother birds keep this warmth by sitting on the eggs and getting off at the right times.

If it is a hot day, the robin might spend only twenty minutes each hour on the eggs. When the night gets chilly, she may sit on the eggs all night.

We usually think that only a mother bird sits on her eggs, but this is only partly true. With some types, the father and mother take turns. A few species are accustomed to having only the father sit on the eggs.

The whole process becomes more tricky because of the need for food. Someone has to go "shopping" and at the same time not leave for too long.

Birds have bare patches underneath them to give warmth and to control the temperature of the nest. If necessary, they can push their bodies harder against the egg to give it more heat. The object is to get the egg warm through to its center. It takes around two weeks for most birds to hatch. Some birds need a certain number of eggs before they start holding the temperature. One type needs two eggs, another may need four.

There are nine thousand different species, or types, of birds. Each kind lays an egg like no other. A robin egg doesn't look like an ostrich egg. A sparrow's egg won't look like a pigeon's. The color, shape, size, or other marks will distinguish one from another.

Eggs are normally laid during the morning.

The differences in sizes are amazing. The huge ostrich lays a two-pound egg. The tiny hummingbird lays an egg that's about a half-inch long.

When the big day comes, the new bird has to do the major portion of the work. Chicks use their young beaks to break open the shell. Some take a few hours while others take several days.

A mother bird goes to a lot of trouble to lay the eggs and hatch them. Now she will search for food to keep her chicks alive. She usually has no interest in stealing anyone else's chicks but is happy with her own.

People who steal from others are just like birds with another bird's chicks—they soon lose interest and don't take care of them. The person who works for what she gets feels good about it and takes better care of it. Stealing is an ugly way to live and a habit that hurts everyone.

102

Like a bird that fills her nest with young she has not hatched and which will soon desert her and fly away, so is the man who gets his wealth by unjust means. Sooner or later he will lose his riches and at the end of his life become a poor old fool.

JEREMIAH 17:11 (TLB)

Do You Remember?

1. What temperature is necessary for most eggs?

2. How long is it before many eggs hatch?

3. What do we think about things we steal?

Stealing hurts everyone.

60 Deep-Sea Diver

One of the South Pole's most interesting animals is the Weddell seal. This huge deep-sea diver can weigh up to nine hundred pounds, and it swims like a minnow.

People may wish they could do what this creature can. This seal can stop breathing for thirty minutes while looking for food. It can dive fifteen hundred feet and catch most fish, including the squid. Some Weddell seals have stayed underwater for forty-five minutes. Humans can't begin to do this.

The secret to such long dives is the seal's ability to change its heartbeat. Normally its heartbeat is 150 beats per minute, but when the seal dives, it lowers its heartbeat to 10 beats a minute. The Weddell seal merely lives off the air in its body.

These seals are born to be fat. They weigh a plump 60 pounds when they are born. In two weeks of feeding on the mother's butterfat milk, junior will increase to 120 pounds. It is a hard job for the mother. While she is feeding a baby seal, she will lose up to 300 pounds.

A mother Weddell means well but isn't terribly intelligent. For some reason she gets confused at the sight of danger. If an animal or human comes near her, she will start killing her young pups. She doesn't seem to understand what she has done. For days the mother stays with her children, even after they are dead.

The seal enjoys ice. In the coldest season it will dig a hole and live under the ice. It uses its teeth to make holes for air, and when it grows older, its teeth are badly worn.

103

In old age the seal looks for a place to retire. It heads for the top of a mountain. Weddell seals have been found thirty-five miles from shore and three thousand feet above sea level. If a young seal is sick or wounded, it heads for the mountains. When it gets better it will return. This gives the seal a chance to get away from a tough life, but it can still enjoy the cold snow and ice.

When we travel to the farthest ends of the earth, the proof of God's work is exciting. The beautiful sunsets, the pure air, the amazing life of little-known creatures are all part of His handiwork. It is a land that richly displays the skillful hand of God.

The psalmist had never been to the Poles, but he would have found God there as easily as in the Garden of Eden, and he never doubted it.

He quiets the raging oceans and all the world's clamor. In the farthest corners of the earth the glorious acts of God shall startle everyone. The dawn and sunset shout for joy!

PSALM 65:7–8 (TLB)

Do You Remember?

1. Why can seals dive so deep?

2. Where do they go to retire?

3. Name two things you think are beautiful in nature.

Thanks for making the earth so interesting.

61 The Friendless Skunk

If you see a small black-and-white animal coming your way, you had better move. It may look lovable and soft, but don't be fooled. Skunks give off a terrible odor.

When they feel frightened, this member of the weasel family has a powerful weapon. It merely turns around, picks up its tail—and look out! Skunks can shoot a spray for ten to fifteen feet.

The smell is so strong it sometimes bothers people a mile away. Often, any clothes in contact with the spray will have to be destroyed. The skunk's weapon is too powerful to take lightly. This explains why few animals even try to attack this unhurried creature.

For some reason, skunks live only in the Americas. This includes North America, Mexico, and South America.

The skunk's color seems to work differently for him than the color of other animals. Some animals are green or brown so they can hide in the forest. Not the skunk. It is black and white—and stands out like spilled grape juice on a rug! The skunk's plan of defense is to be seen. If other animals see it coming, they are happy to move out of its way.

But some people hunt skunks for their fur, and some eat skunk meat.

Often false rumors are spread about skunks. They are clean animals and give off their odor only when afraid. Most skunks do not carry rabies. The few who do have it get it from the bite of another animal.

Many skunks prefer night work. The day is an inviting time to sleep. When they do go out, skunks are usually in search of a good meal. Dinner might consist of a few worms, possibly some bird eggs, maybe a side order of insects. A rat or a mouse would really top off a skunk's evening meal.

Baby skunks are called *kittens*. A healthy mother will have four to six each year.

Skunks can fool us. After they give off their odor, some people think it is safe to go near them. These people are usually sorry. Skunks save a second shot for those who are unwise.

No matter how much some people know, they still do foolish things. Adults and children often hurt themselves doing something they know is dangerous. The smart person listens to good warnings—and obeys them.

Don't waste your breath on a rebel. He will despise the wisest advice.

PROVERBS 23:9 (TLB)

Do You Remember?

1. How far away can the skunk odor be sensed?

2. How does a skunk's color help him?

3. What should we do with good warnings?

We can prevent a lot of pain by listening to good advice.

62 The Jungle in Your Yard

Not all of us have flown off to a thick, scary jungle where lots of fascinating animals live. Someday you might travel to see lions in the wild or howler monkeys racing through the trees or multicolored birds calling in the distance. But for now you might be happy to take a trip to visit the jungle just outside your door. I am talking about that mysterious place we call our yard, where many kinds of amazing creatures live.

Spiders, snakes, wasps, mice, flies, worms, and other creepy things live in the grass and weeds. Some dart around during the daytime, while others scurry around in the dark.

Insects lead a particularly dangerous existence living on a lawn. People might step on them. Children might collect them and put them in a jar. Snakes could eat them for dinner. Birds might sweep down and gobble them up.

Even flies have to watch out. They might land to lay eggs in the grass as gently as possible, but when they turn to take off, the unsuspecting pilot might crash into a spider's web and not be able to escape.

For the fun of it, lie down on the lawn on your belly. Lying still, you will be able to see a wide array of neat creatures making their way around. Some are tiny. Some are large. One moves slowly. The other is scurrying around. One might be chasing something. Another might be running away.

Unfortunately, we think the best parts of nature are in a far-off country. But actually an entire jungle exists only a few feet outside the front door.

God made a wide variety of creatures. Some fly across the sky like airplanes. Others race across the earth as fast as a car. Some are large enough to knock down a small house. Others are small enough to crawl inside our windows even when our windows are closed.

A quick trip to our front lawn or to the empty lot in the neighborhood could help us appreciate how wonderful God is. Watching crawling things in the grass could give us a reason to worship God.

How many are your works, O Lord! In wisdom you made them all; the earth is full of your creatures.

PSALM 104:24 (NIV)

Do You Remember?

1. Name three things that live on your lawn.

2. Have you ever seen a spider on your lawn? What color was it?

3. Do you ever thank God for creating so many interesting things?

Open my eyes to see more of the wonders you have made.

63 If Animals Could Talk

A serious problem occurred at the airport on Midway Island, a tiny island between Hawaii and Japan. Laysan albatrosses built their nests too close to the airstrip. Not wanting to injure the birds, workers carefully caught them and moved the group to the Philippines.

That seemed like a safe distance—4,120 miles from the airfield. Farther than the width of the United States! But in less than thirty days the albatrosses had flown across unfamiliar territory, over the open ocean, and arrived back at Midway Island.

If an albatross could talk, we would ask him a few questions. How could he navigate day and night, good weather and bad, and end up home again? What kind of special equipment did God give them that allows such skill? If we could interview birds, they could tell us something about God's ability.

The ducks of Bali, Indonesia, for instance, could give us some neat information. Every year a man comes to them with a flag tied to a bamboo stick. Immediately twenty or thirty ducks will follow the man as he parades down the road. At the end of their trip they arrive at a rice paddy where the rice has already been harvested.

The ducks waddle into the field and begin eating bugs. After they have picked out all the harmful insects, they follow the man with the stick back home again.

Ducks could tell us something about trust. They know how smart it is to be good followers. We could learn something about following God by watching a white feathery fowl waddle down a road.

Nature doesn't teach us everything about God, but we learn many lessons from things that are outdoors—animals, birds, rocks, things that grow in the ground. Ants teach us about working hard. Lilies tell us not to worry. Lions give us lessons in boldness. Sheep remind us that God thinks everyone is important. A thirsty deer panting by a stream reminds us that we need to let God satisfy our spirits.

Nature is busy talking to us about the reality of God. The animals have lessons to teach that we have not begun to learn. If the animals could talk, we would be amazed to know what God is like.

> *But ask the animals, and they will teach you, or the birds of the air, and they will tell you; or speak to the earth, and it will teach you, or let the fish of the sea inform you.*
>
> **JOB 12:7–8 (NIV)**

Do You Remember?

1. How far did the albatrosses fly to get back home?

2. Can ducks be trusting creatures?

3. Tell three lessons about God from nature.

Your perfect creations remind us to continue following you.

64 Can Fish Breathe?

People would have a few gigantic problems with living in the sea. One problem is the pressure from the water. Most submarines will crush like pop cans if they go down too far. The other problem is air. How are people going to breathe underwater? Presently they can carry their own supply of air, but they can't swim freely like a fish. How can a fish breathe underwater? Or do they breathe?

Fish have special body parts called gills. They are located just behind the head. A fish takes water into its mouth. The water is then forced through the gills. After it passes through the gills, the water is released by openings on its side next to its head. If you pick up a fish, you can see the openings.

While the water passes over the gills, the fish breathes. Its gills take oxygen out of the water and it goes into the bloodstream. The gills also release carbon dioxide, which is carried outside the body.

This is a simple process for the fish. It works just as smoothly for them as air does for us.

If scientists could build mechanical gills on a special helmet, we could take in oxygen and release carbon dioxide, allowing us to breath underwater. If this were possible, people could swim freely without carrying an air tank and surfacing when it runs out. This wouldn't solve all our problems in the sea, but it would be a big step.

It must take a rich imagination for God to create all the marvels of nature. He has given animals special abilities that we barely understand.

Have you ever wondered how people will breathe in heaven? Will there be any air? Will we breathe something special that we have never heard of? Maybe we will live without any need to breathe.

God has created an amazing world. He has planned an even more fascinating heaven.

*For our earthly bodies, the ones we have now that can die, must
be transformed into heavenly bodies that cannot perish but will
live forever.*

1 Corinthians 15:53 (tlb)

Do You Remember?

1. How do gills work?

2. How could people "breathe" underwater?

3. What do you think heaven is like?

Thanks for promising us an amazing tomorrow, God.

65 The Imitating Catbird

How many noises can you imitate? You can probably do a good train whistle or make a sound like a trumpet. If you practice, you might be able to talk like some of your friends, teachers, or favorite television characters.

Maybe you are like the catbird. It's a gray bird with a black patch on its head and red markings underneath its long tail feather. It is only nine inches long and loves to imitate other birds. If you listen carefully on a moonlit night, you might hear a catbird or one of the birds it imitates. How did the catbird get its name? It can sound just like a cat meowing.

Catbirds are often fun to have in your neighborhood. They enjoy eating berries and cherries, but they also like to gobble down plenty of crickets, beetles, and ants. This helps keep the insect population from getting out of control.

In the fall catbirds like to wing their way around the southern United States and Central America. Spring finds them rummaging around North America and southern Canada.

They are much like other songbirds except for this peculiar talent of mimicry. But these great actors are not limited to just bird calls. If you need a frog croak, the catbird can do it.

Each of us has our own way of imitating. We imitate our parents, animals, or neighbors. The Bible encourages us to imitate God. Not just to make noises but to love the way God loves, to share as God shares, to forgive as God forgives.

We all act like someone else sometimes. We don't want to forget to act like God many times.

Be imitators of God, therefore, as dearly loved children and live a life of love, just as Christ loved us and gave himself up for us as a fragrant offering and sacrifice to God.

EPHESIANS 5:1–2 (NIV)

Do You Remember?

1. What can a catbird imitate?

2. How did it get its name?

3. How will you imitate God today?

Love like God loves.

66 Fooling Their Enemies

Life in the wild is tough and unpredictable. At any moment a hawk could swoop down and snatch up a tiny animal, a snake might gulp down a frog, or a bear could pull a fish from the water. To protect themselves and their children, many animals have developed unusual behavior to help keep their young safe.

No technique is more unusual than the one used by the killdeer bird. They have become excellent actors and have often fooled their enemies.

If an attacker comes close to a killdeer's chicks, the mother bird will move away from the nest. It will then begin to drag one wing and act as if it can't fly. In case the attacker doesn't notice, the killdeer will also make loud noises to draw attention away from the chicks.

Frequently the enemy will creep close to the mother, trying to catch it. Suddenly the "injured" killdeer will dart into the air and escape the confused attacker.

Beavers may not be good actors, but their warning system works well. If danger comes close, the beaver beats its flat tail, making a slapping sound and sending its family diving for cover.

Marmots warn their young by giving a sharp whistle. The first one to see trouble gives off a terrible sound and everyone dashes for home.

When a mother bear senses danger, she will try to move her cubs and avoid a fight, if possible. Her method of carrying a cub may not be one we would choose. She grabs the cub's entire head inside her mouth. Without harming the animal, Mother jogs off to a safer den.

Parents are in the protection business too. That explains why they provide care, housing, and food. Unlike animals, people can think through needs and figure out how to meet them.

It's much like the protection God gives us. He watches over us, guards us, and provides the things we need. God cares what happens to us and usually sees to it that we are watched over.

> *For the Lord loves the just and will not forsake his faithful ones. They will be protected forever, but the offspring of the wicked will be cut off.*

PSALM 37:28 (NIV)

Do You Remember?

1. How does a mother killdeer protect her chicks?

2. How does a mother bear carry her cubs?

3. How has God watched over your family?

God always has us in His arms.

112

67 Animal Love

If you ask some people, they would say that animals are just dumb creatures who don't know anything about love. But anyone who has had a pet or has watched animals in the wild knows how much love exists.

When a mother bear even thinks its cubs are in trouble, she immediately risks her life to save them. The bear will attack almost anything to protect her cubs. At that moment she is filled with compassion for her children.

A true story is told of a trapper who caught a female bear in his trap. When he arrived to capture the bear, he saw the bear's mate standing next to her. The male bear was hugging her and crying. The trapper says he never trapped another bear.

Animal lovers believe there is much more than mindless instinct involved. Millions of cat lovers insist that cats develop an attachment to their owners that they share with no one else.

Even if you think that animals don't have feelings like humans do, don't make the mistake of thinking that animals have no feelings at all.

Some animals keep the same mate all of their lives. Wolves and foxes have a lifelong attachment for their spouse, which suggests how much they care.

If we say animals love each other, scientists will start arguing whether that could be possible. However, if we say that "love" means animals care about each other, who can deny that? They feed one another. In some cases they even feed adopted children. Many animals teach their children to hunt, hide, swim, and pick bugs off each other. They understand separation and are happy to be reunited.

Animal love is not human love, but it may be love nevertheless.

Love might be hard to recognize in animals, but it is easy to see in Jesus Christ. Jesus cares what happens to us. That is why He lived, died, and rose from the dead. He cares about you and me.

113

By believing in Jesus Christ as our Savior, we accept the love He gives us.

Greater love has no one than this, that one lay down his life for his friends.

JOHN 15:13 (NIV)

Do You Remember?

1. Have you observed an animal caring for another animal?

2. Tell about the trapper who caught a female bear.

3. Tell about Jesus' love for you.

Love always perseveres.

68 Bird Nest Soup

It's good to try new foods once in a while. I've eaten crayfish, turtle, kiwifruit, liver pudding, and chicken gizzards. Someday I'd like to try alligator meat, squid, or seaweed. Nature offers too much variety for us to limit ourselves, especially if we live in nations where food is plentiful.

One food I'm not sure I can eat is bird nest soup. No doubt it is a fabulous meal, because people are willing to pay forty dollars for one bowlful. It might even be healthful. Many Chinese love to down a good dish of it.

No wonder bird nest soup is expensive. The nests are hard to find and often the supplier has to climb on dangerous cliffs to collect even one nest. His goal is to find a swallow's home. Swallows hide in far-off areas.

If the searcher brings back a pound of top-rate nests, he is paid hundreds of dollars. The more considerate hunters try to avoid nests with eggs in them, but with so much money at stake some don't care what happens to the birds.

Understandably, the thought of eating a nest may not send your taste buds zinging. Fortunately, people don't eat the entire nest. The cook scrubs everything until it is extra clean and saves the part people enjoy the most: the swallow's saliva. When completed, it looks like white strings, but it's stiff and firm.

There's no point in describing the rest of this. It only gets stranger. Those who eat it insist that their skin and complexion improve as well as their health.

If you wanted to do something special to please God, collecting birds' nests might sound like a great idea. He might be impressed with an expensive gift that you risked your life to get. But God isn't looking for riches or daring accomplishments.

What God wants from us is our obedience. If we live our lives by following Him, by being good and kind and loving—doing everything that pleases Him—we are doing exactly what God asks us to do.

If you find an abandoned swallow's nest, give it to a friend. Tell him it is a special treat. But if you want to serve God, simply obey Him. Find out what the Bible says and follow Him.

To obey is better than sacrifice.

1 Samuel 15:22 (niv)

Do You Remember?

1. What is the most unusual food you have eaten?

2. Where are swallows' nests found?

3. Think of something you will do today to obey God.

Following Him is all He asks.

69 Born to Eat

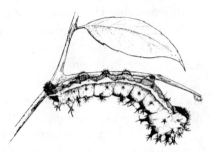

A ll of us enjoy a good meal. It's not only fun to eat but also essential to our health. However, there are some creatures, like the fuzzy caterpillar, that do little else but eat.

We know what caterpillars are. They are the fuzzy little creatures that later turn into moths and butterflies. On their way to adulthood caterpillars like to eat. Eating is their full-time job.

Many begin life as an egg placed on their favorite plant or leaf. When they hatch, the caterpillar will eat its egg and then begin its long journey of trying to munch on everything it can bite.

If the caterpillar finds itself hatched on a leaf that doesn't suit its appetite, the only solution is to move. It uses a silk thread as an elevator and drops rapidly to a plant where the food is more enjoyable.

This continuous eating is both good and bad. On the one hand, caterpillars help remove some overgrowth. Their eating provides an excellent product known as silk. But the caterpillar also manages to destroy millions of dollars' worth of crops each year.

When you eat as much as a caterpillar, you are certain to have clothing problems. Their outfits soon become too tight and they are forced to discard their old clothes. This is called *molting*. Their outer skin falls off and the next layer takes over. The change in clothing could take place from two to ten times while they are caterpillars.

Even the change of clothes is special for some caterpillars. Often they will immediately eat the skin they have outgrown. If they're too busy for skinburgers at the time, insects might later have the clothing for dinner, or it could merely blow away.

Unlike caterpillars, people are not born just to eat. We do many helpful and enjoyable things. A few of us fall into the habit of eating more than we need to. If we do munch and crunch day and night, we could end up with serious health problems later.

God created caterpillars to eat every minute. He expected people to control how much they eat.

He provides you with plenty of food.
ACTS 14:17 (NIV)

Do You Remember?

1. What do caterpillars eat?

2. What happens to the skin the caterpillar outgrows?

3. How can you improve your diet?

Eat to live, don't live to eat.

70 Tough Dandelions

Every spring a massive army of determined homeowners march out to their lawns. Each soldier is armed with knives, hoes, lawn mowers, hoses, and spray cans or bottles of chemicals. The time has arrived again to do battle against the enemy.

At first glance the invaders look innocent. They stand only a few inches high and have a yellow flower. But despite their appearance, these soft buds with green pointed leaves are tough.

Homeowners will spend days hacking, spraying, cutting, and hauling, hoping to eliminate the dandelion. Yet after much widespread war, the dandelion only *seems* to have been defeated. In a few days, more yellow monsters will open their smiling faces. Next spring there may be as many dandelions or more returning to the same lawn.

Each year millions of people work hard and spend thousands of dollars to erase the dandelion. Some residents are successful, but not many.

Dandelions are well and prosperous in most sections of the world. They get their name from a lion's tooth because of the jagged edges on their leaves.

117

You have probably seen neighbors get down on their knees and carefully dig out each dandelion. Next year they will get a chance to dig them out again. Dandelions seem to love being chopped out. They will come back with more plants than were originally removed.

Tired of the useless war, we could make peace with this weed by learning to use it. We could wear them in our hair. Possibly we should cook their leaves and include them for supper as people all over the world do. Some are made into beverages and even turned into medicines.

If you keep fighting dandelions you might win, but few people come out victoriously. Changing our attitude would probably be cheaper and less backbreaking.

Watching the dandelion hang in there under the toughest of circumstances could be an inspiration to all of us. They get knocked down, cut off, poisoned, and hated, but they stand firm.

Christians do the same thing. Sometimes we are insulted, misunderstood, abused, neglected, disliked, and even attacked. But the tough ones hang on. They believe that their faith in Jesus Christ is more important than any hardship. Christians keep coming through no matter what they suffer.

When the storm has swept by, the wicked are gone, but the righteous stand firm forever.

PROVERBS 10:25 (NIV)

Do You Remember?

1. How did the name *dandelion* originate?

2. If the top of a dandelion is cut off, will the plant die?

3. Have you observed a Christian who hung tough through a hard time? Tell about it.

Standing firm as a Christian will bring everlasting peace.

71 Amazing Facts

New Zealand has a gnat that glows in the dark. Called a fungus gnat, it lives in the Wartomo Cave. The larvae—not the adults—use the lights to attract other insects. Curious insects soon become part of the fast-food menu.

Nine-banded armadillos can gulp air to inflate their bodies like footballs. They pump themselves up in order to float across rivers.

Tigers in the wild may eat forty pounds of meat a day. How much does the average person eat?

Bugs live practically everywhere. The petroleum fly actually lays eggs in pools of black oil. Its eggs hatch into larvae that feed on other insects that get trapped in the oil. As the larvae get older, they burrow their way into the dirt next to the oil. There they safely turn into adult petroleum flies.

Kangaroos live only in Australia, but it is believed that they once hopped across Europe, South America, and North America.

When a male avocet (AV-a-set) picks out a girlfriend, he first talks to her only by head movements. No sounds are exchanged—just plenty of nods, jerks, and bounces.

The lowest form of animal is the microscopic amoeba. It has no legs, eyes, or skeletal structure.

Starlings are birds that were brought to America to appear in Shakespearean plays. Those first forty birds multiplied so rapidly that now in one single block in Washington, D.C., there may be as many as ten thousand.

Flying squirrels have flat tails unlike their bushy-tailed relatives. They use them to help guide their glide to the ground and serve as a brake.

These are amazing facts about God's creation. But do you know what is greater than all? That Jesus promised us life after death if we believe in Him.

I am the resurrection and the life. He who believes in me will live, even though he dies; and whoever lives and believes in me will never die. Do you believe this?

JOHN 11:25–26 (NIV)

Do You Remember?

1. How do nine-banded armadillos cross rivers?

2. Tell about the petroleum fly.

3. How does a flying squirrel use its tail?

It's a fact that God wants us for eternity.

72 Noisy Shells

We brought a conch (konk) shell back from one of our trips. My wife, Pat, picked it up on the beach. We shined it ourselves instead of buying an expensive one in a shop.

Conch meat is a common food along the shores of Belize and throughout the islands of the Caribbean. The fisherman cuts out a piece of the shell in the back and is then able to pull the meat out easily. If he pulls slowly, the meat can be pulled out without breaking the back of the shell.

When I was a kid, people told me that if you hold the peach-colored shell to your ear, you can hear the ocean roaring inside. They said the shell had heard the ocean for so long that it would now hold the echo forever. With wide eyes I would hold a shell up and picture the bottom of the ocean with all of its creatures swimming around.

Today I know better, and I am a little sorry I do. If I put my two hands to my ear and cup them closely I can hear that same ocean sound. The reason I can hear a sound is that the air moving inside my hands sounds like ocean waves.

When I hold a conch shell next to my ear, it is the gentle moving air inside the shell that gives the sound. I still want to believe it is the ocean, but I know it isn't true.

Many things go on that we can't see and often can't explain. We see what the wind does or we hear the noise it creates, but we can't see the wind.

God's Spirit is like the wind inside the conch shell or the wind whistling in a canyon. We can't actually see the Holy Spirit, but we can see what He does. The Spirit changes people, guides them, comforts them, speaks to them—even silently. We don't see the Spirit moving from place to place, but He is still there.

Everyone who is born again and becomes a Christian has the Spirit of God working in his life. We don't see the Holy Spirit, but He helps us anyway.

The wind blows wherever it pleases. You hear its sound, but you cannot tell where it comes from or where it is going. So it is with everyone born of the Spirit.

JOHN 3:8 (NIV)

Do You Remember?

1. How do fishermen remove conch meat from the shell?

2. What causes the noise you hear when you put a conch shell to your ear?

3. What has the Holy Spirit done for you?

We can't see you, God, but we know you're here.

121

73 When Animals Retire

Grandparents need to know what they will do when they retire. Where will they live and how will they stay active? Animals need to have a place to retire too.

Some animal lovers have opened retirement centers for animals who need a place to go. These retirement centers have several acres for aging creatures to run freely and live out the rest of their days in peace.

Circus chimps whose performing days are over can run through fields, climb trees, and be cared for. Baby zebras who are unwanted by the zoo where they were born are welcome at these centers. Rhinos would also be welcome at one of these places.

The operators of these retirement centers would rather release the animals and let them enjoy the wild, but the problem is that most animals would have little idea how to survive out there. For years they have received food from trainers and keepers. Some have never spent one night in the rain. They have never hunted for food and are barely able to defend themselves in case of an attack.

Animal lovers all over the world have sacrificed their own money to care for these homeless creatures. Others have worked hard to raise money to support these centers.

Texans seem to have hearts almost as big as their state. Over six hundred ranchers have adopted exotic pets that normally roam in Africa and Asia. The word *texotics* describes the exotic wildlife now being bred in that state.

Homes for wild animals may not be your thing. Not many of us want an orphaned giraffe living in our apartment. Your parents might complain about a thirty-pound vulture in the dining room. Yet it is important that we respect and care for animals. They're part of God's prized creation. And God gives high marks to anyone who treats them well.

A righteous man cares for the needs of his animal.

PROVERBS 12:10 (NIV)

Do You Remember?

1. Why can't zoo animals be released in the wild when they are old?

2. What state has over six hundred ranches that adopt exotic pets?

3. If you have a pet, how do you care for it?

All God's creatures are created and loved by Him.

74 Walking Trees

I f ever there was a tree that liked to be of help, it must be the mangrove. These residents of the tropics not only provide housing for animals, but they also build up the environment by creating more land. When mangroves grow in the right places, they are friends to everyone.

This tree isn't hard to spot because you can see it taking a walk. It's no illusion. A mangrove stretches its long legs out into the water as it plants new seeds.

The trunk remains in the same place but the branches reach out and downward. A branch holds a seed, which opens into a seedling. Mangroves must have salt water. When the branch dips beneath the water it finds the bottom, and soon the seedling catches hold in the mud. From there new legs begin to sprout.

By doing this, the mangrove tree has formed legs, like spider legs, that arch across the water. Before long the branches turn into shopping centers for a large variety of creatures. At first things get trapped. Wood, cans, and leaves become stuck. These are followed by tiny living creatures like snails or sponges.

Higher forms of life, like crabs, begin to shop there for food and houses. Raccoons might join the community to look for both food and shelter.

123

What began as a seedling on a branch, searching for a place to take hold, has now become a busy city. An assortment of birds moves into the area to enjoy the bustling activities.

There are several ways for a mangrove tree to sprout new trees, but walking out into the water is one of the most interesting. If the legs collect objects and silt, as is normal, it will create a new section of land. The area beneath its legs will build up above the water and a new patch of dry land will exist.

Unfortunately this dry land will probably mean the end of the original tree trunk. Salt water is needed to survive, and the creation of more land places the trunk too far away. The mangrove tree puts itself out of business as it walks across the water.

Much of nature is destructive. Volcanoes, storms, and tornadoes can raise havoc on the world. But some of creation is known for the unique way it helps make our environment better.

People fall into the same categories. Some of us choose to tear things apart. At other times we follow the example of God. We look for ways to help, to build up, to make life go better for others. That's the attitude God has.

God has come to help his people.

LUKE 7:16 (NIV)

Do You Remember?

1. Why are mangrove trees called walking trees?

2. How do mangrove trees improve the environment?

3. Name one good thing you will try to do today.

Acts of kindness benefit everyone.

75 Lizard Push-Ups

Have you ever wondered why flies don't turn into ice cubes during the winter or why lizards don't become Popsicles on cold days? Many small creatures *do* die when the thermometer takes a plunge. However, some survive even bitter cold because they have special ways of being protected.

Many insects, especially their larvae, live through the winter because they can change their water and fill up with "antifreeze." Just like our cars, these creatures need a liquid that will not freeze during cold weather. God has made it available.

Their tiny bodies can create a fluid called glycerol. It would take incredibly low temperatures to make this liquid freeze. With the glycerol in place, they look for a warm shelter to help them live through a tough winter.

It's possible that we have a similar fluid our bodies could manufacture, but scientists aren't exactly sure. We are used to putting on coats, turning up the thermostat, and piling on blankets. Our bodies aren't asked to fight extreme cold. Some scientists believe we carry more weight partly because our bodies don't use the fat to fight cold.

Snakes are good at using nature to warm them up. Early in the morning they will crawl out and stretch across the grass. They are allowing the sun to heat their skin. This action, called *basking*, increases their body temperature by several degrees.

Other animals fight the cold by using exercise programs. Men and women can raise their temperature merely by walking, jogging, or chopping wood. Butterflies warm up by doing "wing rotations." Before it begins to fly, a butterfly will vibrate its wings to increase its temperature.

Lizards raise their heat with a workout. The little creatures hop up on a rock and start doing push-ups until they feel warm.

The system doesn't work for every animal and probably shouldn't. If every bug lived through the winter, in a few years we would be overrun with beetles and flies.

People have better systems than animals because our climate control is run by our brains. We can construct heating plants, design clothes, build houses, and manufacture heating pads in ways that animals could never match.

God is in the protection business. He wants people to survive the extreme weather so we can enjoy life and serve Him. If He wanted to, God could change the temperature of the world a few degrees and wipe out a large number of us. Fortunately, His main job is protection, not destruction.

There are many ways we could have been hurt, destroyed, or even frozen. But God works to help and protect us all of our lives.

But let all who take refuge in you be glad; let them ever sing for joy. Spread your protection over them.

PSALM 5:11 (NIV)

Do You Remember?

1. What fluid do insects use to survive the winter?

2. How do butterflies raise their body temperature?

3. How does God protect you?

God's protection makes me feel warm.

76 Turkeys Wear Out

Wild turkeys are back and growing in great numbers in the United States. That's good news because years ago they were so hunted that they almost disappeared. And if they disappear in America they will be gone, since this is the only place the turkey lives naturally in the wild.

Our Pilgrim fathers loved the bird and hunted it freely, but the turkey was too easy to catch. After hundreds of years, many states made it illegal to shoot the bird, and its population began to increase again.

Most of the turkey we eat is a different variety from what the eager Pilgrims enjoyed. Store turkeys come from a group that originated in Mexico. Wild turkeys have a distinctive taste. Part of that comes from the food they eat in the woods.

Wild turkeys are built for short, fast flights. If they sense someone creeping up on them, they can burst into the air with almost no room to take off. Turkeys can reach flight speeds of about forty miles an hour almost immediately. That's remarkable since many birds can't fly much faster.

If a turkey could keep up that speed, it would be amazing for a bird that lives on the ground. The problem is that they can't keep it up. After carrying twenty-five pounds for a short distance, they have to land.

Part of the turkey's problem is its white meat. Birds that can fly long distances have more red pigment in their muscle. The red pigment and oxygen mix to give extra energy. Wild turkeys lack the extra punch.

Not that they are complaining. Turkeys seem more comfortable on the ground. They like to make a mad flight into a tree now and then but are basically content to stay earthbound. Even their nests are simple clearings in a bunch of dried leaves that they have shuffled around.

Though they need only short runways, the lack of ability to endure is a serious problem. If they could fly farther, more of them might live longer. Their quick burst into the air often makes them excellent targets for hunters.

Imagine for a minute that God's love came and went in short, rapid bursts. God would care about you a great deal today, but then He would get tired and stay away for a couple of weeks. He would be enthused, energetic, and helpful for a few hours, but soon He would have to retreat for a long rest.

God is better than that. He stays around day after day. He doesn't tucker out, wear down, or take coffee breaks. Steady as a rock, God hangs in there every day.

His love endures forever.

PSALM 106:1 (NIV)

Do You Remember?

1. Describe a wild turkey's flight.

2. Describe a wild turkey's nest.

3. How would you tell a friend that God's love doesn't ever quit?

Help me to be content just how I am.

77 Lovable Llamas

When you travel west on Interstate 80 in Nebraska, look carefully to the south. Along the highway a farmer keeps a half a dozen or more llamas. They are among the cutest and friendliest animals in nature.

Related to the camel, this hairy, long-necked creature has a slight grin and can wiggle one ear at a time. If it wants to, the llama can be difficult to get along with. It is a good pack animal, but if it's overloaded, the owner has immediate trouble. The llama simply sits down wherever it is and goes on strike. Only after the burden is reduced will the beast agree to stand up.

They make excellent pickup trucks. Llamas stand around five feet tall at the shoulders and can haul equipment or supplies for twenty miles a day. In the United States some hikers use them for trips into the mountains.

It is believed that llamas do not fare well in the wilderness. Most of them throughout the world are owned and cared for by someone. Even the ones we see roaming about loose probably have a home on a ranch or a farm.

Normally we associate the llama with mountains, and they certainly are comfortable in the Andes. However, they function equally well at sea level and find Nebraska no serious hardship.

If a llama becomes angry, it gives off a few warning signs alerting everyone to back away. It will lay those long ears down against its head. And if the llama is especially upset, it knows how to spit like a camel.

No troublemaker, it would rather sunbathe or hum gently to its children as it feeds them.

Llamas are valued for their strong backs. They are also in demand for their milk, their hides, and in some cases their good quality wool. This is especially true of their cousin, the alpaca.

Where did neat animals like this come from? How were they created or put together? We don't understand everything that went into creation or exactly what the process was, but we do know that God commanded that the llama come into existence, and it did.

Birds that imitate frogs, turkeys that take off at forty miles an hour, dolphins that talk, and llamas that can wiggle one ear at a time—these were originally created by our God, who has plenty of imagination.

Let them praise the name of the Lord, for he commanded and they were created.

Psalm 148:5 (niv)

Do You Remember?

1. If a farmer overloads a llama, what happens?

2. Name two ways llamas help people.

3. Name an unusual feature of an animal.

129

We were all created unique by God.

78 Man-Sized Lizards

We didn't see these lizards when we were in Central America, but our friend told us about them. When he took a canoe trip down the river, he saw five-foot-long iguanas, members of the reptile and lizard family. They sat along the side of the bank eating plants, a bit of fruit, and maybe an occasional bird.

My wife and I hope to go back and see these creatures. They look like monsters from a midnight movie.

It wouldn't be polite to say iguanas are ugly. They probably find each other rather attractive. However, iguanas have a frightening appearance. Their outward skin is usually covered with a soft spine that runs from one end to the other.

If you move toward most iguanas, they will hurry to get away. They look like fighters but actually are peace-loving creatures. When people get close, iguanas drop into the water and try to disappear. At night they often hide among the rocks.

It would be fun to see such large animals that don't like to fight but enjoy the peaceful life. If something or someone wants to fight the iguanas, most of them will simply slide away and wait for the pest to leave.

However, not every iguana is shy and retiring. The conolophus (cun-ALL-uh-fuss) loves to charge anything it considers dangerous. It dines on plants and grasshoppers but isn't one to run from a good fight.

Black iguanas also live in Central America and reportedly have miserable dispositions. If they think you are going to attack them, they will try to bite you or knock you over with their long spiny tails. The black iguana is barely two feet long but it can create a lot of pain.

Often we have put too much emphasis on fighting. Quick to pound it out with practically anyone, we think it's tough and cool to battle.

The Bible has a different view. If possible we should avoid trouble, not look for it. Too many people are hurt, too many are afraid, too many are sorry. Whenever we possibly can, we need to live at peace with everyone.

Live in peace with each other.

1 THESSALONIANS 5:13 (NIV)

Do You Remember?

1. Are most iguanas fighters or are they peace lovers?

2. What do iguanas eat?

3. How do you know when to be at peace with someone and when to fight?

Fighting physically only creates more problems.

79 Strange Facts

The dodo was a bird that weighed fifty pounds. They lived on the island of Mauritius, an island in Southwest Asia. None have been seen since 1681.

It may be that the frogmouth bird of Asia and Australia has insects fooled. Some scientists believe the bird merely sits still with its colorful mouth wide open. Insects think it is a flower and fly directly inside.

You could spend the rest of your life studying beetles. There are at least twenty-eight thousand species in North America alone.

A toad can throw its tongue out farther than its body length. Its tongue is sticky and excellent for snagging bugs.

Even animals have a tough time telling poisonous mushrooms from safe ones. If you see dead mice near a group of mushrooms, they probably made the wrong choice.

We all have seen pigeons, but what kind of pigeon? There are well over five hundred different species and subspecies of pigeons in the world.

131

Some scientists believe that hyenas in Africa actually chew through metal cages in order to eat the bait set for leopards.

The Voyager 2 spacecraft shot toward the planet Uranus, traveling at fifty times the speed of a pistol bullet.

Not all creatures develop great hunting skills. Herons are clumsy at collecting mice, insects, crabs, and other foods. Consequently, many herons die during their first year.

Since 1921, many people have died trying to climb Mount Everest. The mountain is 29,028 feet high.

Elephants are the largest land mammals. The second largest are the white rhinos. Some elephants weigh ten thousand pounds or more.

Prairie dogs got their name because they wag their tails and give a quick barking sound.

Giraffes were once called camelopards because people thought they looked like tall camels with leopard spots.

The satin bower bird has a great love for the color blue. Males try to impress their female friends by bringing blue feathers, blue pebbles, and blueberries.

Did you know that we can have a place with God forever if we invite Jesus Christ into our lives and believe in Him?

For God so loved the world that he gave his one and only Son, that whoever believes in him shall not perish but have eternal life.

JOHN 3:16 (NIV)

Do You Remember?

1. What animal can chew through the metal of a trap?

2. Name the largest land mammal.

3. Can you say John 3:16 from memory?

Our personal characteristics make us unique.

80 Horses in the House

What do most of us picture when someone mentions a small horse? We probably imagine a pony or a newborn colt. But there is a type of horse that, when it is full grown, is much smaller than either of these. It is called a miniature horse, and it stands a little over two feet tall at its biggest.

When explorers came to the Americas, they found no horses here. So in 1519, Hernando Cortez brought some in. They proved excellent for transportation, work, wars, and in some cases even eating.

Normally a horse is measured by how many hands high it is. A "hand" measurement is about four inches. Consequently, a twelve-hands-tall horse is forty-eight inches to the base of its neck. Many of the miniature horses are four to eight hands high. You could put the small ones on your lap.

Miniature horses are called Lilliputian horses. The name comes from an island in *Gulliver's Travels* where the people were supposed to be only six inches tall. The island's name was Lilliput.

Having a horse live in your house as a pet may seem like a great idea, but some towns have laws against keeping horses inside a house. Also, a number of horse breeders believe you cannot house-train a horse, even a miniature one. If they have bathroom problems in your house, your parents will probably move them outside very quickly.

God must have had fun creating animals. They come in such a wide variety of amazing looks and different abilities. God allows us to train them, use them for work, and enjoy them. But basically they remain the outstanding products of God's lively imagination.

God made the wild animals according to their kinds, the live-stock according to their kinds, and all the creatures that move along the ground according to their kinds. And God saw that it was good.

GENESIS 1:25 (NIV)

Do You Remember?

1. What are miniature horses called?

2. How tall is a miniature horse?

3. What are some good ways you can use your imagination?

God created everything to have a purpose.

81 Why Do Pandas Somersault?

I f you have two kittens in your house, it's obvious to see that they like to play. Sometimes they wrestle roughly, but neither is out to hurt the other. They tussle, attack, and even bite, but they seldom tear off fur. If you have ever seen two stray cats fight in your yard, you can tell it is much meaner than the way your pets behave with each other.

There is also a similar playfulness among squirrels. When they race after each other up trees and across lawns, it makes you want to join in.

Not all creatures like to play, but a large number spend considerable time tumbling, chasing, hiding, twisting, and pushing with their friends. This recreation time has many terrific results.

When two bears in the wild begin "horsing around," they have no intention of injuring each other. If these mammoth creatures were to forcefully tear into each other, blood and even bones would soon start flying in every direction. But they are careful not to strike other bears with their sharp claws because they know how much damage they could do.

How many animals have we heard of that like to play? Wolves, birds, monkeys, rats, cats, and penguins are only a few of the species that love to frolic.

Animals don't normally tell us why they spend so much time playing, but a few observations could be made. For one thing, playing games is probably a fantastic way to learn how to hunt and defend themselves. Hours of crawling, stalking, lurching, and surprising their friends and relatives evidently puts them in great shape for the tough world they face.

Another obvious reason for play is that it helps their personality adjustment. It appears that the meanest, cruelest, angriest animals in nature usually don't know how to play. They are too uptight to relax and have a good time. This may not be true of every animal, but it certainly proves correct for many.

It does make sense. If we are playing, we definitely are not fighting. Rather, we are busy getting along with our friends.

The sounds of children at play make all of us feel better. It's a sign that things are going well. The same can be said of adults. When they are having a good time together, everyone gets along better.

The Bible uses the idea of children at play as a sure sign that life is going well. When God promised the Jews that Jerusalem would be a happy, peaceful place again, He said children would play in the city streets.

Play isn't just foolishness. God gave it to us to help keep us calm and happy. When we play the right amount, we all get along much better.

The city streets will be filled with boys and girls playing there.

ZECHARIAH 8:5 (NIV)

Do You Remember?

1. What is the advantage of animal play?

2. Name some animals that like to play.

3. How do you play together in your family?

Help me to focus on the joy in life.

135

82 A Blue Jay's Reputation

D o you ever see blue jays hopping around in your backyard? If you live in southern Canada or in the United States east of the Rocky Mountains, you probably have a few close by. The blue jay, with its pretty feathers and peaked hat, will stay with you through the winter. They don't migrate but rather collect food so they can survive even in the snow.

We have a feeder in our backyard outside our kitchen window. We have fun watching the activity. The blue jays perch in our cedar tree. Unfortunately our cats, Bart and Jeff, look at the blue jays as a free lunch. Between the scurrying squirrels, the stalking cats, and sprinting birds, our yard sometimes turns into a battlefield.

The blue jays are a welcome sight, but their reputation could be better. On the one hand they make nature flourish and grow. But at the same time, they have a reputation as destroyers.

One of the blue jay's best contributions to nature comes from its ability to carry seeds and plant them. The noisy bird is a member of the crow family and likes to pick acorns out of oak trees or nuts from other trees. It will then haul its food to a safe place and bury it for a meal later on. During the cold winter the blue jay will return and feast.

Moving nuts all day takes a great deal of energy. The birds might be storing them two miles or more away. Between the number of nuts they stock in the ground and the number they eat to keep flying, the blue jay needs thousands of nuts.

To save himself any unnecessary work, the blue jay checks out the nut before flying away. He rattles the nut in his bill to see if it sounds good. If the nuts don't measure up, he drops them to the ground immediately.

Fortunately for nature, the blue jay can't remember where he hides all the nuts. These nuts that are left then often germinate and produce new trees.

That is the part of the blue jay's reputation most of us like. The other side may be important, but it seems ugly.

To add to their diets, blue jays will raid the nests of other birds and eat their eggs. Sometimes they even eat young chicks. Creatures in nature eat each other all the time, but it still sounds like a terrible thing to do.

Our good reputations are worth having. We work hard and are glad that people realize how kind we can be. But when we mess up or do something awful, we begin to create a bad reputation. Bad reputations are hard to erase. It's much easier to get a good one and keep it.

Or he who hears it may shame you and you will never lose your bad reputation.

PROVERBS 25:10 (NIV)

Do You Remember?

1. Have you seen a blue jay?

2. Tell about blue jays burying nuts.

3. What is a reputation?

Don't let one bad seed tarnish your reputation.

83 High-Priced Mink

Why aren't there any mink in Arizona? Does anybody know the answer? Mink live throughout Canada and the continental United States—except for Arizona. They are so hardy that they can live under practically any conditions, wet or dry, but they don't seem to like that one state.

Mink pelts, or furs, are valuable to some people who enjoy mink coats. It takes a great many pelts to make a single coat, which explains why the finished garment is quite expensive. The pelts used most often come from mink ranches. At last count there were twelve hundred such businesses in the United States.

Trappers collect the small animals, but outdoorsmen don't think the numbers are dropping. The greater threat is home building. When people move close or change the wilderness, the mink is pushed around.

Mink are not picky about where they live. If necessary, they are comfortable in the water and like to dine on fish and crayfish. On dry land they go after a slew of mice, insects, waterfowl, and muskrats. Occasionally they will raid a farmyard and do considerable damage.

The mother takes her kittens hunting—at first for insects and later for the big stuff. Adult mink are so swift that they can sit by a stream bank and yank fast-moving trout right out of the water.

One of the reasons mink have a terrible reputation is their hunting and eating habits. They seem to kill far more than they are able to use for meals. This passion for destroying living things may be way out of control.

A second bad habit customary among mink is their miserable temper. For some reason almost all of them appear to be angry whenever they are around people. At first it would seem that the wild mink is not used to human beings and naturally will lunge at them. However, mink raised in captivity are equally irritable. Many mink keepers say that when they put food in the cage of a mink, the animal would far rather go for the keeper's hand. They prefer attacking and ripping things apart.

Some of us know someone who is as hot-tempered as a mink. He gets angry easily, wants to throw things, and tries to start fights. It makes us nervous to be around him.

It would be good if we could help him calm down. Maybe we could find out what makes him so upset. It would be good to pray for him. But if we can't help our hot-tempered friend, we might need to stay away from him.

People who keep exploding are sooner or later going to hurt themselves and those near them.

Do not make friends with a hot-tempered man, do not associate with one easily angered.

PROVERBS 22:24 (NIV)

Do You Remember?

1. How are mink pelts used?

2. Are mink swift? Tell about it.

3. Do you know someone who is hot-tempered?

Help me to keep a positive attitude all the time.

84 Showing Off for the Girls

Even bats like to look good. And when a flying fox bat is around a female, he shows up in style. First he starts singing and flapping his wings simply to show off. Soon he adds to his beauty by displaying his long, white shoulder fur.

Normally the white shoulder fur is kept hidden in tiny shoulder patches. But they insist on looking their best for the ladies. When they flash their white shoulder fur, the girls know they are special.

When the flying fox bat isn't flirting with the females, he spends his time hunting for fruit or sleeping upside down. Flying fox bats have a vital purpose: Scientists argue that if they were removed, our plant life would be hurt.

There are two reasons why the flying fox bat is being hunted. The first one will surprise you, so tell your stomach to get ready. Many people like to eat bats. I don't know any good recipes for this delicacy, but some say it tastes good.

The second reason they are hunted is because they destroy fruit. Naturally those who want to protect the flying fox bat disagree. They argue that this bat is essential to good plant and tree life.

An active flying fox bat carries pollination from flower to flower. It transports fruit seeds by eating the fruit. The huge baobab (BAY-uh-bab) tree needs this bat to help it pollinate. Figs, breadfruit, and bananas are only a few of the fruit trees that need the services of this nighttime roamer.

Among their own kind, this bat does not lack for company. They hang from tree limbs all day in groups of possibly 150. Others wait in caves for the daylight to go away. When a mother flies, she often carries a young bat tightly against her stomach.

Many people don't want to know the truth about bats because they are too busy being afraid of them. Some people stay away from Christians for the same reasons. They think Christians are stuck-up and just sit around doing nothing.

The Bible tells us to prove our sincerity by doing good things—by helping others, by being kind, by sharing, by being thoughtful. If they see how we treat others, they will learn that our faith in God is real.

Live such good lives among the pagans that, though they accuse you of doing wrong, they may see your good deeds and glorify God on the day he visits us.

1 PETER 2:12 (NIV)

Do You Remember?

1. When does a flying fox bat show its white shoulder fur?

2. Name one reason the bat is hunted.

3. How does the bat help in growing fruit?

Learning about things will prevent false judgment.

85 The Strong Leopard

Leopards are large, beautiful, fast cats that used to live all throughout Africa and Asia. Unfortunately, the huge feline hunter does not mix well with people and therefore has been reduced greatly in numbers.

In most areas it is illegal to hunt leopards for their fur. But since a finished leopard coat might sell in a store for $60,000, poachers still kill the animals and smuggle furs into other countries.

Leopard furs come in several colors. Most are basically tan with dark spots, but they also come in white or black. Black leopards also have spots, but the leopards are already so dark it is hard to see the spots.

At one time leopards roamed around the country of Israel. People in Bible times saw the colorful cats and often wrote about them. Leopards lived in Israel with lions, bears, and wolves. That area was open to wildlife and was probably covered with a considerable amount of trees, bushes, and jungle.

Much like the cats in our yards, the leopard enjoys climbing trees. It can perch on a limb and wait for supper to walk underneath it. Usually the meal consists of goat, sheep, snake, antelope, or jackal. Once it has collected its food, the leopard again puts its tremendous strength to use. Grasping the prey in its teeth, the leopard will carry over one hundred pounds up into a tree. There it will lay the carcass across a limb and keep it to chew on from time to time.

Because of the protection given by many governments, the number of leopards may be growing again. They need so much territory to roam and hunt that it is still hard to keep them separated from people.

The coat of the leopard was given to it for more than beauty, and it is more than just a warm wrap on a cold night in the mountains. The mixture of light color and dark spots makes the leopard difficult to see and protects it from potential enemies—like people.

Like modern man, the prophet Jeremiah was impressed with the gorgeous coat of the leopard. Thinking of the giant cat, Jeremiah asked, "Can a leopard change its spots?" Could a leopard rearrange its spots or drop off a few? Would it be able to stack its spots on top of each other? The answer is obvious. A leopard can't change its spots in any way.

And, Jeremiah said, a person who is used to doing evil cannot turn around and start doing good. That's another reason why we need Jesus Christ. He can forgive us for the things we do wrong. And He can help us do things that are right. We can't do it entirely by ourselves. Not any more than a leopard can change its spots.

Can the Ethiopian change his skin or the leopard its spots? Neither can you do good who are accustomed to doing evil.

JEREMIAH 13:23 (NIV)

1. What does a leopard eat?

2. Describe a leopard's fur.

3. How can a person change from doing wrong to doing right?

Help me to choose the right thing to do.

86 The Dog Wears a Mask

A new breed of animal could be moving toward America. First seen in Asia, these animals have now crossed over Europe. Before long they could be brought across the ocean, where many Americans might see them for the first time.

Called the raccoon dog, it wears a short, black mask similar to the raccoon. However, it isn't closely related. Raccoon dogs are more like foxes. Even if they do become plentiful in America, the raccoon dogs will be hard to find. They roam around at night and sleep during the day.

One of the strange features about these dogs is that they share a bathroom. It isn't really a room, but they have a special place where they go. The area could be from one foot around up to five feet. Early the children (called pups) are taught to go to that one place until they leave home to lead their own lives.

Home is nothing fancy. They don't create complicated dens like a fox does. Rather, they find an opening in some weeds or set up housekeeping inside a tree. If necessary they can live under garages or other buildings.

As with many animals, the fathers play a large role in helping to care for the young. They collect food for their families and spend a great deal of time grooming the pups. Each pup will grow to almost two feet long, not counting a six-inch tail. Most have chunky bodies and weigh around eighteen pounds when they are full grown.

Part of the reason why raccoon dogs are growing in numbers is their appetite for a wide variety of foods. They love a good meal of seafood, including fish or crab. The next day they might dine on fresh bugs or a small bird. They especially like fruit, berries, or a side order of acorns. When seasons change they simply switch diets and still find plenty of food.

Despite the fact that raccoon dogs are hunted for their furs, the animal continues to increase in numbers. Even in areas where cities are being built and expanded, raccoon dogs can be seen in trees or roaming down alleys in the dark. The raccoon dog may not be extra bright like the real raccoon or the fox, but it is smart enough to change with its surroundings. When the weather changes or the streets become paved or trees are cut down, the raccoon dog finds a new way to keep going.

Sometimes all of us have to learn to change. If we keep doing things the same way, we could end up in trouble. If we have been taking things from our parents, we have to change and stop it. If we like to start fights, we have to quit that. If we are in the habit of telling white lies, we have to give them up.

God is pleased to see us change. He is the one who helps us change—we can't do it on our own. Children and adults need to improve their way of living so that we treat each other better and live at peace with God.

I tell you the truth, unless you change and become like little children, you will never enter the kingdom of heaven.

MATTHEW 18:3 (NIV)

Do You Remember?

1. Describe the home of a raccoon dog.

2. What do raccoon dogs eat?

3. A raccoon dog knows how to change when it needs to. What can we learn from this?

It takes strength to change, but there's no reason to fear it.

87 Dump-Truck Ants

My wife, Pat, and I rode in a four-wheel-drive Land Rover across roads with deep ruts and mud holes. We were on our way to Pine Ridge in beautiful Belize. It was our first visit to the Central American country located just south of Mexico on the Caribbean Sea.

Our guide, Peter, knew the area well and had no trouble finding a large anthill six to eight feet wide. Trails of ants were coming from about four directions in straight lines. There were thousands of ants, each carrying a small leaf two or three times its own size.

Racing up and down each line was a larger ant who acted like the boss. It didn't have a leaf but seemed to be busy keeping the other ants in line.

They hustled along. Not exactly running, it looked more like a rapid walk. There was plenty of motion—ants bobbing up and down as they hurried along. The boss ants scurried up the line and then back again as if they were giving silent orders.

The ants were hauling leaves into the gigantic mound and storing them in piles we couldn't see. When the supply was completed, the leaves would be allowed to rot or decompose. Later this would be food.

"Watch this," Peter said. He took a stick, placed it in one of the entrances, and rattled it around.

"Better stand back," he added. "The guard ants will be out."

Within thirty seconds, about twenty huge ants appeared. They were so large their bodies twisted as they walked. Each ant was wide and black and built like a dump truck.

"If they bite you, it will sting like a wasp. They come out to attack beetles or whatever else might try to invade them."

The guard ants (or dump trucks) raced in every direction for a minute. Finding nothing, they retreated inside. Meanwhile, the working ants kept up their quick pace of carrying leaves.

Guards are an excellent idea for all of us. If we don't stay alert and be careful, we can easily end up getting hurt. One of the things God tells us is to guard our tongue. It's easy to say things that could hurt us and our friends.

Christians are careful about what they say. When we begin to repeat a rumor or say something mean, we hurry to catch ourselves. We serve God by controlling our words.

The next time we start to say something ugly, we ought to picture those dump-truck ants. They are hustling to stop anything terrible from happening.

He who guards his mouth and his tongue keeps himself from calamity.

PROVERBS 21:23 (NIV)

Do You Remember?

1. Why do ants collect leaves?

2. What do the guard ants do?

3. Explain "guards for our mouths."

Saying hurtful things affects more people than we think.

88 Leaping Snakes

Our guide used his machete (ma-SHET-ee) to cut a path through the thick, clinging jungle. The large branches, leaves, and vines hung over us, making it difficult for the sun to break through. Our feet could barely find places to step without landing on broken trees and flattened plants.

The short walk was far different from a hike in the forest. We couldn't see very far and the leaves and vines almost smothered us.

In the jungles of Belize there is an abundance of animals, including jaguars, monkeys, snakes, and peccaries (similar to a pig). But many of the animals would rather roam at night. Animals are usually more afraid of us than we are of them. They hide in the dense jungle and normally are not seen by people unless they want to be.

Jungles receive a large amount of rain every year. In order for a healthy jungle to survive, it must have rich soil to support it. These two factors mixed with a generous amount of heat create nearly ideal growing conditions. This environment discourages too many people from living there and allows the flora (plant life) to reach enormous sizes.

The local people in Belize told me about a man who was working in a jungle where leaping snakes live. The leaping viper with fangs as sharp as razors carries a poisonous venom. If a person is bitten by this snake, he will need immediate medical attention. The leaping viper received its name because it can dart through the air the same distance as its length. Since it is three feet long, it can leap one yard.

As the man worked, a leaping viper lunged at him and bit the man through his boot. He was quickly put in a Land Rover and hurried to the capital city of Belmopan. He survived after receiving medicine to resist the poison.

Most snakes are not poisonous and are certainly unlikely to attack a person. However, we have to be careful in unfamiliar areas.

It always makes sense to be careful. When we begin doing foolish things, we easily get hurt. People who disobey God's laws are just like those who walk among snakes—they find out it's easy to be hurt.

But be very careful to keep the commandment and the law that Moses the servant of the Lord gave you.

JOSHUA 22:5 (NIV)

Do You Remember?

1. Describe a jungle.

2. Describe a leaping viper.

3. How do God's laws help us?

Careful people learn God's laws and obey them.

89 A Central American Cave

In Belize we explored a high-ceilinged cave few people get to see. It is located in the mountains near a thousand-foot waterfall. Most tourists don't know it exists. Even the local Indians and nationals seldom travel to this area.

We had to climb down a slippery bank to see the opening to this cathedral-size cave. Long vines hung across the mouth, making it difficult to see inside.

The cave wasn't long. From the entrance we could see the sun shining in from the other side. It had plenty of light so, once past the vine, we didn't need lanterns.

At the bottom of the cave was a sandy area next to a beautiful pool that had been muddied by the recent rains. Normally this water would have been clear.

On the far side of the cave was an amazing stairway. Made of limestone, the steps were almost perfectly shaped. They looked like they had been carefully carved by men, but that is not the case. Over the years the many water levels in the cave have eaten away at the limestone. The water levels have formed at such even depths that it created a nearly perfect set of steps by nature's own hand.

The ceiling of the cave was too high and dark to allow us to see if any bats or other creatures had made homes there. If we had had flashlights and more time, we would have liked to explore it further.

As we stood in the cool, damp cave, a sense of awe overcame us. Its size, its beauty, and even its mystery made us feel that we had found a special place. In unusual, gorgeous places like this, we sense the fact that God is everywhere. He does not live only on top of the earth or high above the clouds. God is found beneath the ground, living where few people ever travel.

God is everywhere we go. He leaves His marks for us to see. No matter where we go or what we do, God will be present and will give signs of His presence if we are looking for them.

In his hand are the depths of the earth.

PSALM 95:4 (NIV)

Do You Remember?

1. Describe the floor of a cave.

2. What is one way that nature helped shape this cave?

3. Does it make you feel good to know God is everywhere? Tell about it.

God is an ever-present Being.

90 Kakapo Paradise

In the dark nights of New Zealand you can still hear the booming sound of the kakapo parrot. Its call rolls across a valley and can be heard for half a mile. For many years this two-foot-long bird lived in its own paradise, enjoying life at a leisurely pace, afraid of little or nothing.

The kakapo grows wings that are of practically no use. Kakapos don't fly but rather poke slowly around the mountains in search of berries and seeds. Their idea of a special treat is to munch on a lizard.

There has never been any reason for them to hurry. A kakapo can live for fifty years if nothing bothers it. They take their time at having chicks. Usually they reproduce only once or twice every ten years.

Kakapos even look content. They weigh a pudgy six pounds, look like feathered penguins, and walk like a happy duck. People don't see them often, but they have been recorded doing their famous booming call.

The good life for the kakapo probably could have continued if they hadn't been invaded. It apparently had no enemies—until human beings arrived one thousand years ago. People brought dogs and rats with them. Soon the defenseless kakapo became a source of food.

Before long, man began cutting down trees, and the kakapo found fewer places to live. People had to have places to live and so did birds, but it looked as if there was no room for this parrot. The number of kakapos dropped so low that only thirty were believed to exist in the world.

Scientists became organized and tried to discover ways that both people and kakapos could survive. They began to hold back the enemies of the parrot.

Kakapos make excellent pets; however, they don't seem to want to have chicks while in captivity. Consequently, scientists are trying to set aside areas where the kakapo can live in the wild and be protected from enemies. There are now possibly one hundred in the world, and their numbers could grow. Unable to fight back, this parrot's best hope rests in people who really care for it.

None of us live in a paradise where there are no enemies. There are people who want to sell us drugs. We often meet someone who wants us to steal. There are many invitations to try alcohol—and then to try other things.

These people act like our friends but really they are enemies. If we say yes we could end up hurt or in trouble.

We have an offer from God. If we are willing to resist our enemies, He will help us fight them off. It may not be easy, but it can be done. We don't have to do it alone because God will give us strength and courage.

With God we will gain the victory, and he will trample down our enemies.

PSALM 60:12 (NIV)

Do You Remember?

1. Can kakapos fly?

2. Why is the kakapo in danger of extinction?

3. Who are enemies to people?

149

Help me to recognize the difference between a friend and an enemy.

91 The Sea Lion Trap

If you have ever gone to a sea animal show, you may have watched a talented sea lion perform. It can learn to bounce a ball on its nose, throw balls back and forth with other lions, and even jump out of the water and sit on a box. In some places you may have even seen them in the wild playing in the water or sunning on the rocks.

Part of the reason why sea lions are fun to train is that they have a natural curiosity. They want to try new things and investigate new places. But that same curiosity sometimes gets them into deadly trouble.

Five species of sea lions live in the world. One of the lesser known is the Hooker's sea lion that lives south of New Zealand. Based on the Campbell and Auckland islands, they led fairly peaceful lives until man and rabbits invaded their territory.

When explorers discovered the sea lions in the early 1800s, the animals were so numerous that they barely fit on the islands. Word soon spread that sea lions were plentiful, and ships from several countries raced there. They slaughtered sea lions so drastically that the population almost disappeared in just twenty-five years.

Hunters stopped coming for the next thirty years and the sea lions lived in peace again. Their numbers increased and before long the islands were covered with eight-hundred-pound sea lions. However, by 1865 the word was out that the lions were back. During the next fifteen years, more boats came and the sea lions were slaughtered again. Finally, the New Zealand government stepped in and began protecting the sea lion.

Government action kept the sea lions safe from man, but that didn't erase the problem of rabbits. Over one hundred years ago the French introduced the feral rabbit to the area. Rabbits do not look as though they could hurt a sea lion, and they don't do it intentionally.

The rabbit builds a home in the ground so it can raise its family. When a sea lion pup sees the hole in the ground, its curiosity rises. It begins to nudge at the opening and check it out. Two or three pups force their way into the rabbit burrow and become stuck. Unable to turn around, they die from lack of air.

People are curious like sea lions. Curiosity is a great gift that no one wants to lose. However, we also need to be careful so we don't get hurt or hurt someone else. That's why God gave us laws—not to be mean, but to help and warn us so we won't get hurt. People who ignore God's instruction are moving toward trouble.

Hear, O Israel, and be careful to obey so that it may go well with you.

DEUTERONOMY 6:3 (NIV)

Do You Remember?

1. Name one reason sea lions can be trained.

2. How is the rabbit dangerous to a sea lion?

3. Do you know someone who is so curious that he goes too far and gets into trouble?

Help me to rein in my curiosity when necessary.

92 The Zoo in Your Library

Don't look now but there could be a host of tiny creatures living in your local library. If you listen carefully, you might even be able to hear them. Some of the noises you hear are creaking wood, but probably not all of them. There may also be small insects making munching noises as they eat.

We call people who read a great deal *bookworms*. But actual bookworms do exist, and they are chewing their way through many libraries.

What does a bookworm consider good eating? That depends on the insect. The spider beetle enjoys gnawing straight through a book. They have been known to chew their way through twenty-five books or more.

151

Other varieties love paper or book glue. Some make a feast of the fungus on the books or the food that sometimes is left by busy readers. For special treats they eat the algae or pollen or mold that books might collect.

Well-lighted libraries with plenty of fresh air have fewer bookworms. The insects look for dark corners with high humidity or dampness. If no one checks out the book for a year or more, the worms (or lice, as they are sometimes called) eat away undisturbed.

Frequently, these destructive monsters are deposited in books as eggs. Later they hatch and, as larvae, begin to eat their way from volume to volume. They are just as much a problem in museums, where they may be more destructive. Making their way into cases and displays, they eat delicate parts of exhibits. You may find the legs or the eyes of creatures on display missing. This probably means the "booklice" have attacked the museum and are eating their way from showcase to showcase.

Don't use the threat of bookworms as an excuse to give up doing your homework. They aren't very harmful to people. Their numbers could be reduced remarkably if we would clean our bookshelves, keep the area dry and well-lighted, and read our books more often.

There is one special book that neither worms nor lice are able to eat or destroy. It's called the Book of Life. We don't know much about it except the Bible says that the names of Christians are written in it. When you ask Jesus Christ to come into your life, your name is recorded. That record is kept forever, and you become part of God's family.

Yes, and I ask you, loyal yokefellow, help these women who have contended at my side in the cause of the gospel, along with Clement and the rest of my fellow workers, whose names are in the book of life.

PHILIPPIANS 4:3 (NIV)

Do You Remember?

1. How do bookworms do damage in libraries?

2. How can bookworms be prevented?

3. What book can't worms and lice destroy?

The Book of Life is a family record of believers who belong to Jesus.

93 Causing Landslides

Squirrels are among God's cutest creatures. You can see them running across telephone wires or sitting on the lawn chewing acorns. They bounce across the yard with their rust-colored tails bobbing up and down.

However, a few squirrels, especially ground squirrels, are not loved everywhere. Ground squirrels don't live in trees but in burrows dug beneath the ground. Normally they make their homes in the desert, on rolling meadows, or on flat prairies. But some dig their homes on the sides of mountains, and this is when people get especially angry.

Ground squirrels look cute and harmless. Their appearance is more like a chipmunk or a prairie dog. They can be red, brown, black, gray, or even white.

Unfortunately, they enjoy large families and are willing to dig wide homes for their many children. A ground squirrel can birth four to twelve young each spring.

As the ground squirrel population rapidly increases, they make their colonies larger until they have dug up much of a mountainside. If a hard rain hits the loose dirt, a landslide can quickly result. When people have built large, expensive homes on those mountainsides, the results can be terrible.

California has a particular problem with hillsides and ground squirrels. During rainstorms, million-dollar homes slide down the hills. If squirrels had not dug homes in these areas, the destruction may not have occurred.

When five hundred squirrels take up residence in one area, the ground can become soft. Squirrels can weaken dams and threaten the homes of hundreds of people. This creates a problem. People don't want to get rid of the squirrels, but they cannot permit the destruction to continue.

The squirrels don't know any better. They don't want to see their burrows or homes washed away either. But even if they fail to understand the destruction they are doing, they still must be stopped.

When people refuse to be careful, we can do a great deal of harm too. If we lie or steal or cheat, we hurt others as well as ourselves. Before we realize what we have done, we have created more problems than we can correct.

But one sinner destroys much good.
ECCLESIASTES 9:18 (NIV)

Do You Remember?

1. What colors can ground squirrels be?

2. How does a ground squirrel do damage?

3. Do you know a person who hurts other people? Tell about it.

Christians don't want to bring pain to themselves or to others.

94 Unusual Facts

Did you know that the praying mantis has only one ear? It is located in the center of the creature's back. Researchers used to believe the mantis was deaf, but now they think it can hear sounds far out of our human range.

Terrible stories have been told of tigers attacking people in India. Over a period of time, a tiger in the district of Champawat killed 436 humans. Some authorities believe that mainly wounded tigers kill people.

Large birds may have as many as twenty-five thousand feathers.

A trained pigeon can travel halfway across the United States and still find its way back home.

Pelicans have a different way of feeding their young. The mother swallows a fish and allows it to partially digest in her stomach. She then brings the food back up into her pouch-beak, where her young eat from it.

It is believed that no two zebras are striped exactly alike. Each has its own pattern, like a human's fingerprints.

A twelve-ton sperm whale eats eight hundred pounds of fish a day.

When a peregrine falcon soars down to grab a small bird, it can reach a speed of 250 miles per hour.

A baby emperor penguin sits on its mother's foot to get a free ride.

The bittern bird is a ventriloquist. Scientists believe it can "throw" its voice to fool attackers.

Centipedes have as many as 173 pairs of legs. The first pair of legs are poisonous claws. The poison is strong enough to make humans sick.

Each of us can know God by believing in His Son, Jesus Christ.

Jesus answered, "I am the way and the truth and the life. No one comes to the Father except through me."

JOHN 14:6 (NIV)

Do You Remember?

1. How may feathers can a large bird have?

2. How does a pelican feed its young?

3. How does a baby emperor penguin get a free ride?

Every person has a purpose.

95 Hiding in the Rocks

Have you ever seen a small mouselike creature spreading leaves on a rock? If you have, it was probably a pika drying its "hay" before storing it for the winter. This six-inch rock-dweller has enough sense to get ready for the long cold months that lie ahead.

Pikas don't hibernate, and often their homes are covered with snow. If they don't store enough to eat, they could starve before spring.

The pika collects plants for its pantry. To stay healthy they have to eat large amounts, which means the haystacks will need to be sizable. A pika will mark off its territory beneath the rocks or boulders and stuff that area with food.

Pikas can be found in many parts of the world. In the United States they are located in the Colorado Rockies and other mountainous regions. Scientists love to argue over whether pikas belong to the rodent or rabbit family.

Because of its size, the pika needs clever ways to protect itself. Basically it is dependent on two forms of warnings: noisy and silent. If a pika sees a hawk flying near, it gives a terrible barking sound. However, if a ground animal enters its territory, silence is the better plan. Weasels will hear the barking and slide between the rocks to hunt the pika.

No matter who the attacker, the pika's best hope of escape is to scurry between the rocks. They aren't large enough to fight back and must depend on a good hiding place.

They have relatives called coneys, or rock hyraxes, which have lived in Syria and Israel. Both Solomon and Jesus were probably familiar with these animals and watched them hustling among the rocks. They have quick feet that adapt easily to the hard surfaces they live on. Some have padded feet with small suction cups that help them climb in different situations.

Proverbs tells us that coneys, the pika-like relative, are creatures with little power. That is why they live among the crags of rocks (Proverbs 30:26). The rocks protect them when they can't defend themselves.

There are many times when we are like the pika or the coney. We can't take care of ourselves. Maybe there are evil people who want to trick us and get us to follow them. Maybe we can feel ourselves being drawn to do something terrible and we don't know if we can resist it.

That's a good time to head directly for the Rock. Our Rock is God and He offers us protection. God, our Rock, will always provide us with a welcome place when we need Him.

The Lord is my rock, my fortress and my deliverer; my God is my rock, in whom I take refuge.

PSALM 18:2 (NIV)

Do You Remember?

1. How does a pika store its winter food supply?

2. How does a pika protect itself?

3. Have you ever needed to find protection in the Rock? Tell about it.

Help me to know when I'm being fooled.

96 Living Dragons

The San Diego Zoo recently tried to raise Komodo dragons, but the experiment fizzled. Both the male and female died without leaving any babies. This was terribly disappointing to scientists because the number of dragons is down to a few thousand and continues to dwindle.

157

Komodos are actually lizards, but they are ugly enough and mean enough to be called dragons. Normally they are found on Komodo Island, an Indonesian territory only 250 miles from Australia. No small creature, they can reach lengths of ten to twelve feet.

When angry, the Komodo puts on a terrifying display. It rears back, thrusts out its tongue, and makes a terrifying hiss. Its armor-looking scales and swinging tail are enough to make you wish a knight were there to rescue you.

It isn't just their appearance that makes people tremble. Komodos are extremely dangerous. They will kill a pig or even a water buffalo. Some even insist that dragons have killed and eaten people.

They may be exciting to study, but they don't sound like great pets. Having a Komodo eat in your house could be more than your parents could handle. Watching a 365-pound lizard eat could be disgusting.

Not picky eaters, with one bite they will tear out the entire side of a dead animal. They gobble down bugs, fur, bones, whatever they manage to rip loose with the flesh. They would think nothing of finishing off an entire goat in one meal. Satisfied, the Komodo would then probably crawl up on your couch and sleep for a week or more while the food settles.

Too bad their parents didn't teach them to control their eating habits. Dragons crunch, tear, and smack at their food. If the selection doesn't agree with them, the Komodos will simply throw up.

We are careful what we eat and how much. The habits we develop while we are young will help keep us healthy as we grow.

If you find honey, eat just enough—too much of it, and you will vomit.

PROVERBS 25:16 (NIV)

Do You Remember?

1. Are Komodo dragons dangerous?

2. Are Komodos really dragons?

3. Think of a way to make your eating patterns more healthful.

Help me to control my feelings of gluttony.

97 The Show-Off Frigate Birds

How many times have you watched someone showing off? Once in a while all of us do it. Even adults like to show off their cars or impress people with how much they know.

Nature is filled with creatures that like to do things to get attention. One of the most famous is the frigate bird. This bird lives in warm climates, looks graceful hovering in the sky, and has a strong seafood diet.

The frigate birds look almost motionless as they float in the air. They hover over an area until they see a fish near the surface, and then they drop down quickly. Sometimes they aren't too particular about where they get their food and will steal the fish that other birds catch.

Frigate birds can grow to three and a half feet long and may have a wingspan of eight feet.

When a male frigate bird wants to show off for the females, he uses a balloon system. There is a wrinkled red pouch located on his throat. He has a method of sucking air into the balloon, and for nearly half an hour he blows it up.

For some reason the girl frigate birds think this is macho and pay more attention to the show-off. That only encourages him. He struts around with his burly chest, making sure everyone sees it. If he feels someone still might miss it, Mr. Frigate Bird flies around like a colorful blimp. His show might go on for hours.

There isn't anything wrong with the frigate bird playing this game. It's part of the bird's natural lifestyle. That's the way God made them. But when it comes to people showing off, it's another story. Sometimes we go too far trying to impress each other. How many times have you tried to show off how much you know?

The Bible tells us to stop showing off our knowledge. It's all right to be smart, but it's wrong to make others feel bad when we show off.

If we want to show something to others, let us show them how much we can love. Let's help our friends; let's think of them first; let's be kind. We can give love to our parents instead of acting like know-it-alls. And they can give love back to us.

Knowledge puffs up, but love builds up.

1 Corinthians 8:1 (niv)

Do You Remember?

1. Explain the frigate bird's balloon system.

2. How big is a frigate bird's wingspan?

3. Name some good things to show others.

Secure people don't feel like they have to show off.

98 Tricky Little Creatures

Animals may not be as smart as people, but they are excellent at pretending and fooling each other. Every day is a struggle for food. They need to know how to get a meal without becoming one themselves. To accomplish that, they often use every trick you can imagine.

The dead-leaf butterfly is a good example of the actor in full costume. They not only have the same color as an old leaf, but they also have a similar ragged edge. When they fly, the dead-leaf butterflies twist their bodies to look like falling leaves.

Bombardier beetles have an unusual method of fighting their enemies. They can squirt a foul-smelling fluid that becomes a puff of smoke when it hits the air, giving them time to escape. A couple shots and practically any creature will back away. They aren't trying to fool anyone. The bombardier beetle really is dangerous.

There is another beetle, a relative of the bombardier. It is a tricky one. It will do a headstand to scare its enemies, which will beat a quick retreat. The pretending beetle then walks away with a grin on its face.

Have you ever leaned against a tree and been surprised when a piece of bark suddenly flew away? It looked like bark, but it was actually the underwing moth, which is almost invisible on tree trunks.

Even the poor firefly has a rough life. Some of its bug relatives can imitate their flashing signals. If a firefly rushes over to answer the phony signal, it could immediately be eaten.

Scientists will continue to argue over exactly how intelligent animals are, but most will agree that animals are clever. An assassin bug is "smart" enough to use the carcass of a termite to draw other termites its way.

Animals are often born with some of their tricks—they didn't learn them—but other forms of imitation may clearly be copied.

Trickery isn't confined to animal forms, though. Many people keep constantly busy trying to fool each other. They even brag about how they cheated someone or lied, as if deceiving a person is a talent they are proud of.

When we play games, it's fun to use tricks, but that isn't how we should treat people in real life.

Do not deceive one another.
Leviticus 19:11 (NIV)

Do You Remember?

1. How does a dead-leaf butterfly trick its enemies?

2. How does a bombardier beetle get away from its enemies?

3. Can you think of ways you will be honest and not try to fool others?

We shouldn't try to deceive others and take advantage of them.

99 The Happy Acrobats

Why do gibbons carry their arms over their heads, wiggling them like loose spaghetti? Are they simply clowns looking for laughs from their friends? No, they don't know what else to do with them.

A gibbon's arms are designed for climbing trees and not for walking. If they allowed their hands to hang down by their sides, as humans do, their knuckles would scrape the ground. They can also keep their balance better by twisting their arms as they hurry along.

If you want to see gifted gibbons at their best, watch them move among the trees. Normally they live in the high branches, where they are as comfortable as any human in a living room. Gibbons don't need nests but prefer to sit on a branch far out from the trunk.

Gibbons don't fight their enemies—they run away. They can race through the branches faster than you or I could run along the ground.

At full speed they can leap twenty-five to thirty-five feet from tree to tree. They are gifted acrobats with amazing hands. A gibbon hand does not have to grab a branch; its hands serve more as hooks. They merely hit the branch and swing on to the next one. Called *brachiation* (bray-kee-AY-shun), this movement greatly increases their speed.

Sailing in the air from tree to tree, the quick gibbon can grab a bird while both are in midflight. He will then hit the next branch in almost perfect timing. If a gibbon needs to haul food to its family, it merely grasps the object in its feet and swings freely with its hands.

We all appreciate seeing talented animals. The gibbon can do a great many things I can't do. I don't carry food in my feet, and any attempts I would make to leap thirty feet from tree to tree would only get me hurt.

Fortunately, we don't need the same talents as these apes. Each of us has abilities and gifts. We aren't jealous of animals and we don't have to be jealous of other people.

We can be happy with the gifts God has given us. We learn to read, work computers, and sing. God has given us so much ability we don't have to envy anyone.

Every good and perfect gift is from above, coming down from the Father of the heavenly lights.

JAMES 1:17 (NIV)

Do You Remember?

1. Why do gibbons carry their arms over their heads when walking?

2. How are their hands used when gibbons swing from tree to tree?

3. Name five things you do well.

God has given all of us gifts.

100 Sweetlips

Some people's names tell us what they look like. Someone might be nicknamed Curly because his hair is curly, or Slim because he's tall and thin. Lefty and Red are some other common nicknames.

In the sea world we have given odd names to many creatures. Usually these names describe the appearance or the behavior of the animal.

We don't know who first called a certain fish sweetlips, but if you could see this fish, you would understand why. A sweetlip naturally has large lips. The fish will leave its lips open and allow little fish called wrasse (ras) to eat from its mouth. The wrasse eats parasites and diseased tissue. It does sweetlips a big favor.

Can you guess how a surgeonfish got its name? It carries small knives. Actually they are sharp spines, but they can cut like a razor. There are one hundred different kinds of surgeonfish, and the strangest is the yellow surgeon. Their spines have jackknives. These knives pop out and then go back into hiding.

Maybe you enjoy hard names. Try pronouncing humuhumunukunuku-apuaa (hoo-muh-hoo-muh-noo-kuh-noo-kuh-ah-puh-WAH-ah). This little creature lives near Hawaii. Its more popular name is the triggerfish.

You need to see the hatchetfish to understand how it got its name. A small fish, it has a tiny tail and a large body. It looks like something that could chop wood.

Many sharks look alike—except for one. The hammerhead shark is different. It has a wide, flat nose. Its eyes are far apart at each end of its nose. Despite its strange appearance, the hammerhead is still a dangerous creature.

Names are labels. We would be at a loss if we didn't have them. Most of the names we have heard we have already forgotten. There are just too many to remember.

Yet one name stands out above all others. The name *Jesus* is special. It means Savior or salvation and applies to the Son of God. His name describes what He is. Jesus is our Savior. His life, death, and resurrection have made it possible for us to live with Him forever.

Someday everyone will bow down before the name of Jesus Christ.

That at the name of Jesus every knee shall bow in heaven and on earth and under the earth.

PHILIPPIANS 2:10 (TLB)

Do You Remember?

1. How did the surgeonfish get its name?

2. What helps sweetlips?

164 3. Why is the name of Jesus important?

There is one name above all others. We thank you for the meaning of your name, Jesus.

101 Saving Ferrets

Everyone thought the black-footed ferret was gone forever. No one had seen the animal in Wyoming for fifteen years. But when a woman reported that her dog had killed an odd animal, scientists hoped it might be the ferret they'd been looking for. And it was.

The search was on again in full force. Money was given by federal, state, and private organizations to find and protect this wiry little creature.

Most searches centered around prairie dog colonies. Black-footed ferrets like to move into a prairie dog's home and eat the occupants.

Finally researchers began to sight ferrets. In Meeteetse, Wyoming, they found nearly forty living in twelve litters. Naturalists then took on the job of preserving the ferret and helping its population grow. This is where the Soviet Union became involved.

Practically every effort to get the ferret to breed in captivity failed. At this point, the zoo in Moscow agreed to help by loaning six Siberian ferrets to the United States. They are the black-footed ferrets' closest relatives. Their hope is to breed the Siberian ferrets with the black-footed ferrets and increase their population.

Why would scientists dedicate so much of their careers to saving this little-known animal that practically no one has seen in the wild? Why would governments spend large sums of money? Why would nations agree to cooperate to save a rare animal that eats prairie dogs? It's because people care what happens to even one of the minor animals in a huge world.

If they care this much for animals, imagine how much God cares for one person. He would do all of this and more to bring one of us to himself. God wants us to be part of His family. That's why He sent His Son to die on the cross. He considered one person, you, so important that God would sacrifice, suffer, search, and work to get us to believe and serve Him.

Suppose one of you has a hundred sheep and loses one of them. Does he not leave the ninety-nine in the open country and go after the lost sheep until he finds it?

LUKE 15:4 (NIV)

I tell you that in the same way there is more rejoicing in heaven over one sinner who repents than over ninety-nine righteous persons who do not need to repent.

LUKE 15:7 (NIV)

Do You Remember?

1. What kind of home does a ferret prefer?

2. How did the Soviet Union cooperate to protect ferrets?

3. How has God shown how valuable you are?

You and I are worth far more than any animal.

102 Wapiti Is King

A lion may be king of the jungle, but the wapiti is king of North America, and it has the crown to prove it. This majestic animal is an elk and a member of the deer family. If you aren't familiar with wapiti, you'll probably confuse them with the larger moose.

The male wapiti's crown consists of a royal rack of antlers that grows every year. The place where the antlers grow is called a pedicel (PED-i-sell). Antlers are different from horns in looks and build. Horns are hollow and can be used as trumpets, containers, and even hearing aids. Antlers are made of solid bone and are heavier and often larger. You never want to insult an elk by saying it has beautiful horns.

A thin layer of skin (soft like velvet) will grow to cover the antlers, which the wapiti will take some time to rub off. Around March an adult wapiti, or white-rumped elk, will shed its antlers. Since he doesn't cast off both sides at once, he could be in an awkward fix for a time. Antlers are heavy, and if only one side is left, the wapiti will have trouble keeping its balance. To correct the problem, the bull will keep stabbing at trees and at the ground, trying to dislodge the remaining half of its crown. When the antlers are gone, he has four or five months to grow a new set.

The people who study antlers give each part a name. The stem coming out of the wapiti head is called a beam; the first branch of the beam is a brow tine, the second is a bez tine, the third is a trez. All of the top branches are surroyals.

Occasionally a wapiti is seen carrying antlers with eight or more tines on each beam; this is considered a true monarch of the outdoors.

Why does a wapiti need antlers? They typically don't use them for self-defense; for most of a wapiti's enemies, a swift kick with their powerful hoofs is enough to send the enemy whimpering.

The big use of these antlers is to fight the other elk during mating season. Mostly it's for show. They don't usually do much harm to each other, but a mock battle is what all of the wapiti seem to expect.

Antlers are crowns to the male wapitis, and they look forward to them each year. God gives people crowns too, but they aren't always the kind you wear on your head. Each child is a crown for his grandparents. Like tines on an antler, children make the elderly and middle-aged feel like royalty.

When children spend time with their grandparents, they usually make them feel like kings and queens.

Children's children are a crown to the aged.

PROVERBS 17:6 (NIV)

1. How are horns and antlers different?

2. How often do wapiti get a new set of antlers?

3. What can you do this week to make your grandparents happy?

When I spend time with my elders, I make them happy.

103 Storks on Your Roof

How did the story about storks bringing babies start? No one can be certain, but it probably began in Europe. Storks made their nests on the roofs of homes in countries like Denmark, Holland, and Germany. Because storks were considered good luck, they were welcomed. Some homeowners even built special platforms on their roofs to encourage the leggy birds to settle with them.

Legends were plentiful about the value of having storks live on your home. They were supposed to keep lightning from striking. Others felt their feathered friends brought financial prosperity. Thousands of storks lived in large cities, making the home-owners feel better.

While those stories were so popular, someone thought they noticed storks around houses just before a baby was born. Since storks were near most houses most of the time, it was easy to believe that storks had something to do with babies. From that began the rumor that storks brought the soul to a newborn baby. How much people actually believed it is hard to say. Maybe it was simply an amusing tale.

168

It was a short jump from the myth that storks bring souls to babies, to the myth that they brought the entire baby. Later it was easier to tell the stork story than tell children where babies really come from.

Even if the story isn't real, the stork is. They can be found on every continent except for Antarctica. Storks look like they walk on stilts and reach a height of four feet. Despite their awkward appearance, they can fly extremely well. Their landings look disjointed, but they manage with reasonable safety.

Storks have an amazing ability to migrate thousands of miles. European storks fly to South Africa, making a round trip of over fourteen thousand miles. While in Africa they live a different lifestyle, as if they were on vacation. Storks live along the rivers, where they lead a rural life. They stay away from rooftop dwellings until they return to their cities in Europe.

As part of their normal route, many storks travel across Israel. The prophet Jeremiah probably saw many of the gangly birds coming and going. He told us we could learn by watching the stork. Unable to read or write, the stork knows exactly what it is supposed to do and does it. Storks have enough sense to migrate when they need to because God created them that way.

You and I were created to obey God, but many of us fail to show the good judgment of a stork. We rebel, sin, disobey, and throw tantrums. Too often we don't have the sense to follow God.

The next time we begin to do something foolish and disobey God, we should say to ourselves, "Even a stork is smart enough to keep God's laws."

Even the stork in the sky knows her appointed seasons, and the dove, the swift and the thrush observe the time of their migration. But my people do not know the requirements of the Lord.

JEREMIAH 8:7 (NIV)

Do You Remember?

1. Describe how the story of storks bringing babies started.

2. Tell about the storks' migration.

3. How does a stork find its way when traveling?

169

We should follow through with what we know is right.

104 Adopted Monkeys

Have you ever seen a picture of an organ grinder on a street corner? As the man grinds or cranks the organ, his monkey on a chain dances around with a tin cup. When it approaches you, the monkey hopes you will throw a coin in the metal container. Better than a picture, maybe you have even seen the man and his monkey in person.

These little monkeys must be the cutest animals in the world. Most often they are the capuchin monkey. Found in Central and South America and on the island of Trinidad, they live in small groups, traveling among the trees looking for food.

If you have ever eaten ice cream and found it smeared all over your face, you can imagine how some of these monkeys look after eating something. They eat and drink from flowers, and one of their favorites contains orange pollen. After drinking from these flowers, the baby capuchins usually have orange sprinkled over their faces. They look comical with their big round eyes and colored cheeks.

Jungles are dangerous places, especially for monkeys. They may have fun climbing trees and sampling exotic foods, but at any second they could be in life-threatening danger from eagles or large roaming cats.

Because of the hardships involved, many of the adult monkeys look out for the young. They help open hard fruit for them and stand guard while they eat it. If an adult tries to steal food, another adult will quickly come to the baby's rescue. When an eagle is sighted, a grown capuchin will begin issuing a warning call for the youngster to scurry for cover. The thoughtful adult will keep his siren going until the eagle has totally left the area.

Frequently a mother capuchin dies or is killed in the cruel jungle. Fortunately another mother will adopt the baby monkey and help guide it into adulthood.

There are a number of reasons why human children are adopted. Every year thousands of adult couples who are waiting for a child to join them adopt a boy or girl.

Every year millions of us at all ages are adopted into the family of God. We become His children by placing our faith in Jesus Christ. God wants all of us to be a part of His family.

He predestined us to be adopted as his sons through Jesus Christ.

EPHESIANS 1:5 (NIV)

Do You Remember?

1. Where do capuchin monkeys live?

2. How do adult monkeys help young monkeys?

3. What do you think it means to be adopted into God's family?

God invites all of us to come to Him.

105 Did You Know?

Female kangaroos are called flyers because they travel so fast. Adult males are boomers. Kangaroo children are joeys.

Elephants are such good swimmers that they can be in the water for as long as six hours at a time.

Fur is really an extra-thick growth of hair.

Cats walk on tiptoe. Their claws are hidden inside their paws but can pop out in a second, ready for battle when danger is near.

Portuguese sailors thought coconuts looked like monkey faces. They named them *coco*, which means *monkey* in Portuguese.

The lynx gets its name from its excellent eyesight. A wild cat, its name is Greek for "keen sight."

Turtles are the only reptiles that are toothless. Sharp beaks, however, can do any biting they may need.

The Irish elk is neither Irish nor an elk.

Ticks and chiggers are not insects but are members of the spider family.

A daddy longlegs has eight legs and belongs to the spider family. If a young one loses a leg, it may be able to grow a new one.

The Australian giant clam weighs up to five hundred pounds.

Elephants are so careful they can crack a coconut shell without cracking the meat.

Unlike many of its cat relatives, the tiger seems to enjoy water. A mother tiger will take her cubs to a stream and teach them how to swim.

If elephants do not wear down their tusks, the ivory will become too heavy to carry.

Reindeer have waterproof coats. The fur holds air and helps keep the animal up as it crosses rivers.

Did you know that Jesus Christ died for everyone—and that includes you?

> *But God demonstrates his own love for us in this: While we were still sinners, Christ died for us.*
>
> **ROMANS 5:8 (NIV)**

Do You Remember?

1. What are kangaroo children called?

2. What animal walks on tiptoe?

3. Which reptile is toothless?

Jesus paid for our sins and prepared a place in heaven for us.

172

106 Deadly Tarantulas?

There aren't many words that can send shivers up your spine, but the name tarantula probably gives you the chills. There are hundreds of scary stories about the hairy little spider with eight eyes.

It's possible that a few people have died from the poison in a tarantula bite, but it can't be many. Tarantulas in South America can be dangerous, but normally a bite from one in the southern United States would only be as harmful as a beesting.

Like most creatures, tarantulas aren't eager to mix with people. Most of the time they hide around the entrances of their burrows, trying to avoid anything they can't eat. If they sense a stranger, the tarantula simply disappears. The idea of attacking a human has probably never occurred to this spider.

The type of food tarantulas usually enjoy is a main course of grasshoppers or beetles. If they become large enough, their diet will include a juicy frog or lizard.

There are thirty kinds of tarantulas in the United States and six hundred varieties worldwide. The thousands of hairs on their bodies serve a double purpose. First, they seem to act as ears. The hairs pick up vibrations. Second, they become weapons. If an animal, like a skunk, sniffs around his burrow, the tarantula shakes off some hairs, which get caught in the attacker's eyes and nose. They make the skunk so miserable it is happy to retreat quickly.

Despite the fairly harmless nature of the tarantula, its reputation as a killer has remained for hundreds of years. Movies have been made and stories written about the hairy-legged tarantula and its ability to kill. Most of the horrible details are imaginary.

Once a false story spreads, it's hard to erase it. That's why it's important not to start them. Too many people have been hurt for years because people were willing to believe a story that was absolutely untrue.

Don't accuse people falsely.

LUKE 3:14 (NIV)

Do You Remember?

1. Are tarantulas in the United States poisonous?

2. What is the purpose of the thousands of hairs on their bodies?

3. How can you prevent false stories from spreading?

Get the facts straight before you believe a story.

107 Mini Pigs

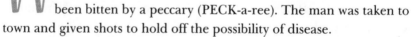

When we were visiting Central America, we heard that a member of a film crew had been bitten by a peccary (PECK-a-ree). The man was taken to town and given shots to hold off the possibility of disease.

The animal that bit him was a small member of the pig family. Peccaries are only three feet long and stand a foot and a half tall at the shoulder. Pigs raised on farms are usually much larger. Peccaries can be found in New Mexico, Texas, and Arizona as well as throughout the tropical countries.

Peccaries are highly sociable creatures that hang around in herds of three to a hundred. The hunter who goes after a peccary must be alert. Instinctively the peccary's friends and relatives will run to protect one of their own.

A herd of peccaries marks off an area they want for their home ground. The territory may equal a total mile. Peccaries might look nearly all alike, but they have a way to distinguish each other. Special musk glands allow them to carry a distinctive odor. Members of their herd can tell from the smell who belongs to their group, and they chase off the others.

Peccaries have four toes on the front feet and three toes on the hind feet; this possibly gives them a firm stance while they root in the ground with their famous snouts.

Peccaries' real strength is the ability to establish a herd and maintain dependence on each other. They are stronger because of their numbers. They are more secure because they can count on each other in case of trouble. Food supplies are easier to keep because they do not allow other peccaries to steal from them.

Peccaries have developed a lifestyle designed to help each other. Christians do something similar. If we have a need, we try to help each other.

Christians don't make good lone wolves. We are more like peccaries, who watch out for members of the herd.

Be completely humble and gentle; be patient, bearing with one another in love. Make every effort to keep the unity of the Spirit through the bond of peace.

Ephesians 4:2–3 (niv)

Do You Remember?

1. Peccaries are members of what family?

2. Tell about peccaries' toes.

3. Tell how Christians you know help each other.

Christians help each other.

108 Tents of Snow

Hunting in temperatures of twenty-five below zero can be dangerous if you don't know how to protect yourself. For hundreds of years the Eskimo, or Inuit, have known how to hunt seals in frozen conditions and yet stay warm at night when they sleep. When they need a warm place to bed down, they just build a tent out of snow, which they call an igluvigak.

Experienced igloo builders can build a snow tent in about an hour. Usually two men work on the structure, cutting out large blocks of snow with a special snow knife. Blocks are stacked leaning inward until they meet at a curved top, reaching twelve feet high. A short tunnel is built to keep the winds out, and often a block of ice is inserted in the wall to allow light in.

Camping on the ice may not sound like motel living, but it can be quite enjoyable. A fire is built on the floor. They don't have water beds, but they spread furs over the ground to create ice beds. The temperature in an igluvigak can reach seventy degrees, making it as warm as your house. A hole in the top of the snow tent provides an opening for fresh air and allows smoke to escape.

Food is seldom a problem. There are no stores for hundreds of miles, but the seals caught during the day are kept in a corner of the igloo set aside for just that purpose. It doesn't take an Inuit mother long to put a tasty meal together from these supplies. A floor space ten feet across gives an entire family plenty of room to operate.

Time changes most things, and the igluvigak is now being replaced with modern tents by most Eskimos, but several Inuits prefer the walls of snow. Often they build them so their children will not forget the ways of their grandparents.

Tents of animal skins, cloth, and snow have been a part of the lives of countless millions. In Bible times people liked to think of God as living in a tent. When they spoke of dying and going to live with God, they pictured a magnificent tent with walls made of rare animal hides and decorated with fine trappings. The center of the structure was God, and they looked forward to being with Him forever.

By believing in Jesus Christ we each have the promise of spending eternity with God. No one knows what the area might look like, but it could be in a spectacular tent. Maybe even one made of snow.

I long to dwell in your tent forever.

Psalm 61:4 (niv)

Do You Remember?

1. What is another name for the Inuit?

2. How is an igluvigak built?

3. How do you picture a home in heaven?

As a Christian, I'm looking forward to spending eternity in heaven.

176

109 A Mean Wolverine

Trappers claim you have to be fast to catch a wolverine. If caught in a steel cage, this forty-pound member of the weasel family will begin to dismantle the trap. When held in a foot trap, it will first try to take the hinges apart, but if that fails, it might chew its toes off.

Any animal this tough is soon respected and feared. Some of the stories about them are hard to check for sure. There aren't many wolverines, and during the summer they go up into the mountains of Montana and other areas to avoid people.

Some scientists believe it is basically a shy, quiet creature. But there is no doubt that when the wolverine turns nasty, it is given plenty of room by most animals.

One account claims a wolverine took the life of a polar bear in battle. Backwoodsmen insist the wolverine knows no fear. When wolverines tear into battle, grunting and slashing, they fight until the death. Razor-sharp teeth and long claws make them champions in most conflicts.

A wolverine's reputation in war is only part of his bad reputation. Trappers insist that the angry animal will try to wreck traps on purpose. Wolverines have been known to eat parts of animals caught in traps and then destroy the rest.

Because wolverines seem so mean, Eskimos call them the Evil One. People don't love the idea of protecting the wolverine because its foul temper makes it undesirable.

That same rule carries over to people. Those who are kind and thoughtful are often welcomed, loved, and admired. The cruel ones are kept at a distance and ignored.

Our behavior has a way of coming back to reward us. Mean people hurt themselves. Good people receive good treatment most of the time.

A kind man benefits himself, but a cruel man brings trouble on himself.

PROVERBS 11:17 (NIV)

Do You Remember?

1. Few people see wolverines. Why is this?

2. What do trappers tell us about wolverines?

3. How can you continue to build a good reputation today?

Doing good brings good things upon me.

110 Flapping Their Funny Feet

All of us want to look attractive. That's why we wash our faces and comb our hair. We wear clothes that are clean and usually neatly pressed. Not many of us want to look like something that fell off a garbage truck.

The booby is a bird that has the same interest we have. It wants to look good for other booby birds. After the bird has been flying and is making a landing, the male booby will try to show the females how sharp he looks. While landing he will start flapping his webbed feet. If she sees his feet flapping, she will think he is one special bird.

His feet are special. The red-footed booby will turn the heads of some females, while the blue-footed ones look great to others. To us non-boobies, he seems to be making a goofy landing, but the bird thinks he's cool.

That's how the booby birds got their name. They act like comedians, so they have earned a name that comes from the Spanish word *bobo*, meaning "clown."

When the booby isn't showing off, it spends most of its time in the air searching for food. Floating high above the water, it stays ready to dive at the first sight of fish. When it attacks, the booby can swim well enough to actually chase a fish underwater. Boobies are fast, strong, and skillful.

Their body structures equip the booby especially well for flight, but they do have some reasons to spend time on the ground. They enjoy raising families in their small, plain nests. When their chicks are first born, the parents remain home to keep their feathered children from wandering away.

Chicks have a natural curiosity; they like to stray off to investigate other nests. While the adventurous spirit is admirable, it's also dangerous. It would be far better for them to stay close and learn from their parents before poking their beaks into places where they might get hurt.

Human beings suffer from the same temptations. We want to get away from home and try things that we know could be harmful. We don't want to listen to anyone. So we keep poking into dangerous situations.

Smart people stay close to home, especially while they are young. There is a great deal to learn and we can learn much of it at home.

Like a bird that strays from its nest is a man who strays from his home.

PROVERBS 27:8 (NIV)

Do You Remember?

1. What is the origin of the name "booby bird"?

2. Why does the booby bird flap its webbed feet when landing?

3. Why does the Bible tell us to listen to our parents' teaching?

If we are looking for trouble, we are sure to find it.

179

111 Horseshoe Crabs and Free Rides

They look a little like old army tanks, and each year they invade the shores of the East Coast of the United States and Mexico. If you aren't used to them, you wonder what kind of prehistoric monster has crawled out of the sea. Millions of horseshoe crabs make their landing each spring.

There isn't anything quite like a horseshoe crab. They aren't really crabs. In fact, if they have relatives, they are spiders and scorpions, but even that's hard to believe since they don't look anything alike.

Also known as the king crab, these awkward creatures have a tough time making it from the sea to dry land. The male, or bull crab, is smaller than its female counterpart. She is over a foot across and better able to climb in and out of the watery holes. Sometimes Mrs. Horseshoe Crab provides free rides. The male clasps his claws to the sides of the female and travels piggyback to the shore. They need each other to keep their life cycle going and aren't too proud to give and accept help.

Stories like this appear frequently in nature. In many cases animals need each other to survive. They provide food, housing, warning calls, bug inspection, transportation, baby-sitting services, and acting lessons.

Most people don't make good loners either. We need warning calls and sometimes a little bug inspection. That explains one of the reasons why God created men and women. The great majority of us need each other.

But for Adam no suitable helper was found. So the Lord God caused the man to fall into a deep sleep; and while he was sleeping, he took one of the man's ribs and closed up the place with flesh.

GENESIS 2:20–21 (NIV)

Do You Remember?

1. Are horseshoe crabs actually crabs?

2. How does the male horseshoe crab depend on the female?

3. Who is probably your best helper right now?

God is extra good at being thoughtful.

112 Ladybugs in Your Refrigerator

When a ladybug lands on your arm, be careful how you brush it off. We don't want to hurt a friend that helps fight harmful bugs. Ladybugs eat a huge number of aphids, mealybugs, whiteflies, green-bugs, and spider mites. Farmers benefit because the red, tan, or black bug will make a feast out of corn earworm or cotton leafworm.

These brightly colored bugs are so useful that some people keep them in a jar in their refrigerator. Ladybugs survive well this way because they hibernate. If houseplants are bothered by aphids, the owner can release the chilled bugs in the living room. After the aphids are eaten, the ladybugs are collected and stored back in the cooler.

A member of the beetle family, one ladybug can eat up to three hundred tiny aphids. But that's only a small part of the way this bug eater is used to keep nature in balance. Every winter workers are sent into the mountains of the western United States to gather hibernating ladybugs. They pick millions and place them in jars. By keeping them at low temperatures, the ladybugs are perfectly safe until they are needed.

When the weather warms up, farmers release these bugs into their fields. Soon they perform the needed job of pest control without using chemicals.

Naturalists have employed ladybugs in apple orchards, potato and sugar-beet fields, and cornfields. It's easier to use chemicals and probably more dependable, but we may be ignoring a tremendous resource. God gave a balance to nature, and in many ways, it still works best today.

God is in the business of helping. He doesn't look for ways to complicate our lives. He isn't trying to see how difficult He can make it. When we look to Him and ask for help, God loves to give it.

Maybe you would like to calm down and study better. God could help you do that. How would you like to forgive your brother? God could help you be more forgiving. Do you ever have trouble with a bad temper? God could help you quiet that down too.

Those are only a few examples. God is a full-time helper who wants us to get in contact with Him. And we don't even have to climb a snowcapped mountain with a jar to find Him.

I lift up my eyes to the hills—where does my help come from?
My help comes from the Lord, the Maker of heaven and earth.

PSALM 121:1–2 (NIV)

Do You Remember?

1. How does a ladybug help keep nature in balance?

2. How do ladybugs help farmers?

3. How has God helped you when you've asked?

God helps us even when we don't ask.

113 The Daily Destroyer

Where are the animals that cause the most destruction in nature? If you want an answer, don't look up for a huge animal; look down at the ground for a small one. Ounce for ounce, the tiny shrew is one of the greatest destroyers in the world.

Typically three to five inches long, shrews love to attack, pounce, kill, and eat. They don't hesitate to fight a creature twice their size, and shrews almost always come out the winners.

They look like mice except for their pointed noses and small ears. The giant otter shrew of Africa reaches two feet in length and enjoys seafood.

Shrews are driven by an incredible need for food. Every day a shrew will eat enough to equal its own weight. That would be like you shoveling down about a hundred pounds of food every day.

These high-strung nervous bodies have no time to relax. They are constantly chewing. To help defeat their victims, the short-tailed shrews of North America have poisonous saliva. After a couple of quick bites, large insects die rapidly. Shrew poison is similar to that found in cobras.

Normally shrews like to attack butterflies, beetles, and slugs, but they have been known to eat rats and snakes. Shrews have a few enemies that like to dine on them, such as great horned owls and bobcats. However, it seems shrews aren't particularly tasty.

Healthy humans have an average pulse rate of seventy-two beats a minute. If you checked a shrew's pulse, it would probably be clipping along at one thousand beats per minute. That may help explain why its life expectancy is only a year and a half. Because of its constant motion, its racing body apparently burns out.

The entire life of shrews seems to be spent tearing things apart. They look out for themselves and don't seem to care about anything else. Some people are much like shrews. All of their lives they aim at satisfying their own appetites.

Christians have wider interests in life. We look out for those in need, we share what we have, and we try to serve God in Jesus Christ.

Their destiny is destruction, their god is their stomach, and their glory is in their shame. Their mind is on earthly things.

PHILIPPIANS 3:19 (NIV)

Do You Remember?

1. How much food does a shrew eat every day?

2. Why does a shrew have such a short life span?

3. Do you know someone who goes out of his way to help others?

183

God keeps us from becoming completely selfish.

114 Repeating Parrots

Off the beaten path in southeast Asia, you might discover a small bird hanging upside down like a bat. It is a hanging parrot, and it has a strange way of sleeping.

If someone mentions a parrot, most of us immediately think of a bird that can talk. That's only a small part of the parrot story. There are over three hundred species of parrots, and many of them lead incredible lifestyles. They are colorful and can use their tongues as an extra hand. Pushing their tongue against their beak, parrots can handle objects with amazing ease.

Even their toes are particularly suited for their needs. Two of their toes point backward, allowing the parrot a good grip on branches.

As with much of nature, the parrot population is in danger as man continues to remove jungles and forests.

Parrots are frequently bought as pets, but protecting them in the wild will continue to be a difficult job for years to come.

There are two varieties—the African gray parrot and the Amazon green parrot—that seem to learn to talk the easiest. However, bird lovers say it is not as simple as people think. Training parrots to talk is a slow task and requires lots of patience. Only after hours of repeating the same words does even the most gifted parrot begin to repeat some of what it hears.

This isn't to suggest that parrots learn a language or can hold a conversation. Rather, they repeat a little bit of what they've heard. Unfortunately, some parrots have been taught to say terrible, ugly, and insulting words.

People aren't much better in the things they say. Often we use some gross and horrible words. They are terms that we repeat without thinking. By using them we may hurt someone's feelings and not realize it.

We are smarter than parrots and can watch what we say. Christians can be careful, choosing words that are fun but not harmful.

Do not let any unwholesome talk come out of your mouths, but only what is helpful for building others up according to their needs, that it may benefit those who listen.

EPHESIANS 4:29 (NIV)

Do You Remember?

1. How do parrots use their tongues?

2. How are their toes suited to sitting on branches?

3. Think of a way you will control what you say today.

God doesn't want us to throw words around carelessly.

115 Never Hug a Grizzly

If you are looking for something soft and cuddly to hug, forget the grizzly bear. The cubs look like friendly pets, but they grow to be some of the toughest animals in nature.

Grizzlies roam in the United States—mostly in Montana, Idaho, Wyoming, Colorado, and Alaska—and in Canada. They grow to be up to eight feet tall and weigh up to eight hundred pounds.

It would be fun to hug a grizzly, but not so fun if it hugged you back. Their claws stretch out to four sharp inches. They can run at the impressive speed of fifteen to twenty miles per hour, but some have been clocked at speeds up to thirty-five miles per hour. Fortunately grizzlies can't typically climb trees—but their cubs can.

Normally the grizzly can live to be from thirty to forty years old. In zoos, they can reach as old as fifty years.

If you did have a huge grizzly as a pet, it wouldn't be hard to feed. It eats practically anything and everything. Scientists call a grizzly bear omnivorous (om-NIV-or-us), which means it eats both vegetables and meat.

In the winter these bears like to sleep because they have so much trouble finding food. They might wake up after a month of snoozing, hunt around for a snack, and head back to bed.

The workers at Yellowstone National Park and Glacier National Park are trying to protect the number of grizzlies, but the job is difficult. Bears don't mix well with people. Because grizzlies eat meat, the sheepherders near the parks and mountains are not fond of bears. The grizzlies don't know enough to stay away, and the ranchers must find some means to protect their livestock.

Fortunately, this problem will not always exist. Someday, after Jesus Christ returns, grizzly bears and livestock will be able to roam in the same field and live together. Then we will all exist together in peace as God intended.

The cow will feed with the bear, their young will lie down together, and the lion will eat straw like the ox.

ISAIAH 11:7 (NIV)

Do You Remember?

1. Tell some facts about where grizzlies live and what sizes they are.

2. Why do grizzlies sleep in the winter?

3. What will it be like when Jesus Christ returns?

God wants all life on earth to live in peace.

186

116 Acorns for Dinner

Can you imagine opening your lunchbox and pulling out a handful of tasty acorns? What if you could walk up to the counter in a fast-food restaurant and ask for a hamburger and an order of acorns?

People used to eat a great many acorns, and some scientists believe we still should. If you choose to eat acorns, the chestnut oak would probably be best. Roasting helps bring out the sweet flavor.

A wide variety of animals and birds depend on acorns for their diets. Insects drill holes in them and deposit eggs so their larvae will have food when they hatch.

One of the most active acorn eaters is the acorn woodpecker. This hard worker drills holes in old fence posts and carefully stuffs an acorn into each space. He has his own vending machine. The woodpecker will simply return and withdraw one as he needs it; that is, if they are still there. Squirrels enjoy stealing these acorns if they can find the right fence post.

There seems to be no honor among the animals that eat acorns. Instead of taking enough time to gather their own, they spend much of their time stealing from each other. Squirrels cart the acorns off from woodpeckers. Bears steal them from squirrels.

All acorns come from oak trees; there are fifty-eight different types of oak trees in the United States.

Oregon and California grow beautiful acorns. The canyon live oak produces an acorn with a bright golden fuzz. When the acorn crop is plentiful, nature seems to prosper. Deer are more plentiful, bears have more cubs, and animals like coyotes have additional small game to eat.

Some animals eat acorns whenever it is convenient. Others store them for winter.

Smart people do the same thing. While they live on earth, they like to do some things that are important not just for today but forever. That is why Christians feed the hungry. It's the reason they clothe children and help educate the poor. They know they are doing good things that will be valuable to God—forever.

> *Tell them to use their money to do good. They should be rich in good works and should give happily to those in need, always being ready to share with others whatever God has given them. By doing this they will be storing up real treasure for themselves in heaven—it is the only safe investment for eternity!*
>
> **1 TIMOTHY 6:18–19** (TLB)

Do You Remember?

1. How does a woodpecker store acorns?

2. How many different types of oak trees are there in the United States?

3. What are some things Christians can do that are important forever?

Helping others is important to God too.

117 Which Animal Is This?

Standing next to one of my favorite places on earth, I checked out the changes near the dam. The water was high that day, though sometimes it is terribly low. During some seasons families bring inner tubes and float along the waterway.

This was a good day for the birds flying over the dam to soar low over the water and pick up fish for dinner. Fishermen stood nearby, trying to snatch food for their big red coolers.

As I stood there surveying the territory, I happened to look at my feet. To my surprise, my eyes suddenly focused on a green, spotted, pudgy, even slimy-looking monster about one foot long. Resting comfortably on the damp ground, neither my new friend nor I bolted and ran away.

We just kind of looked each other over.

My first reaction was that this was a snake, but it wasn't exactly shaped like a snake. It had plenty of time to run away, but it didn't. It also could have bitten me by now, but evidently I wasn't on its regular menu.

Slowly I walked away, convinced I was the champion. It wasn't going to be my lunch and, thank heavens, I wasn't going to be his.

Looking back and comparing pictures with my memory I changed my mind about my aquatic buddy. This was no snake at all. This was a tiger salamander.

This creature loves to wiggle around in watery districts. Its idea of munching snacks is to gobble down a cheek full of pond insects. Even cooked, most of us wouldn't overeat on this rare treat.

The salamander I had a run-in with was going through a transformation. It was leaving its childlike stage and becoming an adult. You aren't a salamander, but you still travel through a transformation. Someday you won't be a child at all anymore.

And you won't have to eat pond insects to become an adult. Now, that's good news.

Over and over God might change our attitudes. He may not change our hair or our number of legs or give us a third ear. But God might change us from an angry person into a loving individual. He might remove our frowns and replace them with a happy look.

This would be a transformation of our personality. He can change us in ways he never changed the salamander.

> . . . because the Lord had filled them with joy by changing the attitude of the king of Assyria.
>
> **EZRA 6:22 (NIV)**

Do You Remember?

1. Where is your favorite place in nature?

2. How have you changed?

3. Have you noticed other people change?

God makes all kinds of new creatures.

189

118 House Hunting

Almost all creatures need a good place to live. They need a dry place to hide from the rain or a high place to keep them safe from enemies. That is why most animals and birds spend much of their time building homes and nests. They want to protect themselves and their newborn children.

The wren is one of the busiest birds when it comes to preparing a home. It is the father wren's job to prepare a good place to live. Usually the mother bird refuses to have anything to do with him until he has a place ready.

In the early spring the father wren starts to look for housing. He is searching for something already made, but he would like to redecorate it himself. House hunting takes him to rusty tin cans, abandoned birdhouses, and even other birds' nests.

Once he discovers the right dwelling, he begins to furnish it to match his taste. Twigs, sticks, string, and other materials are added until it looks comfortable.

However, the wren knows that his work is not finished. He must find a couple more houses and decorate them too. The female wren will want to inspect several of his houses before she makes her final decision.

When his job is complete, the wren starts singing in hopes the female will come to his "open house." If she agrees to live in one of the houses, she will then select some feathers of her own choosing and rearrange the nest. Only then will she agree to lay her eggs.

This is far from being the end of the father's work. He must now serve as the protector of the eggs. After they hatch, he joins Mother in the endless search for food for the chicks. They comb the area for every insect they can find. For a solid month they will continue their search. Each will gather over a hundred pieces of food.

After the chicks are old enough to feed themselves, the father wren starts all over again. He begins to redecorate in hopes of beginning another set of chicks that same summer.

Just as birds need places to live, so do human beings. We not only need a home in this world, but we also want a home in heaven. Jesus told us that there are many places to live with our heavenly Father. He promised to go to heaven and prepare a place for us to live forever. We don't know what "homes" will be like in heaven, but we believe that our Father has some great places for us. By believing in Jesus Christ, you and I reserve a place in heaven.

There are many homes up there where my Father lives, and I am going to prepare them for your coming. When everything is ready, then I will come and get you.

JOHN 14:2–3 (TLB)

Do You Remember?

1. How does a wren prepare a house?

2. What does a male wren do after he has prepared the nests?

3. What do you think your home in heaven will be like?

God the Father will take care of everything for us.

119 Walking on Water

If you saw an animal walking on water, you would have to look twice. You would rub your eyes, stare, and step closer to get a better look. Everyone knows that something cannot walk on water. And yet something does.

We are talking about the small water shrew, a six-inch-long creature that lives around shallow pools. Half its size is its tail, but the busy shrew eats all the time. That's why it keeps on the move in constant search of food. At least that is one reason. It also keeps moving because trout and other fish would like to eat this speedy animal.

When the water shrew has its choice, it likes to dine on water spiders and a few small fish. However, usually it will eat almost anything that gets in its path.

Since most of its time is spent around the water, this shrew has learned how to use the water to its advantage. The water shrew can dive or merely take a casual float across the pond. But its most amazing feat is walking on top of the water.

The water shrew doesn't just give the appearance of walking on water—and it isn't fooling everyone by tiptoeing across the rocks either. Its feet are made in such a special way that it can actually stay on top of the water.

The bottoms of the water shrew's feet are covered with tiny hairs. Small air bubbles become trapped in these hairs as if there were small balloons on the soles of its feet.

When a shrew races across the water, it is traveling at a high speed. Its speed plus the balloons under its feet allow the shrew to stay on top of the water.

Since a water shrew can shoot quickly over the top of the water, it can surprise most of its victims and grab them before they know what is coming.

Walking on water is almost impossible, but the small water shrew is an exciting exception. Ships are also exceptions because of the way they are built. It is especially unusual when we hear of a human who can walk on top of water without anything to help him. Jesus Christ was able to walk on water not because He had balloons under His feet or because He knew where the rocks were. Jesus could walk on water because God helped Him. Jesus had the power to make waves calm down, make lame children walk, and cause the blind to see. Many people followed Jesus because they believed He had a special power from God and yet He was still kind, loving, and forgiving.

192

He saw that they were in serious trouble, rowing hard and struggling against the wind and waves. About three o'clock in the morning he walked out to them on the water.

MARK 6:48 (TLB)

1. Name an amazing thing about the water shrew.

2. What does the water shrew eat?

3. Name an amazing thing that Jesus Christ has done.

Jesus does amazing things for us every day.

120 Playing in the Snow

Parents might groan a little when they see snow beginning to fall. But there are so many good uses for the white fluff that snow must be one of God's best gifts.

Eskimos learn to accept snow as a friend. Instead of slowing down their lives, it actually speeds things up. They use snow as a highway. With their dogsleds and snowmobiles, they can get around much faster if the ground is covered with snow.

Snow also works to protect their homes from the terrible cold of the north. If snow is packed against a house, it helps keep the cold air out and it locks the warm air in. Snow holds air between its flakes and refuses to allow colder air to push past it.

Snow provides an excellent playground for people of all ages as well as for animals. Without snow we couldn't make snowballs, build snowmen, ride sleds, or go skiing.

While you and I are playing on top of the snow, some of nature's animals are traveling beneath it. Beavers spend their winters under the snow-covered ice, coming up for short trips. The holes they leave lead to their snug living quarters.

Some tiny rodents live under the snow and try to avoid coming up too often. Foxes, owls, and hawks wait for any small animal to poke its head above the snow. Without the snow cover, many of these little creatures would be captured easily by their enemies.

193

Snow is an excellent source of water in many parts of the north. If it melts slowly, the earth receives moisture to help the vegetation in the spring. However, if too much snow melts quickly, some areas begin to flood.

The beautiful snowflake takes on a great change after it settles on the ground. Often six-sided, flakes become granular after they hit the ground. The heat of the earth plus evaporation cause them to shrink and change form.

Snow has an extra benefit that we sometimes forget. Because snow closes roads, cancels schools, and makes airplanes stay on the ground, families can spend the evening together drinking hot chocolate and getting to know each other better. We have to stop hurrying around and think about what is really important in life. It gives us a chance to think about the majesty of God and spend time with the people we love.

For he directs the snow, the showers, and storm to fall upon the earth. Man's work stops at such a time so that all men everywhere may recognize his power.

JOB 37:6–7 (TLB)

Do You Remember?

1. How does snow help the Eskimos?

2. Think of an animal and the way snow helps it.

3. What do you like best about snow?

Sometimes we need to stop and think about what a blessing life is.

121 The Bad-Luck Bird

Hundreds of years ago the magpie got a bad reputation, and this reputation has hung on. Stories are easy to start but they are tough to get rid of.

The story of the magpie bird probably got started because of its neatness and attractiveness. In some forgotten conversation, an individual suggested that the magpie was a close friend of Satan and probably worked for him.

Once the rumor started, it was easy to prove. Someone said that every Friday magpies left for a secret meeting with the devil. People looked around on Fridays and guess what? It did seem hard to find a magpie just before the weekend. Maybe there was some truth to this story.

And had anyone noticed the magpie's tongue? It sort of looked like it was dripping blood.

With evidence like this and the willingness to believe anything, some people told these tales to their children, who in turn told them to *their* children.

The superstitious stories jumped the Atlantic Ocean, and when early Americans saw magpies they became afraid. They believed the magpie could bring them bad luck. If farmers saw magpies in their fields, some thought their crops would fail. And naturally a few crops did fail. When mothers saw magpies flying near their homes, some were frightened that one of their children might die. And naturally a few children did die.

As you might imagine, few people wanted magpies around. If someone saw one, he might shoot it, throw stones at it, or even try to cast a net over it. They were going to kill the "devil bird" and all its relatives.

Today the white magpie, the black magpie, and their relatives live fairly normal bird lives. They face all the natural dangers other birds encounter, but the deep superstition no longer follows them.

Often we say things when we don't really know the facts. Hurting the reputation of a bird is bad enough, but frequently we injure the lives of people by unkind words. It's a shame to injure human beings simply because we enjoy saying evil things.

A good man thinks before he speaks; the evil man pours out his evil words without a thought.

PROVERBS 15:28 (TLB)

Do You Remember?

1. What are some stories that were told about magpies?

2. What was the nickname of the magpie?

3. Have you known someone who was hurt by what someone else said about him?

As Christians we should guard our tongues.

122 What Good Are Mushrooms?

196 Mushrooms can taste good and they can have beautiful colors, but what is their real job in the woods? Probably their most important role is to attach themselves to dead logs and slowly take them apart. If it were not for mushrooms, the forest would be stacked with old wood.

A mushroom is a fungus and therefore gives off spores. Sometimes the spores grow in patches and look like snow, but an individual spore is too small to be seen without a microscope.

Spores have an amazing ability to get around. Some have been found as high as thirty-five thousand feet up. That is as high as the large commercial planes fly.

When a spore finds a place to attach to, it soon begins to grow. Mushrooms do not need light, so they are often tucked away in dark corners or under leaves. Some will build slowly as strands come together. Others, like shaggy ink cap mushrooms, seem to jump up overnight.

Called "saprophytes," mushrooms must take their valuable food from the dying forest. They have no green leaves to help them. By reaching into dead wood they pull out important food sources. Robbed of its strength, the dead log will begin to decay and fall apart.

People enjoy eating mushrooms on pizzas and other good foods. However, mushrooms can be very dangerous if you eat the wrong kinds. Even if you think you can tell edible from nonedible mushrooms, it is still easy to be fooled.

It would be best if you never ate mushrooms from a field unless you first checked with your parents. The wrong mushrooms can make you terribly sick.

In many ways that is exactly why the Bible is like our parents. It gives us warnings so we can avoid trouble. Without some direction, it's easy to make terrible mistakes. The Bible has wisdom, direction, and love. As the Word of God, the Bible leads us so we can get the best out of life.

I am not writing about these things to make you ashamed, but to warn and counsel you as beloved children.

1 CORINTHIANS 4:14 (TLB)

Do You Remember?

1. What is the most important role of mushrooms?

2. Do mushrooms need light to grow?

3. How is the Bible a guide for you?

The Bible can guide me to choose between right and wrong.

123 Turtles Are Tanks

Turtles are one of the more popular pets among children. In order to discuss turtles, we should begin by learning two words. The carapace (CARE-a-pace) is the camper or top shell, which comes in a variety of colors and shapes. Its color helps the turtle hide in a bush or in water. The shell is connected to the turtle's body, and the turtle cannot step out of it.

The second word is *plastron* (PLAS-trin). This is the bottom plate of bone that covers the turtle's chest. It too is part of the turtle's body.

If you see a box turtle hiding in the forest, look for its trapdoor. When the box turtle pulls itself into its shell, a door closes to cover its head for protection. It sticks its head out of the door to feast on beetles, spiders, and other choice delights.

One of the main reasons turtles survive in a crowded, polluted world is their ability to change eating habits. When man polluted rivers and killed shellfish, the map turtle simply switched diets and ate insects and dead fish.

Most turtles we see range from a few inches in length up to a foot long. However, a few rare turtles become massive. The famous giant tortoise reaches an amazing four feet in length and weighs in at nearly five hundred pounds. Members of this species have lived for more than one hundred years.

Another large variety is the sea-going loggerhead turtle. More a submarine than a tank, it supports its five-hundred-pound body by eating such delicacies as the man-of-war, which looks a lot like a jellyfish.

Among the more famous turtles is the snapping turtle. While most turtles cannot hurt you, this one could make a nasty wound. Found on both land and water, its snap is quick and strong.

If a turtle tried to fight, it would leave itself open to getting hurt. Should it try to run away, the turtle would be easily caught. Usually a turtle will merely draw its head and legs inside its shell and wait for the attacker to go away. An animal might yell at the turtle and jump on it, but the rock-like creature just sits tight.

It refuses to be moved. When the enemy is done ranting and raving, it will get disgusted and leave. But the green tank keeps its cool and stands its ground. It wins almost every time.

Sometimes Christians would do well to imitate turtles. We don't need to back down and we don't need to run. Christians can draw a line and say, "I won't do that," or "I must do this." Christians can do what they know is right no matter what other people do.

Put on all of God's armor so that you will be able to stand safe against all strategies and tricks of Satan.
EPHESIANS 6:11 (TLB)

Do You Remember?

1. Tell about a turtle's top shell.

2. Tell about a box turtle's trapdoor.

3. Tell how you have stood your ground as a Christian.

As a Christian, I don't need to back down.

124 What Guides the Butterfly?

Usually we think of butterflies as weak little creatures that float around flowers. If we understood them better, we would realize how tough they really are.

One big surprise may be to discover that they are fighters. If another butterfly drifts into their territory, a bruising battle may break out. The war can become so violent that their wings can be torn and the butterfly left unable to take to the air.

These large-winged beauties cannot afford to sit around and enjoy nature. Nectar is their food and they must move constantly to find enough. This hunt serves nature well as the butterfly also picks up pollen and transfers it from plant to plant.

A painted lady butterfly will sit gently on a flower and put its long tube tongue to work. Drinking up the nectar, the butterfly brushes against the pinhead-size pollen. Pollen must be transported to another plant within a couple of hours. Drifting off to the next flower, the butterfly leaves the pollen with the flower. This union allows seeds to form.

Sometimes their work of cross-pollination takes butterflies to unusual places. In the summer, the meadows near the Arctic Circle also need to swap pollen. When their time arrives, butterflies will carry out the job.

One of nature's most beautiful butterflies, the monarch, makes it a point to stay away from cold areas. If freezing weather hits the monarch, it can't possibly survive. That's why they keep moving south as cool temperatures start chasing them. They believe Canada is a good place to visit but they wouldn't want to live there.

Their trips south have been traced and their winter resort area discovered. Monarchs are aiming for sunny Mexico. Once there, they will set up quarters in the mountains. Millions of monarchs live in the trees and wait to head back north. Some of their friends lounge around Florida and California.

Scientists do not yet fully understand how a simple butterfly can find its way to Mexico and back to Canada. The insect does not seem capable of making the trip. Nevertheless, God has put some sort of guidance system in this fragile creature, and it does a great job from year to year.

People also need guidance. We need to recognize good and evil so we can choose between the two. If we are Christians, God lives inside us to be our guide. He helps us pick and choose when decisions become really hard.

For this great God is our God forever and ever. He will be our guide until we die.

PSALM 48:14 (TLB)

200

Do You Remember?

1. What is the food of butterflies?

2. Where do monarchs spend the winter?

3. How do you know when God is guiding you?

God helps me make decisions.

125 The Missing Python

How hard would it be to lose a nine-foot-long python snake? Well, it happened in a town in Nebraska, and as you might guess, the neighbors were a little concerned.

Where could a nine-foot python hide? Practically anywhere it wants to. Because of its color and ability to slide into small places, pythons are difficult to see unless they choose to come out. This snake was found beneath a tree in a local backyard.

Pythons are one of the most amazing and mysterious snakes. They are not, however, completely harmless. A child in Iowa was reportedly killed by just such a creature. Despite the friendly nature of some animals, many can become dangerous at the most unexpected times.

Snakes continue to hold our attention for several reasons. One reason is that many stories have been told about snakes that are fascinating but not necessarily true. Some people believe snake eyes have a strange power. Many people believe that most snakes are deadly and must be killed on sight.

Naturally we should stay away from any snake if we don't know what kind it is. However, most snakes are harmless. The problem is that we don't know enough about them to be able to tell the good ones from the bad.

If you want to study snakes, a python would be as interesting as any. Pythons are long and like to climb trees. They are not poisonous but have a tight grip and can crush small animals. Many of its prey are small enough to swallow in one gulp.

A python can be a beautiful creature. The longest ones span thirty feet. That would make ten of your longest steps. Sometime step off ten *long* strides in front of your house and try to imagine how long some of these reptiles are.

We have many fears about snakes. Some of our fears are based on facts, but most are myths. God has promised us a day when all creatures will live in perfect peace. We will have nothing to fear from snakes and they will have nothing to fear from us. It will be a good time of harmony in the world.

Babies will crawl safely among poisonous snakes, and a little child who puts his hand in a nest of deadly adders will pull it out unharmed.

ISAIAH 11:8 (TLB)

Do You Remember?

1. Are the majority of snakes harmless or harmful?

2. How long can pythons get?

3. Describe the time, as you picture it will be, when nature will be in harmony.

There is nothing to fear in heaven.

126 A Hippo's Lullaby

How would you like a two-thousand-pound hippopotamus to sing you to sleep at night? You wouldn't want it to cradle you in its arms. A hippopotamus's good-night kiss might be a little more than you would enjoy.

Would you settle for the pudgy cheeks of a pigmy hippo, weighing in at an ample five hundred pounds? This smaller edition could wring you out like a soggy washcloth.

While all the squeezing and snuggling is going on, the hippo could also sing you to sleep at no extra charge.

A hippopotamus might move slowly on dry land, but in water it's a different story. Hippos are aggressive in a river and will move rapidly to your side.

My wife and I stayed in a cabin next to the Mara River in Africa where hippos frolicked, wrestled, and sang through the night. We were thankful for the strong fence that kept us separated from the large-mouth monsters.

We didn't want them climbing the riverbank at any time. Neither did we want to stumble into their territory.

There may be no more dangerous animal in all the wilderness. They definitely don't like people, except maybe to nibble on for lunch or a midnight snack. We weren't meant to spend much time rolling around and playing together.

For spending so much time in the water, you might expect them to suffer a terrible sunburn. But no need to worry. Each hippo carries an ample supply of sunscreen. It never has to shop at the local store for a tube of lotion; instead, it carries a large supply of pink oily mucus in its own body. Automatically it squeezes whatever it needs onto its skin. It is then ready for a carefree day in and out of the water.

It's hard to say if Job ever saw a hippopotamus, let alone heard one sing. Maybe he did. But it is certainly possible that he heard songs in the night. And, of course, God may have sent those tunes wafting through the night.

You might enjoy hearing a song before the light goes out, and just maybe a song will come to mind as you drop off to sleep.

But no one says, "Where is God my Maker who gives songs in the night?"

JOB 35:10 (NIV)

Do You Remember?

1. Why is it called a pigmy hippo?

2. Why doesn't a hippopotamus suffer from sunburn?

3. Why do people enjoy songs in the night?

It is peaceful just knowing God is around.

127 What Good Is a Dead Tree?

Have you ever looked at a small log and thought how dead and still it was? But it's not really still—if you picked it up, you'd find hundreds of bugs and insects crawling around on the ground. It looked lifeless, but underneath a tiny world bustled about.

The same thing may be true of the dead tree you drive past on the way to school each day. All of its leaves are gone, but that doesn't mean there is no life there. Both inside and out there could be a wide variety of living creatures.

If a tree is dead and still standing, scientists call it a snag. You might want to leave a snag standing on your property because of all the good it is able to do. In fact, some animals would far rather have a big snag around than a tall healthy tree.

The eruption of Mount Saint Helens left thousands of snag trees. Soon afterward creatures began to inhabit those trees and are flourishing today.

The loose bark of a snag makes it an excellent home for many insects. A number of beetles like to snuggle under the bark and lay their eggs. Ants also find the soft wood easy living quarters for their young.

Since insects enjoy living in a dead tree, birds will also find it attractive. Some birds, like the woodpecker, stick around searching for meals in the soft wood. Other birds enjoy snags because of their height. Hawks use them as towers so they can scan the nearby territory.

By removing all dead trees, we also chase away many of the valuable insect-eating birds. If we leave some snags, we furnish the birds with dependable feeding grounds. The birds return the favor by cleaning up other insects in your area.

Birds such as owls, chickadees, nuthatches, wrens, and woodpeckers may want to live near your house, and an inviting dead tree could make that possible.

When squirrels can find a suitable hole in a snag, they may move in and store their food for the winter. Raccoons will look it over too to use for a den. Before long this "dead" tree can become a sizeable apartment house.

If conditions are correct, a dead log could turn into stone. This is called petrified wood. Slowly, each particle in the wood is replaced by other particles, most of which are supplied by water washing lime into the log. As stone washes in and wood washes out, the log still holds its original form. Eventually it ends up as a stone log, but this takes many, many years.

Nature has many ways of taking things that are dead and using them for life again. Vegetation becomes food for other plants. Dead trees fall to the ground, and after long periods of time become coal. Seeds go under the soil, die, and become beautiful plants.

People die too. If they believe in Jesus Christ, they stay alive in heaven. A person who places his or her faith in Christ will live forever with God and His Son.

Death becomes life. It happens often in the woods and fields. It also happens among people. Those who die trusting in Jesus Christ continue to live—forever.

Jesus told her, "I am the one who raises the dead and gives them life again. Anyone who believes in me, even though he dies like anyone else, shall live again."

JOHN 11:25 (TLB)

Do You Remember?

1. What is a snag?

2. How does a dead tree provide homes for insects and animals?

3. What do you think this means: "Now we know that if the earthly tent we live in is destroyed, we have a building from God, an eternal house in heaven, not built by human hands" (2 Corinthians 5:1 NIV)?

205

I'm looking forward to eternal life with my Father.

128 Look at the Facts

Hummingbirds do not hum. They move their wings so fast that a humming sound is made. Those swift little wings race at four thousand beats each minute.

A baby sea otter can float long before it can swim. The air trapped in its fur helps hold the otter up.

A walrus has four hundred whiskers that help it feel the bottom of the sea when it searches for food. Because of restrictions on walrus hunting, their numbers have tripled in recent years.

To make sure they do not get stuck in their own webs, spiders also spin unsticky threads, which they carefully walk on to cross the sticky parts.

Tigons have a tiger and a lion for parents.

Some prairie dogs are big smoochers. Those that live in the same colony evidently greet each other with a kiss and a few brushes of the nose.

A blue whale's tongue weighs the same as about fifty people do.

The porcupine quill is really made of hair. The hairs have grown together to form stiff sharp swords.

Moss does not always grow on the north side of a tree. It will form on the side with the least sunlight. Often that is the north side.

Approximately two thousand meteors hit the earth every day. A meteor hit Arizona and left a hole 575 feet deep. That is deeper than the Washington Monument is high.

Miracles were recorded in the Bible so that you will believe the man Jesus is the Son of God.

> *Jesus' disciples saw him do many other miracles besides the ones told about in this book, but these are recorded so that you will believe that he is the Messiah, the Son of God, and that believing in him you will have life.*

JOHN 20:30–31 (TLB)

1. Name two unusual facts you learned about nature.

2. What are two miracles in the Bible?

3. Why do you think Jesus performed miracles?

I believe in Jesus' miracles.

129 Not Looking for Trouble

If a hedgehog had its way, it would live every day in quiet and peace. A low-key figure, a hedgehog doesn't even like to work in unpleasant weather. If the animal gets too hot, it gives up most activities; if it should turn cold, the hedgehog will take the first opportunity to hibernate.

But don't let this relaxed creature fool you. If anything wants to do battle, the hedgehog will turn immediately into a mean fighting machine. It is equipped with sharp teeth and quills like a porcupine. A hedgehog moves slowly but is not afraid to swim a stream or climb a tree. In fact, it isn't afraid to do many things since it has tough skin and can roll into a ball that makes it practically impossible to hurt.

Like porcupines, hedgehogs cannot throw their quills, but they are painful weapons. Every once in a while they like to shine them up, possibly just to frighten enemies. A hedgehog will begin by licking smooth objects, like rocks, until its mouth is watering with saliva. It will then reach around and lick each of its sharp quills. Maybe they are merely trying to stay clean, or possibly they are showing off their swords.

Occasionally a hedgehog will be attacked by a snake, but it doesn't get too excited about the creeping creature. Often a hedgehog will tease and let the snake try to get it, which might look like easy work to the attacker, but the snake soon learns the hedgehog is very tough. The hedgehog plays his

207

own form of tag until finally the snake lies down exhausted. At that point the hedgehog goes over and makes short work of the snake. A snake may have high hopes of what it will do, but it will probably end up as dinner.

Many of us have never seen a hedgehog. These creatures live mostly in China, Europe, Great Britain, and Africa.

Animals are much like people. Some creatures are ill-tempered and get angry at practically anything. Other animals are content with a calm nature. The hedgehog is one of those; it is a lover of peace.

We don't prove we're strong by starting fights. People who live to quarrel must be pretty miserable characters. Jesus believed that those who work for peace are wiser than those who try to start fights.

Happy are those who strive for peace—they shall be called the sons of God.

MATTHEW 5:9 (TLB)

Do You Remember?

1. How does a hedgehog spend the winter?

2. How does a hedgehog defend itself?

3. Do you know someone who is a lover of peace? Explain.

Living at peace is much closer to how God intended for people to live.

130 Fathers Make a Difference

208

You can find all sorts of fathers in nature: fathers who raise their own young, to dads who have absolutely nothing to do with them. Some make excellent parents who prove patient and caring with their babies.

For instance, who takes the youngsters for rides in the poison dart frog family? The father is the one who packs junior on his back and gives him a trip to the local pond.

And who enjoys wrestling with baby baboon? It's the father who gets down in the dirt and tumbles around.

The emu is a prime example of father care. The fathers devote two years to the process of training their chicks. They give special instruction in searching for food and in the art of dodging enemies.

Father wolf takes his job seriously too. Not only does he hunt for food for the family, but he teaches his pups to do the same. He is not content to push his young out into the world but takes time to train them.

Sandpipers seem to designate most of the food gathering chores to Father. He assumes the baby chicks are his and not the mother's, since she lays eggs for several males.

The Siamese fighting fish is a proud and hard-working father. He builds a nest out of bubbles. Each bubble is thick because it is made from mucus. Father constructs this nest near the surface of the water and places eggs from the female inside. While they are waiting to hatch, the Siamese keeps a close guard over the eggs. He remains near in case any danger threatens. Not content to leave his eggs to chance, this parent wants to help usher them into this world.

Not all of us are fortunate enough to have a father living with us, but those who are have good reason to thank God. Fathers, like mothers, can be very caring and can help us do things.

It feels good to have a father around with whom you can share time and do things together. Thank God for your father if you have one. If you don't, then God has promised to be a special Father to you, and you can thank Him for that.

209

My son, how I will rejoice if you become a man of common sense. Yes, my heart will thrill to your thoughtful, wise words.

PROVERBS 23:15 (TLB)

Do You Remember?

1. What does the Siamese fighting fish build his nest from?

2. Name two animal fathers and what they do for their children.

3. Name one trait that makes a good dad.

No matter what, our Father in heaven waits for us.

131 Our Eyes Fool Us

Many animals look like something else when you first see them. That's why we rub our eyes and take a second look.

It is said that the first person to see a manatee believed he had seen a mermaid. He actually believed he was looking at a female person who lived in the sea. He needed to rub his eyes and take a closer peek.

That person needed a nap and probably a visit to the ship's eye doctor.

The same was true of some of the people who saw the first buffalo in western America. Of course, these are actually bison. But since early travelers had never seen a bison or a water buffalo, they got confused easily.

Someone yelled, "Buffalo!" and we have been calling them that ever since. The fact is they don't seem to mind whether you call them bison or buffalo. They seldom laugh at visitors anyway.

When I was in Kenya, Africa, I checked it out to see how much they looked alike. A water buffalo stood in my path and twisted its head from side to side. I wasn't sure what it might do next, so I hoped it would hurry up and get into the perfect pose.

"Come on," I whispered, "a little more to the left."

Snap! I clicked the camera and took off running for the jeep. I couldn't imagine myself wrestling with an overgrown barrel-chested, twisted-horned beast.

As we drove off I didn't even look back to see if it was still standing there. Fortunately the picture turned out perfect.

This time I didn't have to depend on my eyes. The photo hangs on my wall, giving proof of what I saw.

Life is filled with people of all ages who would like to fool us. They tell us about a good place to go when it is really a bad place. They insist this is an excellent thing to buy when it is actually not worth having. They encourage us to follow the group of people, but we will only wind up cheated or robbed.

Smart people know right away that a manatee is not a mermaid. They keep their eyes open and see what is going on around them.

May your eyes see what is right.

PSALM 17:2 (NIV)

Do You Remember?

1. Name one place where bison live.

2. Name one place where water buffalo live.

3. What kind of people would like to fool us?

May our heavenly Father help us keep our eyes wide open.

132 Ants Keep Livestock

I f you want to study nature, you don't have to travel to foreign lands. You don't have to climb a snow-capped mountain or descend into a huge canyon. You can spend many happy hours sitting on the ground, watching ants go about their lives. Ants do far more interesting things than most people realize.

Take for instance the dairy ant. You can call it that because it actually keeps other insects in order to use their "milk." They keep miniature livestock, feed them, protect them, and live off the little creatures.

The livestock are called aphids, small lice that live on plants. Usually people try to get rid of them because they feed off the plant juices. The tiny aphid has two small tubes leading from its body. From those tubes ants are able to take a sweet-tasting liquid. The ants enjoy the healthy "honeydew."

Somehow in their insect world the aphid and the ant work out a deal they both enjoy. The ants build a house for the aphids, where they are protected and allowed to carry on their daily tasks. In turn, the aphids serve as dairy cows for the ants.

No one knows how the ant figured out this system or why the aphids first trusted the ant, but it has gone on for many centuries. The ant builds a structure out of string-like plant parts. After the ant has woven a "barn" or "shed," the aphids happily move into their new home.

If you have carpenter ants, watch them climbing branches that are covered with tiny insects. The carpenter ant will gently stroke the aphid with its antennae. Feeling relaxed and comfortable, the aphid gives off a pleasant-tasting liquid, which the ant is happy to drink.

Because aphids are important to ants, they are generally treated well. The ant makes sure plenty of food, housing, and protection are provided.

If you visit Mexico you can see a similar sight with caterpillars rather than aphids. Here not only do the ants keep the blue butterfly larva in pens, but at night they take the caterpillars out to graze. The ants lead the caterpillars to croton plants to feed. When they are done, the ants return them to their pens.

The ants milk these creatures for their honeydew in the same way the aphids are used.

Ants would be foolish to ignore the aphids that provide food, just as we would be silly to leave milk out on the table to spoil or forget to place meat in the refrigerator. Smart people take care of the things that are important to them.

God is concerned that we take good care of the things we have. If we are wasteful and thoughtless, we could end up having to do without. Ants watch over the aphids because they need them. People need to be just as careful with the things they consider valuable.

For the man who uses well what he is given shall be given more, and he shall have abundance.

MATTHEW 25:29 (TLB)

Do You Remember?

1. Describe the dairy ant and its livestock.

2. What are some things you do to be careful about not wasting?

3. Could you go for one month without buying anything new and instead fix up and use what you already have?

It's important to take good care of things.

133 Why Finches Don't Freeze

Any self-respecting bird should have enough sense to fly south in the winter. However, many of our feathered friends prefer snow instead of the beach. They can be found perched in leafless trees in parks, forests, and backyards all over the north.

The key question to scientists is, How do birds keep from freezing to death in such cold climates? Some birds die during the winter, but many others survive quite well.

Like people, birds have learned to adapt to the frigid north. Each variety has developed its own ingenious system. A few birds put on winter coats by growing a thicker layer of feathers. Some find excellent shelters and build homes protected from wind.

Other birds, like the finch, look within themselves for the extra heat needed to survive. The finch shivers to keep warm, and its tiny heart beats five hundred times a minute! Shivering isn't too difficult to understand. That is exactly what you and I do when our bodies try to fight against the cold.

When we shiver, our muscles contract to produce body heat. If we're not moving, our insides need to move to create warmth.

213

The small finch loses heat quickly because it has a little body. Large birds can stay warm longer and can skip meals if necessary. Finches are not so fortunate. In order for them to shiver so much, they must constantly find food. Food supplies the fuel that allows their muscles to contract or move. It is the contracting muscles that supply heat.

In some of the worst weather, the finch is able to stay comfortable inside. It supplies its own heat and therefore can survive.

When we face tough times, we often need to find strength from inside. A teacher might yell at you. The neighbor's dog chases you. A mean kid takes the ball and throws it on the roof. Life can be cold and hard.

God understands that some days are rough. This is one of the reasons He decided to send the Holy Spirit to live inside of us. The Holy Spirit makes us feel better, calms us down, and becomes our constant comforter.

But when the Father sends the Comforter instead of me—and by the Comforter I mean the Holy Spirit—he will teach you much, as well as remind you of everything I myself have told you.

JOHN 14:26 (TLB)

Do You Remember?

1. Name ways birds adapt to cold weather.

2. How does a finch keep warm?

3. How does God help us face tough times?

214 ***God has not left us alone.***

134 How Much Wood Does a Woodchuck Chuck?

The famous tongue twister asks the question, How much wood would a woodchuck chuck if a woodchuck could chuck wood? Well, a woodchuck doesn't chuck wood! In fact, it isn't even a woodchuck; it's a groundhog. Early Americans misunderstood the Indian name for the groundhog, and many of us have been misnaming it ever since.

Those who did get the name correct decided the groundhog was a good weatherman. That is why many people believe that if a groundhog sees its shadow on February 2 in Punxsutawney, Pennsylvania, winter will last six more weeks. Actually, this date is too early for any sane groundhog to poke its nose out.

If a groundhog has its way, it will spend most of the day digging and eating. By fall it hopes to be stuffed so it can sleep or hibernate through the winter. They are not accustomed to storing food for the frozen season. Overeating is closer to their style.

To carry out their favorite hobby of eating, they have a great set of teeth. Much of their day is spent grinding down vegetation.

Life is not always peaceful for our furry friend. For one thing, groundhogs can be fairly rough on each other. One or two tend to take over and are soon telling everyone else what to do.

A more serious problem is the fox. Faster and perhaps smarter than the groundhog, the fox frequently cuts down groundhog numbers. The danger presented by the fox may be the reason the groundhog often sits upright, looking alertly around.

However, when it does this, it is left wide open for human hunters. A groundhog sitting on its back legs makes it a perfect target for gunshots.

Living underground has definite advantages. A groundhog's apartment has both front and back doors. It needs two entrances in case a fox makes it uncomfortable. While the fox snoops at one door, the groundhog is gone out the other. Some burrows have half a dozen entrances or more.

Called a burrow, the living quarters drop six feet beneath the surface and wind around for forty-five feet. There are several rooms where different members can either hide or hibernate.

To provide this type of housing, groundhogs spend a great deal of time digging. They remove hundreds of pounds of dirt in order to construct a home. Fortunately they carry their own earth-moving equipment. Their front legs serve as diggers while their hind feet throw the dirt out of the hole. Their front feet have especially sharp claws.

Because of their need to dig, groundhogs have been disliked for centuries. When a farmer's prize cow steps into a groundhog's hole and injures its leg, the farmer may become furious.

Despite its unpopularity the groundhog must continue to dig; otherwise it will have no place to raise its family. But at the same time, the farmer cannot have the invader tearing up his place.

Constant diggers will never be popular. Neither will people who keep digging into the personal lives of others. Some of us like to dig up dirt about others. We like to hear gossip and spread stories that make others look bad.

God wants us to stay away from dirt digging. We can help each other far more if we say nice things rather than spread ugly stories about other human beings.

An ungodly man diggeth up evil, and in his lips there is as a burning fire.

Proverbs 16:27 (kjv)

Do You Remember?

216

1. What is the correct name for a woodchuck?

2. What is the main enemy of the groundhog?

3. Describe a groundhog home.

Help me to control my tongue.

135 Stuck Up a Tree

Maybe you're one of the millions of Americans who love cats. Any cat lover can tell you what an excellent animal a cat can be. They can sit in your lap while you read or follow you from room to room to keep you company, and they are energetic wrestlers. A piece of string or a ball is all you need for entertainment.

When a child first gets a kitten, he needs some simple instructions on how to treat it. We had one friend who came home after work and opened the refrigerator door, and his cat jumped out. After that he had a long talk with his son. Another family heard some thumping in their clothes dryer. They arrived just in time to rescue their kittens.

Most of the time children and kittens mix well. Kittens provide an outstanding opportunity to teach about responsibility and mutual caring.

Kittens like to purr; it usually means they are happy or content. It might also mean you're doing a good job of feeding, watering, and caring for it.

One of the activities a kitten enjoys most is to have its fur stroked and rubbed. A gentle touch tells the kitten that you care and everything is fine. Stroking a kitten is also good for people. Touching tends to calm us down and make us feel at peace.

Cats are fortunate if they can be raised by their mothers. They have some of the most considerate mothers in nature. Not only do mother cats feed their kittens, but they also keep them clean. Using her tongue for a washcloth, Mother sees to it that her kittens are dirt-free from head to tail.

A mother cat will teach her kittens to stalk birds or mice. She will show them how to stretch their bodies out as they tiptoe under a tree, and she

217

will teach them the difficult art of backing down a tree. Not a skill easily mastered, it is one that most cats will need. If the cat fails to learn this, some poor pet owner will have to haul out his ladder and rescue his timid friend.

Kittens that have mothers to help them grow up are fortunate. Children who have mothers may be even more fortunate. Mothers can be loving, listening, and helpful. They can teach us to care for our things, to bake, and to brush our teeth. Mothers can remind us of things we forget like books, jackets, and saying thank you. And when you need it the most, they are terrific at giving hugs.

If you have a good mother, maybe you will want to tell her so. And don't forget to thank God for her too.

Her children stand and bless her; so does her husband.

PROVERBS 31:28 (TLB)

Do You Remember?

1. Name three things a mother cat teaches her kittens.

2. What animal do you think is the best pet?

3. What do you like most about mothers?

My mother is a blessing.

136 The Strange Platypus

Many of us can't stand being different. We don't want to wear a shirt that has an odd pattern on it. Our shoes might look a little strange, but we won't wear them if they're totally out of style. And as we grow older, it might seem very important that we become like everybody else in school.

If fitting in is your number one goal, you ought to be grateful that you weren't born a platypus. They don't fit in with many other animals.

To begin with, the duck-billed platypus has a flat nose and webbed front feet, so it looks like a duck. But it is certainly not a duck.

A platypus walks like a duck, searches for food like a duck, and often swims like a duck; but this is no duck. This is a strange animal that lives in Australia, munches on insects, and likes to store food in its tail.

We will want to keep our distance from the male platypus. The hind legs carry a real poison. With one swift sweep, it can inject that poison into anything that gets too close.

Among its many oddities, this creature uses an electrical system that connects in its body and allows the animal to swim with its eyes closed. It can sense what is around it without seeing the other animals or the terrain.

With so much to do, you might think the male platypus wouldn't have time to look for a girlfriend or a wife. But finding a mate is one of its main jobs. If it needs to, it is willing to fight and even shoot a bit of poison in order to win the heart of a special female.

The truth is, you couldn't be a platypus if you wanted to be. Even if you loved eating small insect larvae and crawling on your belly in the mud, carrying poison around in your body might be more than enough to make you sick. You have to be special if you want to be a platypus. Human beings never qualify to make this change. That's why we might enjoy being like others yet still want to be a little different.

Jesus was often a stranger to others. That was all right. Sometimes it is even better to be a stranger.

I was a stranger and you invited me in.

MATTHEW 25:35 (NIV)

Do You Remember?

1. Where does a platypus usually live?

2. How is a platypus like a duck?

3. Sometimes do you like being different?

My God is not like others.

137 Squirrels Are Acrobats

I f you have squirrels living in your backyard, you are a fortunate person. You don't have to hike for miles into the forest to see nature at its best.

Squirrels put on one of the best shows in town. Without spending a dime you can sit inside your living room and watch their crazy antics.

They are excellent at climbing trees and leaping from one branch to another. Have you ever watched two squirrels chasing each other through the trees? They move so quickly they are hard to follow, but you can certainly hear the noise as they rattle the leaves and tear along. In a flash they can switch branches or reverse direction and be gone again.

If you want to see a champion acrobat, you have to find a flying squirrel. Actually they do more hang gliding than flying, but they do travel through the air. However, they are pretty much restricted to night flights.

As a good investigative scientist, you will also want to take note of where your squirrels live. This one could be tricky. Do your squirrels live in the hollow of a tree? They are likely to live in trees until the weather gets nice. Squirrels will then often build summer homes in the form of nests. Check to see if you can find both bird nests and squirrel nests in your yard.

No study would be complete without checking out the squirrels' food supply. They have two pressing jobs to keep up with. The first one is to find enough food to eat each day and the second is to store up meals for the winter.

Generally speaking, squirrels collect nuts. They also enjoy a large selection of corn, wheat, and fruit.

If you watch closely you might be able to see the fast-fingered little creature burying its cache in the ground. It will spend a great deal of time storing up for tomorrow, and the squirrel is wise to do it. Later, it will have an amazing ability to find that exact spot and dig up the food, even if it is buried under the snow. How does a squirrel do it? Can it smell the nuts buried there? Does it somehow recognize the scenery? Has its mind marked off the area in some mathematical dimension? We don't know, but God knows.

Storing up so we can have food for tomorrow is a solid principle people are smart to follow. The bad thing is that some people spend all of their time collecting goods for tomorrow. They forget to share the things they have with people who need them.

Jesus seemed concerned over people who gather things only for themselves. He encouraged us to share our possessions with others.

Don't store up treasures here on earth where they can erode away or may be stolen. Store them in heaven where they will never lose their value and are safe from thieves. If your profits are in heaven, your heart will be there too.

MATTHEW 6:19–21 (TLB)

Do You Remember?

1. Where do squirrels live in winter? In summer?

2. Where do squirrels store their food?

3. How do we store up treasure in heaven?

Sharing with others makes God happy.

138 Sheep Living in the Mountains

Not all sheep live on level pastures with rolling green fields. Many wander among high mountain ranges and almost tiptoe across dangerous cliffs. They leap over rocks where one false step would lead to certain death. And despite their excellent ability, some do fall and are injured or killed.

Their experience and knowledge of rough mountains becomes one of their better defenses. If they are attacked by a bear, coyote, wolf, eagle, or other predator, the mountain sheep will head directly for the most dangerous part of the cliffs. There they will climb around on the most treacherous rocks to discourage their attacker.

We can only guess why sheep choose to live in the mountains, but some of the benefits of mountain living seem obvious.

Sheep remain within easy strolling distance of small mountain fields of lush grass. And yet when the need arises, they can scurry to the safety of the rugged terrain close by.

Water is generally no problem at these heights. Some mountains have snow nearly year-round. As it melts, the snow furnishes streams and lakes.

With all of their assets, mountain ranges are not without their problems. When the severe winter sets in, many sheep perish from the harsh elements. Newborn lambs frequently fail to live through their first winter.

Many lambs like to play with each other. They will butt heads and jump over rocks. Sometimes they drift away from the older sheep as they play, and a sneaky coyote watches and hopes it can add a lamb to its dinner.

Fortunately, most lambs begin to sense the danger and realize they have strayed. Quickly and safely they hustle after the others; there is protection in numbers.

The Bible describes us as being like sheep. We stray away from God when we sin or do things that are wrong. Fortunately Jesus died to pay for all our sins. We have strayed, but we are welcome back into the presence of God because Jesus died for us.

We—every one of us—have strayed away like sheep! We, who left God's paths to follow our own. Yet God laid on him the guilt and sins of every one of us!

ISAIAH 53:6 (TLB)

Do You Remember?

222

1. Why do sheep like to live in mountains?

2. How is water supplied in the mountains?

3. How are people like sheep?

God, help me find my way back when I have strayed.

139 Monkeys With Large Noses

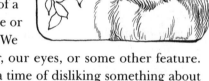

As we grow up, we begin to look at ourselves, and we might not like what we see. We stand in front of a mirror and we stare at our nose or we start to think our ears are too big. We may not even like our chin, our hair, our eyes, or some other feature. Almost all young people go through a time of disliking something about their face.

If a young person were a proboscis monkey, he would have a serious problem. This monkey comes into the world with a small nose, but it grows rapidly. By the time the monkey is full-grown, its nose is so long and wide that it covers part of the monkey's mouth. Sometimes it has to push its nose aside in order to eat.

The proboscis makes good use of its prominent nose. It uses it as a very loud horn. If another monkey moves into its territory, the proboscis gives a couple of loud bursts through its nose. That sound sends a message telling others they had better clear out quickly.

The proboscis monkey is hard to find outside of zoos. Far-off Borneo is the only place they can be found in the wild. Borneo is located approximately halfway between Australia and Asia. Because it lives in a hot climate, one of the proboscis monkey's favorite recreations is to take a swim in a local river to cool off.

None of us looks like a proboscis monkey; most of us have normal features that we can be happy with. As we grow older, we usually stop worrying about ears and noses because we realize how little they really matter. Honesty is more important than dimples. Love means more than curly hair. Friends are more valuable than dark eyebrows.

King Solomon looked at the woman he loved and told her that her nose was like the tower of Lebanon. Solomon was one of the wisest men who ever lived, and he adored the good-sized nose on the woman he loved.

Our features are not ugly. They are simply parts of a very interesting person.

Your nose is shapely like the tower of Lebanon overlooking Damascus.

SONG OF SOLOMON 7:4 (TLB)

Do You Remember?

1. What does a proboscis monkey use his nose for?

2. Where does the proboscis monkey live?

3. What would you tell someone who thinks he is ugly?

I am happy with what God gave me.

140 When Elephants Get Thirsty

When an elephant wants a drink of water, it has a big problem. An animal that big can't get by on a few sips from a puddle. A good drink of cold water on a hot day might mean thirty-five gallons of water. (Try to imagine yourself drinking thirty-five gallons of milk at the table tonight!)

Since the world is 70 percent water, you may think there would be no trouble finding plenty to drink. However, many people and animals die each year because there is not enough water to raise crops or to drink.

There are many reasons why some people do not have enough water. It may have been too hot in that land for too long, so ponds evaporated. There may not have been much rain and the rivers dried up. Possibly there has been war and people are not free to move around to get water.

Elephants not only need water to keep their insides working, but they must get huge amounts of water for their outsides. An elephant is a gigantic physical machine. On a hot day it is easy for this machine to overheat. Human bodies can also overheat. That is why we drink water, perspire, take cool baths, and look for shady places. If we overheat, we'll get sick.

To stay healthy, elephants look for a good watering hole. Ideally they want to find enough water to stand in and take a shower. They carry an excellent shower hose with them: Their trunk can suck up a large supply of water. The elephant then points the hose over its back and lets the water gush.

Mother elephants like to help out their young. That's why they spray their children with a short shower too. As the small ones grow, they get better at showering themselves.

In dry areas, the search for water is a constant problem. Elephants wander in small herds from hole to hole looking for more. If they run out of places to look, the elephants turn to another plan. They begin digging holes in the ground in search of water.

Not very adept at using shovels, a desperate elephant will use practically any part of its body to dig. Tusks, trunk, and feet each become valuable tools in its search for water.

Finally the elephant will find a small collection of water or at least some soggy mud. Their determination to find water is the only reason some of these huge machines survive.

As long as we live, the need for water will control our lives. Both animals and people dare not wander too far from this valuable liquid. We can go much longer without food than we can without water.

When Jesus spoke to a woman at a well, He offered her living water. He told her she would never be thirsty again; He promised her eternal life. Eternal life would be like having a spring inside her and she would never run out of water.

Jesus lived and died so that you could believe in Him and live forever. You will never run out of life—even after you die.

"But the water I give them," he said, "becomes a perpetual spring within them, watering them forever with eternal life."

JOHN 4:14 (TLB)

Do You Remember?

1. How much water does an elephant drink on a hot day?

2. Why do some parts of the world not have enough water?

3. What did Jesus say about water?

Eternal life never runs out.

141 Fur Coat for Your House

Last year we painted our house. Before we applied the paint, we spent many days scraping the wood. We even sanded down the front door. After we had scraped the wood, we could see all the problems the house had.

Some of the wood had termite damage we needed to repair. Other places had nicks where things had bumped the house over the years. In other areas the wood had become stained or rotted because of the weather. We spent a lot of days trying to repair the damage to the building.

A few scientists believe we are putting the wrong material on houses. They would like to see a company manufacture artificial fur. It would be like fitting a gigantic fur coat over your house.

Before you laugh too loudly, you should know that there are scientists who are experimenting with this idea. They came up with the idea by studying polar bears. A polar bear's fur is excellent at trapping heat from the sun and carrying warmth into the animal's skin.

That ability is precisely why a polar bear looks white. Its fur is not really white; when photographed with a special camera, we can see that the fur is transparent and the skin is black.

Consequently, a professor has worked hard at trying to create a thread that acts like the hair of a polar bear. He would like to lay that fake fur on the roof of a house and possibly spread a little more around the sides of the building. The fake hair would collect rays from the sun and carry warmth into the house.

So far the government hasn't become excited about fur coats for houses. They do not want to give money to experiment in the overcoat business. But if some material like this could be developed, it could serve two purposes. It would keep homes warm and it would hide the nicks, cuts, dents, and stains that are on houses. We could cover them like we cover old furniture.

This is what God does when He covers our sins. We have all done things that were wrong. But God is willing to cover our sins with His love. Then our sins are gone. God does not see them anymore because He has forgiven them.

And forgiven the sins of your people—yes, covered over each one.
PSALM 85:2 (TLB)

Do You Remember?

1. Where does the idea of a fur coat for your house come from?

2. What color is a polar bear really?

3. How can we have our sins covered over?

God reaches out and covers us with His love.

142 Marmots Like to Play

It would be interesting to make a list of how many animals enjoy playing: otters, kittens, dolphins, foxes, and all kinds of cubs and pups. You could add many others. One creature who takes time out for fun is the marmot.

This little rodent leads a short, rugged, dangerous life. With that kind of pressure it needs to find ways to relax.

Its name comes from French and means "mountain mouse." If you ever take the cog railroad up Pikes Peak in Colorado, you will probably see them sitting along the rocks, staring at the strange tourists riding the train.

Although their name means "mouse," marmots can weigh up to twenty-five pounds. Their front teeth, long hair, and full tails give them the appearance of beavers.

The marmots of Olympic National Park in Washington State are often called "whistle pigs" because of the security system they have adopted. When a colony of marmots is outside its burrow, one of the members serves as a lookout. It watches the area for any possible enemies.

Marmots do not lack for enemies. Hawks, eagles, mountain lions, and coyotes would all like to include a marmot in their daily menu. If the lookout sights one of these creatures or any other intruder, it gives off a whistle designed to startle the deepest sleeper.

Hurriedly, the marmots race for the safety of their homes and wait for the predators to leave. Predators are anything that destroy or eat animals. Many animals are predators.

Even without enemies the marmot has a rough life. The winters are snow-packed and many do not survive winter's hibernation. Because of the cold in their high altitudes, marmots can spend only a mere five months in the open air.

But no one has ever heard the marmots complain. They are too busy getting the most out of life. Marmots love lying in the sun catching a few rays. They seem to enjoy the other marmots that live in their colony.

When time allows, they like to find other marmots and wrestle in the grass. In friendly play, two of them will rise up on their back legs and lock arms. If possible, they will tussle until one tosses its opponent into the twigs. He then gets up and happily goes at it again.

Life can be harsh for all of us. We don't have predators looking for us, but there is sickness, disaster, disappointment, and failure. When time allows, we ought to get in some playfulness. God gave us a sense of humor and the ability to laugh. It would be a shame to waste it.

And Sarah declared, "God has brought me laughter! All who hear about this shall rejoice with me."

GENESIS 21:6 (TLB)

Do You Remember?

1. What is a predator?

2. How does the lookout warn the other marmots?

3. What activity do marmots have that we should copy?

Life doesn't need to be so serious all the time.

143 The Arctic Fox

Most of us can find food in our kitchens, but animals do not have life this easy. Many have to move from place to place in a constant search for food.

The arctic fox is a good example of a constant food shopper. Food becomes scarce in the cold arctic areas with temperatures dropping to negative 60 degrees or less. To survive, the fox has grown a long white fur coat.

The desire to survive may drive this animal one thousand miles and back again. The fox is in a dangerous position. If it stays put, it may soon run out of food. If it moves around, it is likely to become a victim to human or animal hunters.

Not every arctic fox goes south to escape the cold. The southern areas are filled with danger. There are many animals and people who love to hunt this lovely little creature. A number of arctic fox will travel north to within fifty miles of the North Pole.

Moving north would seem like certain death, but the fox often manages to survive. The land is frozen, with practically no plant or animal life, but the arctic fox is a tough and smart creature, and it turns up food in places where it is hard to imagine.

They aren't picky eaters because they can't afford to be. It is believed they can find food buried several feet under the ice. Frozen conditions have forced them to learn how to wait for food. A fox can dig a hole in the ice and place its snow-white body into the space. When a small animal comes by, the fox lunges out against its victim. Fortunately, an arctic fox carries extra body fat and can go up to three weeks without food.

The arctic fox is happy to eat dead sea animals that have washed ashore. Seals and whales are likely to become part of their diet.

In the spring the foxes that survive return to their home areas. Many have died but others have won at the challenging game of searching for food.

Nature can be harsh for animals; life can be just as cruel to human beings. Millions of people live in a continuous search for food. They dig through garbage cans. Some beg on the streets for food. Many babies die for lack of milk and food.

Jesus knew we would always have hungry—even starving—people with us. That is why He taught us to feed those who are starving.

> *For I was hungry and you fed me; I was thirsty and you gave me water; I was a stranger and you invited me into your homes.*
>
> **MATTHEW 25:35** (TLB)

Do You Remember?

1. What color is the arctic fox?

2. What is one of the hardest jobs for the arctic fox?

3. What has your family done to help starving people?

Be grateful for the food you eat.

144 The Mighty Amazon

Do you like adventure? Would you enjoy traveling on a river filled with dangerous fish? How about seeing hundreds of thousands of insects, many of which have never been named? Would you like to ride a boat four thousand miles without ever leaving the same river? Can you tolerate terribly high humidity where all day long you are dripping wet?

If you answered yes to these questions, you may be ready to explore the famous Amazon River. Located in South America, it is born in the high

Peruvian Andes. Winding its way across massive Brazil, the Amazon finally pours its cargo into the mighty Atlantic Ocean.

Before you buy a plane ticket and head for the jungles of Amazonia, you should know what to expect. Take a camera along in case you spot a dolphin arcing out of the freshwater river. And don't forget to keep your hands in the boat in case you ride over some piranhas. A long-blade machete will come in handy if you decide to walk into the jungle. Most of the area is so seldom traveled that it is nearly impossible to make your way through the thick overgrowth.

There is no need to worry about being lonely even during the night. The insects would not think of leaving you alone, and the monkeys are willing to chat with you all night long. Monkeys will also keep you company during the day with their bright faces and circus tricks.

If you are tired of garter snakes in your backyard, you will be surprised at the reptiles that crowd the jungle. The anaconda, possibly the world's longest snake at thirty feet long, would be pleased to meet you. Bushmasters are smaller snakes that are attracted to a human's body heat. Snakes find the jungle a good place to live and raise their children.

Under almost ideal conditions, large, beautiful trees have prospered along the Amazon. Prized varieties such as cedar stretch majestically toward heaven. Trees provide homes for an almost endless number of animals. Some of the trees are decked with gorgeous orchids growing freely on their trunks.

As you move lazily along the river and drink in some of its wonders, you might think of Psalm 1:3. The verse speaks of those who follow God. Christians are like the healthy, towering trees by the river. Their lives are full and satisfying because "they delight in doing everything God wants them to do."

They are like trees along a riverbank bearing luscious fruit each season without fail. Their leaves shall never wither, and all they do shall prosper.

PSALM 1:3 (TLB)

Do You Remember?

1. Where is the Amazon River located?

2. Name some animals found in that region.

3. How are Christians like trees, according to Psalm 1?

I am a child of God, and I yearn to make Him happy.

145 How Smart Are You?

When you go to school and study with other students, you might start to wonder how smart you are. You might even compare yourself with the other students in the class. Some people do their math faster than you do. But you may write better sentences than someone else in the class.

Soon you find out that you may be smart in one subject and not as smart in another. Everyone is smart at different things because God made people to be intelligent in one way or another. An animal might be very smart in one thing and not as smart in another. But God definitely made you smart.

An arctic tern can't read a book, but it can do some things that most people can't do. This bird leaves home at the age of six weeks; it flies eleven thousand miles from home and returns the next summer to the same nesting area. In navigation, a tern is extra smart.

Some people argue that the dolphin is nature's most intelligent animal outside of man. Dolphins do seem to have talents for language that are very unusual. They have little difficulty talking to each other and are able to learn a vocabulary and grammar. A dolphin may not be able to fly a plane, but a dolphin is still smart.

Bees aren't dummies either. When a bee tells its fellow bees where to find nectar, the message needs to be correct. A special dance tells other bees which direction to fly and exactly how far to go, yet bees in another county might not be able to understand the language of this particular bee. Some scientists believe a bee's language is the most complicated in the world outside of human beings.

It's true that a bee can't fill out an income tax form, but a bee is still smart. Bees understand something about geometry. The hives they build are often made of little sections created at precise mathematical angles.

All of us are smart in one way or another. And because we are smart, we are able to think about God and what He means to us. We aren't smart enough to totally understand God, but we are intelligent enough to believe in Him. Because we can think about God, we are able to come to Him and believe in His Son Jesus Christ.

I thought about the wrong direction in which I was headed,
and turned around and came running back to you.

PSALM 119:59 (TLB)

Do You Remember?

1. What special ability does an arctic tern have?

2. What special ability does a dolphin have?

3. What special ability do you have?

We are so close to God.

146 The Skunk Pig

The next time you're in Texas, Arizona, or New Mexico, look for the javelina (hava-LEE-na). Weighing about thirty pounds, this short skunk pig can be found chewing on a prickly pear cactus.

Javelinas are neither skunks nor pigs, but they have reputations for acting like both. The only reason they remind people of skunks is their ability to give off a gagging odor. This terrible smell may not be given to frighten attackers, but it is strong enough to do the job. Its real purpose is probably to warn fellow javelinas to head for cover.

Their reputation for being pigs will make sense after merely one look at them. Javelinas have flat noses almost exactly like pig snouts. They have

233

even developed grunts like pigs. Consequently, people in the area often call them desert pigs.

If you study them more closely, the javelina turns out to be related to the boar. They can be found throughout Central and South America.

These little pig-like creatures probably got their name because of the sharp tusks that stick out of their mouths. To some, the tusks look like javelins.

Despite the terrible stories told about vicious javelina attacks, few if any of them are true. When a javelina sees a human being, it seems to have only one instinct— to get away as quickly as possible.

With all of the study that has been done on the javelina, we might expect some of the stories to go away. However, once an animal gets a bad reputation, it can take decades or even hundreds of years for it to go away, if ever. Many of the terrible things we believe about animals are not true; most of the time we simply don't know any better.

The Bible tells us that dead flies will make something even as pleasant as perfume smell awful. In the same way, a very good person could do one bad thing, and the bad thing will always be remembered.

Javelinas have bad reputations they do not deserve. Some people have bad reputations they do not deserve either. They may have made one or two mistakes, but that doesn't make them a bad person.

Often we need to forget something that a person has done and like him for the good person he is today.

> *As dead flies give perfume a bad smell, so a little folly out-weighs wisdom and honor.*
>
> **ECCLESIASTES 10:1 (NIV)**

Do You Remember?

234

1. Why is the javelina called a skunk pig?

2. Where did the name *javelina* come from?

3. Do you know someone who has a bad reputation that you think doesn't deserve it?

Consider a person for who he is, not who he was.

147 Swinging Monkeys

Do you ever wish you could travel through the trees like a monkey? Would you enjoy swinging from branch to branch, going hundreds of yards without even touching the ground?

Not every monkey is at home flipping through the jungle, but a number of them seem to love it. Gibbons almost skip from tree to tree without stepping on the ground. They swing from branch to branch with such ease that they barely take time to touch each branch.

A few monkeys are so good at space travel, they use their tails to help them swing along. The spider monkey puts its tail to work like a fifth hand. Not only can he move quickly, but his tail is so talented it can pick fruit just like a hand with fingers.

If a spider monkey should happen to tumble from a tree, its tail can reach out to rescue it. It will grasp a limb and immediately lock itself around the wood.

This tail is called prehensile. That means the tail is used as an extra limb or a fifth hand. When you visit the zoo, watch to see which monkeys use their tails as extra limbs.

When a colobus (CALL-uh-bus) monkey grows tired of tree living, it has a unique way of getting down. Like a fearless skydiver, the colobus simply hurls itself into the air. Dropping the distance of a four-story building, the monkey merely spreads open its arms and legs and lands almost as gently as a butterfly.

Should you grow tired of regular monkeys—the ones that eat bananas and merely show off their teeth—take a trip to Asia. The Philippine macaque has developed a taste for seafood. It likes to hang around the water, and when it becomes hungry enough, it will dive in and pull up a crab. Unafraid of the crab's claws, the monkey has a feast.

None of the animals are really related to us. Some animals seem much more intelligent than the apes or monkeys. Some animals know far more about the world and navigation. They are better at building homes. Some animals can communicate better. A few are healthier. Even rodents and pigeons can perform some activities that chimpanzees cannot begin to comprehend.

Among God's creatures *man* is unique. There is no animal like us, and we are not like other animals. We see similarities between ourselves and some creatures, but we are not the same. God breathed life into human beings in a special way in order to make us His children.

> *Then God said, "Let us make a man—someone like ourselves,*
> *to be the master of all life upon the earth and in the skies and*
> *in the seas."*

GENESIS 1:26 (TLB)

Do You Remember?

1. What does prehensile mean?

2. How does a colobus monkey get down from a high spot?

3. What is the main difference between man and animals?

We are unique creatures to God.

148 How Good Is Your Memory?

Have you ever had trouble finding your books when it was time to go to school? Frantically you searched everywhere—behind the couch, in the closet, under the kitchen table. Finally you saw the stack and remembered that was exactly where you had left them.

Animals may not be as intelligent as humans, but some of them have amazing memories. Many animals can place food in the ground and find it months later just as if they carried a well-drawn map.

If you want to see an excellent memory at work, you could begin by watching a bird called the nutcracker. In September you can find them picking at pinecones in the western part of the United States. These pinecones begin to open in the fall, exposing their seeds. It looks like the pine tree wants birds to come along and take the seeds.

A nutcracker has a long bill and a small pouch. The bird eats as it works, and it also stuffs seeds into its pouch. It then flies away, often for miles, before reaching its hiding place.

When the nutcracker finds an area it likes, it pecks a small hole in the ground no more than an inch deep. The bird will deposit half a dozen seeds in its underground cupboard. The place is covered over and a tiny object is laid on the spot. A twig or a small stone will mark the spot. Working steadily, the nutcracker will bury many thousands of seeds in thousands of tiny holes.

Months later, often after a tough winter, a nutcracker is able to travel for miles and find the exact location of its seed deposits. Even though there are other stores of food around, the nutcracker will find only the ones it hid.

A nutcracker's memory is not perfect, but it will find most of the seeds it buried. Fortunately, it does not find all of them because sometimes the seeds that are left in the ground become new pine trees.

These little birds cannot think the same way people think, but there is something remarkable about the memory God has given them. God knows that memories are important to both animals and people.

We don't get hit by cars because we remember to look both ways before we cross the street. We don't hit our heads if we remember to duck when we go through small places.

No one has a better memory than God himself. It is hard to imagine what life would be like if God forgot something. It would be terrible if one day He couldn't remember where He put the world.

Fortunately, God remembers each one of us. He remembers we are weak and He remembers to love us each day of our lives. God doesn't misplace people.

He remembered our utter weakness, for his loving-kindness continues forever.

PSALM 136:23 (TLB)

Do You Remember?

1. How does the nutcracker help the pine tree?

2. Tell how the nutcracker stores food.

3. Name one reason you are thankful for the memory God gives you.

237

Not a day goes by when God doesn't love us.

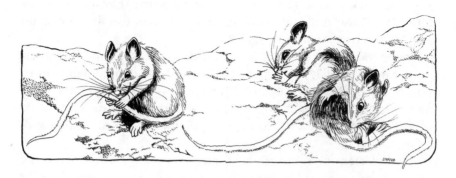

149 Cleaning Animals

I f you were an elephant and you needed a bath, you would have a big problem. A bathtub for elephants would be almost the size of a truck. Fortunately they don't need a tub. Elephants can take refreshing showers by using their trunks. They can also enjoy a hot dust bath. Throwing dust on themselves seems to get the most insects off. Their next step is to use a tree for a towel. After a few rough brushes against a tree trunk, most small pests decide to leave the big bather alone.

Practically every creature finds some way to clean itself. If you have a birdbath in your yard, your feathered friends can freshen up on a hot day. Some birds enjoy baths so much that they will take them even while it's raining. On hot days they use the baths to cool off and to take a drink. If you want to draw birds into your yard, a feeder and a bath will help a great deal.

Kittens take baths in a different way. They use their tongues and paws to scrub their faces and even behind their ears. Cats often lick each other to help out at bath time.

Most animals are cleaner than we give them credit for. They spend much time grooming and washing. Frequently their idea of clean is different from ours, but looking good and feeling good is important in the world of nature.

Geckos are lizards that have a serious problem. They have no eyelids. What can they do if they get dirt in their eyes? Fortunately geckos have long tongues that they use to clean out their eyes.

Baboons like to give each other dry baths. They do it by picking at each other to remove any matter that doesn't belong there. Sometimes they seem to groom each other merely for the pleasure of being near someone they like, much as children often comb their parents' hair.

Mice have reputations for being dirty, and in some ways they certainly are. Some carry diseases that can be dangerous to human beings. Despite these problems, they are personally extremely clean. Much of their spare time is dedicated to licking their paws and removing any leftover food or dirt.

People are also concerned about cleanliness. We spend a great deal of time keeping our bodies clean. Many of us spend enormous amounts of money to make sure we smell good.

The hardest part for man to clean is his soul. We can't see it or touch it. The only way we can reach the soul and cleanse it is to ask Jesus Christ to take care of the job.

But if we confess our sins to him, he can be depended on to for-give us and to cleanse us from every wrong.

1 JOHN 1:9 (TLB)

Do You Remember?

1. How do elephants take baths?

2. How does a gecko lizard clean its eyes?

3. How does a person cleanse his soul from sin?

It takes work to clean the outside and the inside.

150 Dogs Are Friends

Dogs can be special friends, and they have frequently come to the aid of people in serious trouble. For years the famous Saint Bernard dogs were used to help travelers in the Alps. A monastery at the Great Saint Bernard Pass kept the dogs, and when a blizzard struck the area, they were sent out to find stranded victims. A dog named Barry is credited with saving over forty people in a ten-year period.

In the 1960s a tunnel was dug through the Alps, so Saint Bernards were no longer needed as before. Usually the dogs are kept in the valley during the snowy season; however, they are still brought up to the mon-astery for the tourists to see.

Occasionally you will see a large, beautiful Saint Bernard. Friendly and kind, they enjoy being with children and belonging to happy families.

Another dog that is a friend to man is the handsome German shepherd. He makes a popular seeing-eye dog because of his good common sense. A German shepherd has an excellent memory. He is willing to do what he is told if he is trained properly; however, if you command a German shepherd to go forward and there is danger ahead, he will refuse to move. More than a guide dog, he is also capable of thinking through a situation.

Many dog trainers agree that if you want your dog to be your friend, the best way to train it is with kindness. Rewards, encouragement, gentleness, and soft words let the animal know you really like it. When you like an animal, that animal is probably going to like you too.

Dogs enjoy being around kind people. People want to be around kind people too. Harshness, yelling, rudeness, and anger chase others away. Kindness makes us fun to be around.

Kindness makes a man attractive.

Proverbs 19:22 (TLB)

Do You Remember?

1. Name three ways that dogs are useful.

2. What special ability does a German shepherd have?

3. What is the best attitude if you want friends?

I want to be a person others want to be around.

151 The Moose Is Back

Moose have a tough time because of their size. As man keeps moving into the wilderness, there are fewer places for this stately animal to live. The adult male weighs up to fifteen hundred pounds, and its antlers may stretch six feet across.

Natural enemies present plenty of danger to the moose. Black bears and wolves attack the calves and the older moose, thinning out their population.

In New England, a terrible threat to the moose is the brain worm. This creature finds its way to the moose's brain and terrorizes the animal's nervous system. Soon moose are confused and helpless, becoming easy victims for winter, other animals, and man.

Man is the far greater enemy of the moose. If we hunt them without limitations, we tend to remove too many moose. Fortunately laws exist to control hunters from becoming carried away. These in turn help the hunter by guaranteeing that moose will be around to hunt in the future.

Another difficulty for the moose has been the destruction of protected areas where they live. As man builds in these regions, the moose are forced to retreat to areas where they have difficulty finding enough food.

However, the practices that had almost ruined the moose population have now turned around. The moose is making a comeback. Fifty years ago the moose population in Maine had dropped to a mere two thousand. Today they have rebounded to an amazing twenty-five thousand. The Alaskan wilderness is home to thousands more.

Careful planning has demonstrated that there is room for both man and animals to live on this planet. Many animals now exist in record numbers, and so do people. God is happy when man lives peaceably with animals. Animals provide food, clothing, companionship, and a sense of wonder to human beings. We must in turn provide territories where God's creatures can live and roam.

Your righteousness is like the mighty mountains, your justice like the great deep. O Lord, you preserve both man and beast.

PSALM 36:6 (NIV)

Do You Remember?

1. What are some enemies of the moose?

2. What is the good news for moose?

3. Do you think God is interested in preserving animals? Why do you think that?

Animals need to be protected.

152 Wild Horses

If you ever visit the mountains of Colorado, be sure to go horseback riding. Galloping up and down the hills and looking out across the valleys from horseback is a great way to enjoy the outdoors.

Not every horse lives with people. There are still quite a few that run wild across the plains and mountains of America. Some of these horses have been turned loose by their owners. Others have run away from ranches. Many have never been in captivity.

Wild horses run in herds. The young male horses are called colts. Young females are fillies. Adult females are mares and adult males are stallions.

Among wild horse herds, there is a definite order of leadership. Normally the commander is the stallion, who runs at the rear of the herd. A mare will travel at the front as the second leader. The herd consists of mares and colts. When a colt becomes a stallion, he is usually forced by the leader to leave the herd. This places pressure on a stallion to collect some mares and begin his own herd.

Many people envy wild horses' ability to run freely. Wild horses may well be happy without the restraints of fences and corrals, but it is a dangerous life, since they could be destroyed by other animals, shot by man, injured by other horses, or possibly starved to death.

However, the freedom for the wild horses to run and even to struggle for themselves has been defended by many people. One of the most famous defenders of wild horses was a fifth-grade boy. This young boy led a fight to save the herds. Repeatedly he wrote to many congressmen describing the plight of wild horses. Finally Congress passed a law protecting them. Today it is illegal to kill or otherwise hurt a horse living in the wild.

Our society is filled with stories of young people who have spoken up and made a difference. God realizes the value of young people and has often used them. You don't have to wait until you're an adult before you have anything worth saying. Today, *you* are making a difference.

> *Don't let anyone think little of you because you are young. Be their ideal; let them follow the way you teach and live; be a pattern for them in your love, your faith, and your clean thoughts.*
>
> **1 TIMOTHY 4:12** (TLB)

Do You Remember?

1. What are the names for the following: a young male horse, a young female horse, an adult male horse, an adult female horse?

2. How did a fifth-grade boy help wild horses?

3. Tell about a young person whom you know and how he has shown his love for God.

Age makes no difference in the importance to God.

153 Do Roadrunners Go "Beep Beep"?

If you wander into the deserts of Texas and Arizona, you might soon find yourself in a hot race with a fleet-footed roadrunner.

At top speed, the roadrunner hits fifteen to twenty miles an hour. That means they run a mile every three minutes. Their running style is helped along by coasting through the air. Since they probably do not run too great a distance, they need to find ways of escape. Unafraid of the prickly cactus, they think nothing of scurrying in among the stickers to get away or to grab a quick bite of lunch.

Related to cuckoos, they stand less than one foot high and reach two feet in length. Their ability to race across the desert floor among the brush has caught the eye of amused onlookers.

In their hurry, the roadrunner may be looking for a snack. A couple of juicy lizards will make its stomach feel good. If it gets lucky, it might find a tasty baby rattlesnake. Insects make up a large part of a roadrunner's menu. Confident little creatures, they do not hesitate to munch on mice and tarantulas. Their choice of delicacies helps considerably in keeping the pest population under control.

It is unlikely that roadrunners actually make "beep beep" noises. However, they are noisy. They make such a wide variety of sounds that you might wonder what's heading in your direction. By smacking its bill together in rapid motion, it can sound like a broken dinner bell.

Roadrunners hurry across the ground because they have a great deal to do. They move quickly to get food, to get back to their children, and to avoid danger.

Most of us can move rapidly if there is something we really want to do. We hurry to catch planes, we hustle to birthday parties, we make a mad dash to kick a can. The writer of Psalms said he was in a hurry to get close to God. That was important to him. The sooner he could get it done, the better.

Some people are that way. They're in a hurry to learn more about God. They race to do what He wants. They move quickly to ask Him for His help. Getting close to God is something that should be done rapidly.

The Lord is a strong fortress. The godly run to him and are safe.

PROVERBS 18:10 (TLB)

Do You Remember?

1. How fast can roadrunners travel?

2. What is one of the many noises a roadrunner makes?

3. Name a few things you should hurry to do.

There are things in life that are worth chasing after.

154 It's Cooler at the Beach

In the hot summer, most of us like to spend a day at the beach. What is it that makes a lake, ocean, or river a great place to be on a warm day?

If you stand near the water, you are often in the middle of a refreshing breeze. The sandy beach is hot. The air above that sand naturally goes up because hot air is lighter and moves upward. Just above the water there is cool air. As the hot air over the sand moves up, the cool air over the water moves in to take its place. The gentle wind you feel moving off the water is what we call a breeze. You feel much better because the temperature by the water is kept lower by the cool-air movement.

Not only does this happen next to the water, but you can often feel it half a mile away. If you are driving toward a lake, you can frequently feel the cool breeze long before you reach the water.

245

Winds can be destructive, but most of the time we are happy to feel a gentle breeze. Part of the reason the equator is so warm is because of its lack of wind. The hot air around the middle of the earth moves straight up instead of going east or west. The middle band of the equator is called the doldrums. Sometimes we use this word to mean dull, listless, even despondent. There is little movement; everything sort of sits around.

Air movement is exactly what causes the famous monsoon season of Asia with its continual rain. As the land heats up, it makes a huge amount of air go up. When that air rises, it calls for a massive need for cool air. Wind comes from thousands of miles away to take the place of the hot air that has risen. As that air moves across oceans, it picks up moisture. Arriving at its destination, the newly cool and moist air dumps its rain on the ground. And it keeps dumping and keeps dumping. Some areas that received almost no rain one month could be drenched with over two feet the next.

Areas that frequently have monsoon seasons suffer from terrible extremes of parching heat and soaking storms. They get plenty of rain, but unfortunately they sometimes get it at the wrong time.

By setting the world in motion and by giving us changing temperatures, God has provided us with the gift of wind. In the right amount it gives us coolness at the beaches as well as rain and dryness in their season. Out of His treasure chest of marvelous works, God has given the wind as one of His greatest gifts.

He makes mists rise throughout the earth and sends the lightning to bring down the rain; and sends the winds from his treasuries.

PSALM 135:7 (TLB)

Do You Remember?

1. What creates a cool breeze at a beach?

2. Why is the air so hot at the equator?

3. What good comes from winds?

Everything is a gift from God.

155 Avoid This Animal

High on my list of undesirable characters is the gruesome hyena. Frankly, just the thought of them sends chills up my back.

If you dislike someone you haven't even met, it's called prejudice. I have a terrible prejudice against the ugly little hyena. Consider some of the facts about hyenas for yourself.

They spend their nights looking for dead bodies of other animals. If one can find a dead zebra or buffalo, it can spend a couple weeks chewing on its body. It will eat the flesh, crack open the bones, and then finish it off for dessert. When hyenas travel in a group, they may complete their meal much more quickly.

You aren't likely to meet a hyena unless you live in Africa or Asia. Some hyenas have spots on their bodies while others have stripes. Probably their most famous trademark is their blood-curdling laugh. It's not really a laugh, and it's doubtful that this scavenger has much of a sense of humor.

Recently it has been discovered that hyenas enjoy a wider diet than just carcasses. They appreciate four or five dozen crocodile eggs for breakfast if they get the chance. Hyenas are also willing to kill game, especially if it's weak or young and straying from its herd.

Gazelles, wildebeest, and zebra can be found on their menu of living game. After the kill, they may have to fight other animals in order to eat their prize.

Not restricted to fine dining, a hyena is willing to sink its teeth into a truck and bite into a generator. In some circumstances, a hyena will attack a human being.

Hyenas are good mothers who patiently feed and care for their cubs. Some will supply milk for their playful little offspring for almost a year and a half.

When I saw a hyena in Kenya, I did not want to get close. In my mind I know there are many other animals that eat carcasses. I also know that some of the ugliest animals are also some of the most cuddly and lovable. But until I get to know hyenas a bit better, I think I'll keep my distance.

The same thing is true of people. We need to stay away from strangers until we know more about them. They may turn out to be terrific, but we can't be sure—not yet. Children need to be especially careful. The safest way to meet new adults is after your parents have met them first.

Avoid their haunts—turn away, go somewhere else, for evil men can't sleep until they've done their evil deed for the day. They can't rest unless they cause someone to stumble and fall.

PROVERBS 4:15–16 (TLB)

Do You Remember?

1. What do hyenas eat?

2. Are hyenas good mothers?

3. Why should you be careful about strangers?

Some people want to hurt others; it pays to be careful.

156 Do Spiders Have Ears?

Do spiders have ears? If not, how do they hear?

The answer to the first question is easy: Spiders don't have ears. Question number two is the tough one. It may be that spiders can't hear at all. However, another possibility is that they "hear" vibrations or sound movements through the tiny hairs on their bodies. These hairs contain nerves and could send sound waves through the spider's system.

There are so many spiders in the world that we only see a small percentage of them. A few spiders like to work alone, but most of the forty thousand species of spiders would rather live in groups. They squeeze into tight spaces all over the world. Not only do they like to take over buildings, basements, and attics, but they love the outdoors. If you walk into almost any field, you will be in the middle of thousands of spiders.

In some areas spiders prefer to cooperate in building one huge web. Often thousands of spiders will work together to construct a gigantic net. Frequently a large colony of spiders will consist of five to eight thousand members. In a few cases they have reached a hundred thousand in number.

Spiders are not as friendly as ants or bees, who all work together as one big family. Rather, spiders make webs much as quilts are made. Each spider makes its own section of the web and then they tie them together. If any part of the web becomes broken, it is each spider's responsibility to repair only its own section.

When a victim gets caught in part of the web, the meal belongs to the builder of that part alone. If there is a misunderstanding over who owns the food or what the boundary line is, a terrible fight can break out between neighbor spiders.

A colony or community of spiders is found more often in areas where there is plenty of moisture and trees. These areas offer more food and consequently will support a greater number of spiders. In dry, barren regions, fewer spiders live together.

Despite the difficulties of working together, the benefits are excellent. Because spiders manage to get along, they build a much larger web than they could do alone. A large web means food for each spider. It is easier for an insect to escape from a single web, but a group web is a much better trap. A bigger web is also more likely to capture insects of greater size.

Early in the morning, just before most of us awake, the colony of spiders finishes repairing their gigantic web. They have added touches to the net all night, and they scurry around to make sure it is finished.

As day breaks, members of the group sit back and take it easy. They are waiting for the rewards of their labor, and when food arrives, they will be glad they managed to work together.

God made people to also work together. Some individuals seem to get along alone, but not most of us. We need each other. We help others when they are sad; we help each other celebrate when we are happy. If we stick close to each other, life goes better. Thank God for giving us relatives, **249** friends, and other Christians to help us when we need it.

All the believers were together and had everything in common. Selling their possessions and goods, they gave to anyone as he had need.

ACTS 2:44–45 (NIV)

1. Why do spiders build webs?

2. How do spiders work together?

3. How do we help each other?

We are better off in the company of other Christians.

157 Monkeys Need Monkeys

Why do we enjoy watching monkeys? Probably because they are a great deal like us. They stand up, they climb, and they seem to have a good time playing. No doubt they are fairly intelligent, but they are not as smart as their ape relatives.

Not every monkey likes to frolic around in the trees. Generally speaking, we can divide monkeys into two basic categories: those that live in trees and those that move on the ground. The tree dwellers live in Central and South America. Ground monkeys are normally found in Africa and Asia. Almost all monkeys sleep in trees.

Because of their separate living conditions, they face different enemies. Red colobus monkeys in Africa live in savannas. These are low-lying areas with few trees. Colobus monkeys have to watch out for crocodiles and pythons. At the slightest indication of danger, they shout warning calls and everyone scrambles.

Tree monkeys have a number of enemies such as jaguars, but they are also concerned with birds that fly in the sky. At any moment an eagle or similar bird could sweep out of the air and snatch a baby monkey. Living in the wild is extremely dangerous for any variety.

Danger is one of the reasons why monkeys live in groups. With two hundred kinds of monkeys, most of them can still be put into three types: the family groups, the many-male groups, and the single-male groups.

Marmosets, the smallest monkeys in the world (about the size of a mouse), are part of a family group, complete with one father and mother. The red colobus lives in a troop led by several males. Patas monkeys are headed by one male and his harem.

Monkeys are smart to live in groups because they need each other. When death occurs, the children that survive are adopted into other families. Monkeys spend many hours, up to six a day, grooming each other and picking off bugs. When predators approach, monkeys call out an alarm that sends all the monkeys to a safety zone.

Groups can be great. People need each other as much as monkeys, and maybe more. Christians get together in churches, youth groups, and Bible studies because people have a hard time making it alone.

We call this fellowship, and it means we love and depend on each other. We encourage, teach, laugh, cry, listen, and sing together because it's a bummer being alone.

We proclaim to you what we have seen and heard, so that you also may have fellowship with us. And our fellowship is with the Father and with his Son, Jesus Christ.

1 JOHN 1:3 (NIV)

Do You Remember?

1. Describe the three types of monkeys.

2. How do monkeys help each other?

3. How is your Christian group important to you?

Our faith grows by sharing with Christians who are hanging together.

158 The Brave Pigeon

When you visit Washington, D.C., be sure to go to the Smithsonian Institution. Its buildings have so many things to see that you will want to spend several days there. Whatever else you have to miss, be sure to see Cher Ami. Cher Ami is a pigeon who has been there for many years. The pigeon is stuffed to serve as a reminder of genuine bravery by one of God's small creatures.

During World War I, communications were not as good as they are now. Consequently, if a message had to get through enemy lines, carrier pigeons were often used. It was dangerous work, and many pigeons were wounded and killed.

One battle in the war left a group of American soldiers trapped by the enemy. They tried to get messages out, but they were unsuccessful. Every carrier pigeon they sent was killed by the heavy fire.

Finally, the pigeon Cher Ami was chosen. The all-important note was tied to its leg and the pigeon was released to go for help. Extremely thick fire broke loose all around Cher Ami, and the pigeon was struck in the leg with a piece of metal. Refusing to quit, Cher Ami pushed through the air and continued its long journey.

Almost half an hour later, courageous Cher Ami arrived at its destination. The pigeon's leg was torn and the note it carried barely hung on to its torn muscles.

We can't say how much Cher Ami knew about what it was doing, but we do know it stuck to the job. This famous pigeon knew it was supposed to travel from one point to another, and Cher Ami refused to allow even gunfire to stop it. That was a tremendous amount of courage, whether Cher Ami knew it or not.

Courage is a rare and important characteristic. It's hard to have enough courage to say no when you know you should. But people do it even though it is tough.

It's also hard to say yes when you know you should. It's difficult to help out, to reach out, to share with others. You might be rejected, made fun of, or even insulted.

A person has to have courage to follow the teaching of the Bible and Jesus Christ, and when people do it, they feel great because they know it is right.

Be ye therefore very courageous to keep and to do all that is written in the book of the Law of Moses.

JOSHUA 23:6 (KJV)

Do You Remember?

1. Tell about Cher Ami.

2. Define courage.

3. Tell about some act of courage you have seen.

I have enough courage to stand up for what I believe in.

159 Some Snakes Are Wimps

Most snakes are harmless creatures wiggling across the ground looking for a meal. Usually they are happy to gulp down a mouse now and then, or maybe swallow a frog for dessert. If they need a bedtime snack, they might sample a couple of earthworms. Generally speaking, life is dull for them.

If a snake gets any excitement at all, it will probably come from a frightened woman with a garden hoe. If it lives in an open area, eagles might try to grab it. Lately, highways, construction sites, and huge farm equipment have made its life pretty uncomfortable.

What many of us see in our yards is the harmless garter or garden snake. Many of these are olive green, brown, or black, complete with a racing stripe along their sides.

253

Garter snakes seldom get over three feet long. In most cases, if a person finds a garter snake in the grass, a high-speed race begins immediately. The person tears off in one direction and the snake shoots off in the other. Neither wants anything to do with the other.

Some yards are the happy hunting grounds of the famous hognose snake. This snake likes to pretend it is dangerous, but in reality it could barely hurt a human being at all.

If you surprise a hognose snake, it goes right into its mean act. The hognose will puff up its body and spread its neck to look like a cobra. It even makes a hissing noise in hopes of sending you into the house screaming.

But the hognose snake is a wimp. If a person runs away, this snake crawls proudly away thinking it is pretty tough. However, if you yell at the hognose it will fold up like an old chair. It will roll over on its back and pretend to be dead. Now it hopes you will walk away and leave it alone.

Temptation is much like the hognose snake. At first it looks tough. You think, *It would be all right to steal that* or *I had better lie and get out of this mess.* It sounds good and we think we can't turn it down, but maybe we should.

Like the hognose, temptation looks tough at first. But temptation is also a wimp. If we tell it to go away, it does. If we give in to temptation, it feels powerful.

The Bible tells us that we should tell temptation to take a hike. If we do, it will roll over and play dead, just like the hognose snake.

So give yourselves humbly to God. Resist the devil and he will flee from you.

James 4:7 (TLB)

Do You Remember?

1. What does a garter snake do if it sees a person?

2. What does a hognose snake do if it is frightened?

3. What should a person do when he meets temptation?

254 *Help me to not give in to temptation.*

160 Counting Fish Scales

I f fish could talk to human beings, they would have unbelievable stories to tell. Fish have seen beautiful sights that we can only try to imagine. But they could also tell horrible tales that we don't want to think about.

Some fish have been living underwater for a long time. With many, it is nearly impossible to tell how old they really are. Without gray hair or receding hairlines, it is hard to even guess. However, a fish's scales are one way to estimate its age.

Much like the rings in a tree trunk, a fish's scales grow as it grows. Each year they extend a little farther. Counting the number of times they have stretched out helps determine its age. Often it takes a capable biologist to do this.

We can do this with a dead fish, but don't try to examine the scales on a pet. Fish have an oil-like liquid covering their scales. If we rub that oil off, the fish loses a protection it must have. It would also be unwise to push, pull, or squish its scales, since they need to be in order.

When you do examine a set of scales, notice the way they overlap each other in neat fashion. Like feathers or roof tiles, they are tightly fitted to keep practically everything out. Many fish do not have scales, and some varieties have only part of their bodies covered with scales. A few mammals, like the pangolin anteater, have scales also.

If properly cared for, some fish live many years. Though few live this long, some goldfish could possibly live to celebrate their twenty-fifth birthday. The biggest obstacle to reaching old age is other creatures that want to eat them. When cared for properly, a catfish could live for sixty years.

Fish must see some unforgettable sights. They have seen diamond rings sink aimlessly to the bottom. Some have watched gigantic ships sink past them. Others have looked at men and women as they swam by in scuba outfits.

If fish could talk, they could tell you that God has been good. Nature is a living testimony that God is real. The next time you see a fish, say to yourself, "That fish has seen some of God's ability that I will never see." Even the fish knows that God is good.

Who doesn't know that the Lord does things like that? Ask the dumbest beast—he knows that it is so; ask the birds—they will tell you; or let the earth teach you, or the fish of the sea.

JOB 12:7–9 (TLB)

Do You Remember?

1. How can a biologist determine the age of a fish?

2. What is the biggest obstacle to a fish reaching old age?

3. How does nature show that God is good?

God has given us all we need.

161 When the Sting Is Gone

Some people are allergic to beestings and can become very sick. A small number of people die from such stings. Those who have had bad reactions often carry medicine in their car or in their purse in case they get stung.

For most of us a beesting is painful, but the pain will soon go away. Once we are stung, we are very careful to keep a good distance from bees or anything else that can sting.

If a honeybee should sting you, you don't have to worry about the bee anymore. The action of stinging you actually killed it. However, you might still want to keep an eye on its relatives.

You may have seen hornets or wasps flying around houses or barns. They often build their homes high up in doorways or in attics. The bad thing about a hornet or wasp is that they do not die when they sting. They could be on the prowl for you a second time. It might be better if your parents could remove the hornet nest from near your house.

If you live in certain warm climates, you have an extra creature to watch out for. It is called a scorpion, and it carries a nasty sting in its tail. Most scorpions are only a couple of inches long, but they can give you a lot of pain.

Normally scorpions avoid people. However, if attacked or surprised, they defend themselves very quickly. Their sting will hurt, but they do not carry enough poison to kill a person in good health.

Avoiding the heat of the day, many scorpions prefer to hide during the day and go hunting in the early evening. Scorpions have a pair of sharp, crablike pinchers which they use to hold their prey while they zap them with the stinger in their tail.

Maybe Paul had the scorpion in mind when he wrote about death. He told us the Christian no longer has to fear the sting of death. It is still there, but the pain is gone; death has lost its sting. A scorpion without a stinger would still be there, but we would have little to fear.

O death, where then your victory? Where then your sting? For sin—the sting that causes death—will all be gone; and the law, which reveals our sins, will no longer be our judge.

1 Corinthians 15:55 (TLB)

Do You Remember?

1. Can a honeybee sting you twice?

2. Where do hornets build nests?

3. What does Paul say about the sting of death?

Jesus Christ has made sure that death cannot hurt the believer.

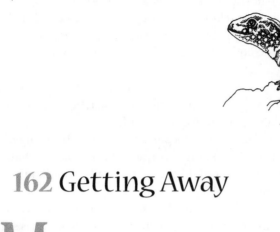

162 Getting Away

Many times animals need to get away from danger, and some creatures have amazing ways to escape.

One of the most unusual ways to escape is the method used by several lizards, like the green anole. If a bird sweeps down and grabs this reptile by the tail, the green anole will simply drop its tail. The surprised bird will be left hanging there disappointed while the lizard runs away.

You might feel sorry for the green anole, but don't worry too much about it. If left in peace, this lizard will begin growing a new tail for another bird or snake to pull off.

Lizards are not the only creatures that have great ways to escape danger. Another great getaway artist is the snowshoe hare. It looks much like a rabbit and lives in cold areas of the north. When conditions are extremely cold, the snowshoe has white fur and travels across the snow as if it were a ghost. However, when the temperature warms up and daylight appears for more hours, this hare turns a shade of brown.

Despite its ability to change colors, life is still dangerous for the snowshoe. Often its best chance to survive is to run. That is when its big feet come in handy. Its feet are four to six inches long, which is very large for its size. Oversized feet allow them to run across the top of snow at speeds up to twenty-five miles per hour. Many of their enemies merely sink into the snow with each step. While the hunting animal is stuck in deep snow, the snowshoe goes bouncing across the top, sometimes reaching nearly twelve feet with each bound.

There are many ways to avoid danger, but often the best way is simply to run. Some situations become very threatening if you stay around just to see what will happen.

Running away from trouble is sometimes the best thing to do. If necessary, say no, but definitely aim your feet for the door.

Run from anything that gives you the evil thoughts that young men often have, but stay close to anything that makes you want to do right.

2 TIMOTHY 2:22 (TLB)

Do You Remember?

1. How does the green anole lizard escape danger?

2. How does the snowshoe hare escape danger?

3. How can young people escape an invitation to do wrong?

Help me to do the right thing when trouble is around.

163 The Mantis Parent

Nature has many good parents. Some animals care for their young and will fight to keep them safe. But not the praying mantis. It usually leaves its newborn alone to face whatever trouble there is in life.

The praying mantis received its name because it looks like it could be praying. Its hands are folded at its face, and its head is slightly bowed. But looks can fool us. Actually, the mantis can be extremely tough, and in its own world is feared by many creatures.

One of the reasons many people like the praying mantis is because it loves to eat insects. Some farmers like to have them around just to cut down on the number of insects in their fields.

The praying mantis menu does not call for dead or cooked insects either. They enjoy their meals fresh and alive. The mantis is patient for a good dinner and will merely wait in the leaves until a tasty morsel comes by. Not a picky eater, it will be happy with a Japanese beetle, a bee, a moth, a grasshopper, a wasp, or practically any buglike creature.

When its victim comes close, the mantis jumps on the insect's back. Holding it firmly in its strong forelegs, the praying mantis takes a few well-aimed bites out of its prey, and the rest is strictly mealtime.

The mantis has to be careful, however. Skunks, birds, and monkeys like to fill out their diet with a couple of choice mantises.

Most of us have seen a praying mantis, but there is much more to the story than we might think. There are eighteen hundred different varieties of mantises, and they live in most of the world. They come in a large assortment of colors, everything from green to gray to brown to brilliant pink.

It all sounds like gruesome business, insects attacking and eating each other, but that is the natural cycle. If the praying mantis, bird, reptile, and others did not eat insects, we would soon be overrun with bugs destroying our crops, plants, and trees. God has apparently sent them here to hold the lower creatures in check.

The praying mantis may be good at many things, but it appears that as a parent, it gets especially poor grades. They are excellent at reproducing but seem to lack basic parental skills. A praying mantis makes no attempt to protect its eggs. After the eggs are hatched, the tiny insects are left to struggle for themselves. The result is confusion for the newborn, which can be easily eaten.

It comes as no surprise that the mantis family is not close. In most cases the female mantis ate the father mantis long before the eggs hatched.

Children who have good parents have a great deal to thank God for. That's exactly what God wanted us to have—parents who are caring, patient, kind, and loving.

When you grow up, you may have the chance to be just that type of parent. God had a terrific idea when He created good parents. They watch carefully over their children.

Rather, bring them up with the loving discipline the Lord himself approves, with suggestions and godly advice.

EPHESIANS 6:4 (TLB)

Do You Remember?

1. Where did the name praying mantis come from?

2. Why do farmers like praying mantises?

3. What kind of parent do you want to be?

Thank God for good parents.

164 Building Stone Houses

All of us know of animals that build their own homes. Some collect twigs to make nests and add a bit of straw to give comfort. There are wasps that construct homes of mud or clay. One of the most unusual homebuilders is the caddis fly, which builds an underwater home out of pebbles and glues them together for strength.

A mother caddis will lay hundreds of eggs in the water. She looks much like a butterfly but usually lacks the bright colors. There are three thousand different types of caddises. The caddis spends most of its life as a youngster. It is in the larva stage for an entire year, but may live less than a month as an adult.

Not every caddis larva builds a strong home. Some are content with nests. But if you build a home in a mountain stream, you had better make sure the stones will stick together. This is where the caddis's special glue kit comes in handy. An unusual cement-like paste comes out of its head, and the caddis applies this to the stones. The glue is water-resistant and strong enough to hold underwater.

When the young caddis starts to construct its home, it begins by looking for bright-colored pebbles. Red, white, and black stones are gathered for the project, and other shiny objects might be added.

A baby caddis fly would be an easy victim for any fish that wandered along. In fact, a caddis's main purpose may be food for other fish. But while many creatures would simply hide in any place that is open, the caddis would rather have a stable home that is built correctly and offers the most protection.

You might see a caddis fly if you visit the mountains, but you have to know what to look for. As adults they leave the water and fly. They look a great deal like moths.

How does a baby or larva caddis know how to build a stone house and glue it together? Somehow God placed an instinct in the caddis that allows it to drive toward that goal. And since it already has the glue in its head, this becomes the natural urge to follow.

If a caddis is to depend on its stone house, the cement or glue has to hold. It must be adhesive and yet water-resistant at the same time. If it did not hold, the house could crumble and fish would eat the caddises.

When some things do not hold, the result is often disaster. The Bible tells us to hold on to the good and godly things in life. If we let go and start reaching for things that are evil, our lives will soon start to crumble.

Jesus is like the glue. By following Him we can hold on to what is good.

Test everything. Hold on to the good.
1 Thessalonians 5:21 (niv)

Do You Remember?

1. Where does the caddis carry its glue supply?

2. Describe the caddis's home.

3. What good things can you hold on to?

Christ helps us to hold on.

165 The Young Deer

There aren't many animals as cute as the white-tailed baby deer. Called fawns, they are usually born in the spring and stay close to their mother for almost a year. The fawn's spots help it hide while it is young. By September the spots begin to disappear and the deer takes on an adult appearance.

If you have ever seen a deer standing in a field, you know how captivating they look. In the Midwest you'll occasionally see a deer bounding among the trees. Sometimes they will stand on a dirt road and stare as your car approaches.

The correct terms for deer are the fawn, the doe, and the buck. A fawn is a baby deer like Bambi. A doe is a female adult or a mother deer. A buck is an adult male or a father.

A buck grows an impressive-looking set of antlers. Every year its antlers fall off and it grows a new set. With so many antlers being dropped every year, why aren't there plenty to be found in the woods? The main reason is that nature provides many creatures to tidy up. A number of animals, including rabbits and mice, enjoy munching on tough antlers. If you're lucky enough to find a set, you know the animals have not had time to finish them off.

When a fawn is born, it has a close relationship with its mother. At first an awkward youngster, the fawn soon develops strong enough legs to wander around by itself. The mother keeps a close eye on the new offspring. If a fawn roams too far or gets too close to danger, the doe is quick to call its child back. The mother will really scold the fawn so it will not do it again. Sometimes the mother deer will give the fawn a sharp smack with its head—nothing long or abusive, just enough to get the fawn's attention. Sometimes fawns need to be stopped simply for their own good.

Their need for good discipline from their parents is much the same as our needs. There are many troubles and dangers that could hurt you if you didn't have parents to warn you.

Sometimes mere words are not enough—discipline is needed.
For the words may not be heeded.

PROVERBS 29:19 (TLB)

Do You Remember?

1. What is a fawn? A doe? A buck?

2. Why don't we find many deer antlers in the woods?

3. If you were a parent, how would you discipline your child?

My parents discipline me because they love me.

166 Even Lions Get the Blues

What kind of troubles could a lion have? They're huge beasts that can leap across two cars and take most animals down. Lions seem to lead peaceful lives. It isn't often that any creature wants to start a fight with one of these giant, muscular cats.

Female lions are able to spend much of their time lying near water holes and playing with their cubs. Cubs enjoy a little bit of roughhousing.

Lions like the feeling of closeness. When it sleeps, a lion often has a paw or its head up against another lion. Meeting in the open, they like to rub heads. Generally, lions live in extended families called prides. The group will consist of five or more females, their cubs, and usually one adult male. Some lions travel in pairs, but most want to join prides.

Most of the time lions look like they're on vacation. Lying around and sleeping is their idea of a great day. If they could read newspapers, they would be just like many human parents on Sunday afternoons. Often they spend as little as four hours a day doing any real activity.

It isn't easy to keep a lion's stomach full. A single meal for an adult male may consist of fifty pounds of meat. The lioness is smaller and often makes a better hunter than the male. However, hunting isn't the only way to get food. Lions can turn into first-class bullies. If another animal has brought game down, the lion will move in and force the original hunter away.

Since the lion is the king of the beasts, one would think lions have it made. However, life is not only tough for the lion—it is also extremely dangerous.

One of the big troubles a lion faces is drought. If no rain comes, both water and food become scarce. Some of the animals that lions hunt starve to death. Others wander miles away to find food. This in turn causes the lion to travel to support itself and its cubs. Desperate for food, a few lions do starve.

Even in good weather lions have trouble finding food. Many of the animals they hunt are decreasing in numbers, causing hardship on the pride.

When a lion finds a prey, it is by no means certain to catch it. A lion might chase twenty animals before it is able to catch one, and it may have to share that meal with ten other lions. There is no end to the shopping they need to do.

It would look like a lion is in control during a chase, but that isn't always the case. A prey will try to run away from a lion, naturally, but if the cat gets close, he might get kicked. Many lions lose an eye or some teeth or get broken bones from trying to take down an animal. When a lion is wounded, it has to take time to heal. During that time it's nearly impossible to find food.

All of us have troubles. Even if you were the king of the beasts, on some days things would be rough. No matter how old you are, you will always face troubles once in a while.

We need to give our problems to someone else to handle for us. Unlike lions, we can take them to Christ and ask Him to help us with them. When we do, God hears us and helps us through our troubles.

> *I am radiant with joy because of your mercy, for you have listened to my troubles and have seen the crisis in my soul.*
>
> **PSALM 31:7 (TLB)**

Do You Remember?

1. What is a pride and what does it consist of?

2. What are some troubles a lion faces?

3. How can Christ help you when you face troubles?

Help me to keep my head up even on bad days.

167 Who Loves Mosquitoes?

When a mosquito lands on your arm, you know exactly why it's there. The puny pest is going to run its tube into your flesh so it can draw out your blood. If the mosquito's eggs are to develop, it must have blood. It would prefer animal blood, but it will settle for yours.

The tube that pierced your flesh is no simple instrument. Part of it does the cutting. Part draws out blood. And another part pours in mosquito saliva. The saliva keeps your blood from clogging in his tube.

Mosquito saliva is something your body doesn't want. Saliva causes the swelling and itching that most of us experience. People are different, and some will hardly swell at all. Others react to the saliva with large bumps on their skin.

It is the saliva that carries a number of sicknesses that can be deadly to humans. Yellow fever, malaria, and encephalitis are a few of the killer diseases mosquitoes carry.

The world is not in danger of running out of mosquitoes anytime soon. One female can lay four hundred eggs at one time, and she'll do that several times in one summer. We won't run out of a variety of mosquitoes either: There are over two thousand different species. My personal favorites are the ones that do not hunt for blood.

Mosquitoes are excellent fliers. They have all the ability of a helicopter plus more. They can hover over an area, go up and down, or take off in a flash. In a struggle, they become outstanding fighter pilots. Darting in and out, they are tough for humans to catch in flight.

Fortunately, birds, frogs, and fish have less trouble catching mosquitoes. They feed on them regularly. One-third of all mosquitoes are eaten within one day of hatching. However, their rate of reproducing is so high that their numbers remain large.

These little pests seem to be drawn to man because they like our breath. The feel of warm, moist carbon dioxide convinces the mosquito that you must have a good supply of luscious blood in you.

Despite all the problems mosquitoes represent, there is good news. Many people and animals used to die from the diseases carried by these insects. Today, medicine has been able to control these diseases. We can thank God that many of us are safe. But there are areas in the world where mosquitoes still cause illness and death. Maybe we can help missionaries and doctors deliver the medicines and protective nets necessary to wipe out these horrible sicknesses.

Always give thanks for everything to our God and Father in the name of our Lord Jesus Christ.

EPHESIANS 5:20 (TLB)

Do You Remember?

1. What causes swelling from a mosquito bite?

2. What animals feed on mosquitoes?

3. Why are mosquitoes drawn to man?

I am thankful for my health.

168 The Wiry Weasel

No one likes to be called a weasel. This cousin to the skunk has a bad reputation for sneaking around and, in many areas, wiggling into chicken coops. They kill chickens, frequently destroying more than they really need for food.

Because of their long, flexible bodies (which are about six to eighteen inces long), weasels are hard to keep out. Twisting their thin frames, they can squeeze through openings only a few inches wide.

In the wild, weasels play an important role in keeping other animal populations from growing too large. They love to eat mice, snakes, and frogs. Even a few meals of rabbit or squirrel are nice.

An aggressive hunter, the weasel will chase mice between rocks and race through hollow logs. If they have to, they will push their wiry bodies into the homes of mice, looking for food.

After emptying a mouse house, the weasel may choose to convert it into a den for its family. They line the interior with feathers and fur previously worn by their victims.

Weasels are difficult to see during the winter because of the subways they build through the snow. Preferring to travel at night, they can move great distances through these tunnels without fear of being caught by humans. They also need not fear their toughest enemy, the great horned owl. But if caught in the open, the weasel is picked off by the owl.

One type of weasel, the ermine (ER-min), turns white in the winter, and the fur is considered valuable to man.

People would probably have a fairly high opinion of weasels if it were not for their nasty habit of stealing chickens. Chicken theft has given weasels a bad name. It's a hard reputation to get rid of. Bad names stick.

People seem to have the same trouble with names. Once you get a bad reputation, it's really hard to get rid of. A thief or a liar or a gossip is a title that's difficult to shake. The person may become a Christian and change entirely. Nevertheless, the name might hang on.

It's far better to keep your name clean in the first place.

If you must choose, take a good name rather than great riches; for to be held in loving esteem is better than silver and gold.

Proverbs 22:1 (TLB)

Do You Remember?

1. Why are weasels hard to keep out of chicken coops?

2. What else besides chickens do they eat?

3. How do you get a good reputation?

Help me to stay out of trouble.

169 Can Quicksand Swallow You?

Few parts of nature sound as terrible as the thought of quicksand. We often picture a person walking out onto a sandy area and suddenly being pulled beneath the sand.

Before we let our imagination run away with us, we should look at this a bit closer. First, consider a couple of facts. People and animals have died in quicksand. However, quicksand is not exactly what many of us believe. Some seacoasts, streams, and rivers have soft spots we call quicksand. These areas are a mixture of sand and water. Their surface *looks* firm, and a casual walker or wader may think it will support his weight. Yet when a person steps on that spot, the sand gives way and the person starts to sink. As he sinks, sand will rise to the top, but the sand is not capable of actually sucking a person under.

To survive, the victim needs to simply lie on his back. He will float on the watery sand just as he would on water. Most of those who die in quicksand probably did not know they could have floated.

Books and movies have given horrible descriptions of the mysterious power of quicksand, but you have little to fear.

Today construction goes on in quicksand. Builders use specially designed foundations to hold their structures. Others add chemicals to help change the thickness of the sand.

There are dangers in the rivers and seas we visit. However, there are not as many as we hear about. The more we learn about nature, the more safely we can enjoy it. Old myths and exaggerations aren't much help to anyone.

The same principle is true about God. Many things are said about Him that are not true. When we learn what God is really like, it is easier to love Him and feel His love for us.

And you will know the truth, and the truth will set you free.

JOHN 8:32 (TLB)

Do You Remember?

1. How can a person survive if he is in quicksand?

2. How are buildings constructed in quicksand?

3. What are some ways to learn more facts about God?

Understanding Jesus Christ is a big step to knowing the truth about God.

170 The Intelligent Raven

What do you think of when you hear the word *raven*? Do you picture a thief stealing crops? Do you imagine a blackbird so smart it can talk? Maybe you think of a scout leading people to find food.

All of these ideas about ravens plus many more are true. The raven can live in the bitter cold of the Arctic or in the heat of southern Mexico. They can build nests in the Sahara Desert or live comfortably in the Himalayan Mountains.

Ravens make good pets for those who like to study birds. They can be taught to say words, and some owners insist they know what they are saying. A raven can also be trained to perform tricks; however, don't be surprised if it steals your rings. They have a terrible reputation for "borrowing" things that do not belong to them.

If you have something a raven really wants, it may find another raven to help fool you. One raven will get your attention by doing tricks for you. While you watch its antics in amazement, the second raven will quietly sneak up behind you and steal the object it wants.

Ravens have also been known to make deals. If you have food it wants, the raven might bring you an object in exchange. It could deliver a stone or a stick. If you decide to deal with the raven, it might bring you a second one.

Are ravens smart enough to lead people to find food? That's a hard one to answer. Some hunters insist it's true. They will follow ravens and as a result find a herd of animals. What really happened? Did the ravens accidentally pass over hunters on their way to a herd? Or did they want people to see them fly over? Possibly they wanted the people to follow and hunt the animals so the ravens could feed on the remains.

Some hunters believe the ravens led them. Therefore, they leave some meat as a reward for the black birds.

It will surprise some to learn that the ravens are good parents and family members. A raven mates with one bird for life. The relationship can last for fifteen years or more.

They are also excellent parents to a nest of very demanding youngsters. Since the young are constantly crying for food, the parents must make as many as forty-five trips daily from their nest in search of food.

Despite this constant need for food, ravens do not seem to go hungry. The number of ravens in the world remains high, as God has provided them with good sense and plenty of food.

It's hard to picture a raven perched on a telephone pole worrying about its next meal. Jesus had trouble imagining worry lines on a bird's forehead. He told us the raven doesn't have half the ability we have, and yet it doesn't fret about surviving. God takes care of the raven's needs. He is also willing to meet the needs of people who trust Him.

Look at the ravens—they don't plant or harvest or have barns to store away their food, and yet they get along all right—for God feeds them. And you are far more valuable to him than any birds!

Luke 12:24 (TLB)

Do You Remember?

1. How do two ravens work together to fool a person?

2. Are ravens good parents?

3. How did Jesus use the ravens to teach His followers?

We can place our worries with God.

171 Black Widow Spiders at Work

Do you ever feel useless? Do you have days when you feel as if you can't do anything right? We all feel that way sometimes. Fortunately you are really one of the most useful of all of God's creations. There are so many things you can do and enjoy.

If you want to talk about something useless, imagine the middle strand in one thread of a spider's web. What good could anything that tiny possibly be? Well, science has found an important use for this almost invisible piece of material.

When companies build surveying instruments, they need a thin thread to use for the crosshair. A crosshair marks the middle of their lens.

You might think any piece of thread would serve for this job, but that's not correct. A human hair is eighty times thicker than a thread from a spider web.

The exact spider web the company is looking for belongs to the black widow spider. Their web strands are so thin that most people have trouble seeing them. That works perfectly for the surveyor's instrument, since the thread is magnified thirty times its actual size. Despite its thinness, the thread is tough and will not break easily.

Even a spider web is thicker than the company really wants. When they find a web, they must carefully pull the thread apart. It is the tiny center part they are really looking for.

Since a black widow spider is extremely poisonous, the worker has to handle it carefully. If the spider doesn't feel like spinning a web, the worker gets one of the strangest jobs in the world. He has to gently and carefully rub the belly of the spider. Soon the happy little spider begins spinning out its web.

You are never useless, even if you sometimes feel that way. There are too many things you can do. There are too many people you can help. There are too many ways you can serve God.

And you are more valuable than many, many middle strands from a black widow spider's web.

Serve the Lord with gladness.

PSALM 100:2 (KJV)

Do You Remember?

1. How is the middle strand of a black widow spider's web used in industry?

2. Why was it chosen?

3. Name five ways you are useful to others.

We are all so very important to God.

172 Chimps Are Comedians

Have you watched chimpanzees running around in a zoo? Maybe you have seen them in an outdoor show. They can roller-skate, ride motorcycles, and wear strange clothing. Do chimps realize they are being funny, or are they doing it by accident?

Those who have studied chimpanzees for years have decided that chimps know exactly what they are doing. They enjoy being ridiculous; they like to make people laugh.

Even chimps that do not live around people like to be a clown for themselves and other chimpanzees. They don't have to be taught to act funny. As tiny babies, they begin making faces and playing games. Mother chimps play peek-a-boo with their babies and send them into long giggling attacks.

As they grow older, chimps like to tease each other. They try to make other chimpanzees laugh and often collapse in laughter while they are trying. By no means sad-faced comedians, they get caught up in the action and laugh as loudly as anyone. Chimps have expressive faces and use them to communicate a wide range of emotions.

Chimpanzees are considered one of the most intelligent animals. They are fairly easy to train and seem to learn a wide range of human activities. They can be taught to dress themselves and brush their teeth. One chimp was able to master the game of tic-tac-toe.

But there are several reasons to keep a safe distance from chimpanzees. For one thing, they can have bad tempers and are much stronger than humans. Another reason is their surprising humor. At any moment a chimp might gulp a mouthful of water and then playfully spit it all over the people watching. It will then laugh loud and long at the soaked victims.

Laughter is an important part of a healthy, happy life. Maybe that's why God created it. When it doesn't hurt anyone, laughter makes people feel good about themselves and about others. Possibly God watches us and laughs every once in a while.

A time to laugh.

ECCLESIASTES 3:4 (TLB)

Do You Remember?

1. Name one thing a chimp can be taught to do.

2. Besides the chimp, name another member of the ape family.

3. Tell about a situation where you and your family have laughed together.

Laughter lifts my spirit.

173 Gecko Stars

In recent years, geckos have become famous television stars. On the tube they talk, have a British accent, and are fairly funny. Most of us would like to meet one, especially if it is like the pleasant little characters we see on TV.

Living in our yards, the lizard is actually our friend. It likes to eat the things that bother us.

A good lunch for a gecko might consist of two or three insects and a bouncy spider. While we might prefer a taco, it likes something that runs across the floor or races around on our ceiling.

Geckos prefer outside living, but inside works well too. If you see a pile of old bricks or a load of stones, look carefully for a green creepy-crawly. Just like a human, geckos enjoy sunbathing whenever the opportunity lends itself.

One amazing biblical law taught us to not eat weasels or rats. We probably won't spend a great deal of time arguing over that one. However, some people do eat rats and have for a long time.

Yuck! Let's move on.

The same passage of Scripture teaches us to not eat geckos, monitor lizards, and wall lizards (Leviticus 11:29–30). I think I'll pass on that diet also.

Smart people do not eat everything they can eat. For instance, it sounds exciting to eat bugs and spiders, but some bugs could make us miserably sick. I have eaten chocolate-covered bugs, but I'm not about to begin picking them up off the ground or snatch a flying insect out of the air.

We will probably have geckos around for a long time. They even live in kings' palaces, and the royal families can't get rid of them. If we have them, we might as well be gecko friendly.

A lizard can be caught in the hand, yet it is found in kings' palaces.

PROVERBS 30:28 (NIV)

Do You Remember?

1. Do geckos roam around your house or your yard?

2. What would a good gecko lunch be?

3. Why would God make a cute animal?

God's universe is filled with variety and lovable creatures.

174 Water Fountains in the Desert

Some places look so hot and dry that you have to wonder how anything lives there. Nights are better in these areas because they usually cool down in the darkness. But daytime heat leaves everything tired and weak.

Fortunately most tiny creatures find a way to survive even in the worst of conditions. The fog-basking beetle is a clever desert dweller. If you look under dried leaves and turn dead branches over, you would never find a pop machine or a water cooler. But this beetle needs to find something to drink—and often.

Beetles may not exactly think, but they are able to create. They noticed that at night, the air where they live changes. Fog and mist sometimes move across the dark. But it would be pretty hard to drink the fog, and the mist doesn't amount to enough to actually swallow.

Like most inventors, beetles probably tried several ideas before they found one that worked. When fog touched a beetle's body under the right conditions, it would condense and become water. But how does a little bug get enough to meet its needs?

Why not turn their bodies into water fountains? There must be a way.

For some reason the beetle decided to stand on its head when the fog rolled its way. Beautiful idea! That way water would form on its athletic body and slide downhill into its mouth. The beetle would become its own water fountain.

No cups to throw away. No plastic bottles to collect and recycle. The beetle had its own delivery system.

That's the way God made us. He made us to eat and drink. And in order to do that, He let us create or invent lots of ways to get that done.

I know that there is nothing better for men than to be happy and do good while they live. That everyone may eat and drink, and find satisfaction in all his toil—this is the gift of God.

ECCLESIASTES 3:13 (NIV)

Do You Remember?

1. What rolls toward the beetle at night?

2. What does the beetle stand on?

3. How does God supply water for you?

God is loving and meets our needs.

175 A Living Trash Can

Most families have someone who will eat almost anything and eat almost anywhere. There is also a shark that will eat almost anything. It would love to munch on a rubber boat for lunch. If it finds an empty can, it will give it a few bites hoping it will become a quick dessert. And how about that old swimsuit floating just beneath the surface? Maybe that would go great with a cardboard box for a snack.

Actually, the shark likes to bite now and see what it thinks later. An oil-soaked rag might turn into a treat, or the shark might spit it right back up. Maybe it was the wrong flavor. But don't worry. It will try another juicy cloth later.

That's how it got its nickname. It is called the ocean trash can. In some ways it does a great service for the environment. There would be a lot more junk and debris cluttering up the shorelines and ocean bottoms if it were not for this constant eater.

If your parents want to buy a garbage disposal, ask them if they want to get a trash can shark instead. Imagine keeping this creature in a backyard pool. Once a day your job could be to dump the trash where your shark could get a fresh meal.

All of us know how important it is to stay clean. If we don't keep our kitchen clean or wear clothing that has been washed, we could get sick. That's why we wash fruit before we eat it. That's why we place our trash outside the house.

We aren't the only ones interested in cleanliness. God is concerned that we be clean on the inside as well as the outside. He wants our sins and mistakes to be forgiven and washed away. God wants to remove everything we might have done that was mean or nasty or without thought.

He must be a great God to volunteer to pick up everything we have ever done wrong.

As far as the east is from the west, so far has he removed our transgressions from us.

PSALM 103:12 (NIV)

Do You Remember?

1. Do you have a relative who eats almost anything? Who is it?

2. What do you not like to eat?

3. How far have our sins been removed?

Our heavenly Father is the great sin remover.

176 Why Do They Have Tails?

The cheetahs we saw in Africa had tails, and they definitely needed them. Not only did they use their tails to chase off bugs and to keep warm at night, but they used them to help keep their balance.

How can a cheetah run at full speed, leap into the air, land on the roof of a small vehicle, and not fall off? In large part it is because it has a tail. You or I don't have a tail, but actually we don't need one.

Some cats are better at using their tails than are other cats. Normally at night a cat will pull its tail in close to the body. This will keep it warm as the temperature drops.

However, sometimes a snow leopard or similar cat will forget and leave its tail sticking out. An animal or a human hunter will be overjoyed to discover a tail hanging outside of a bushy area. Quickly the hunter will attack. Soon the cat will be on its way to becoming dinner at someone's campsite. The hide, tail, and head will be hurrying down the road to be sewn into an expensive fur coat.

A tail is just one of a large cat's valuable parts. But like most of us, a cat can forget to take care of itself. It can leave that beautiful tail out for just anyone to find.

The same would be true if we don't take care of our minds. Our minds are great computers. Our mind is responsible for much of our ability to keep our balance. Our head holds our brain, and our brain protects our speech and our talent to read well or do math problems. People who mess with drugs take chances that they will injure important parts of themselves.

There are millions of people who can no longer think straight because they failed to protect their body parts.

And the peace of God, which transcends all understanding, will guard your hearts and your minds in Christ Jesus.

PHILIPPIANS 4:7 (NIV)

Do You Remember?

1. What is one of the main reasons that cats have tails?

2. What might happen if a cat leaves its tail out at night?

3. How might we hurt our minds?

Help us think like Christ.

177 The Great Pretenders

I don't have to travel into the forest or the jungle in search of wild animals. Sometimes they come wandering into my garage—and I live in a town.

One summer I put water dishes outside for my cats. But late one night I turned on the garage light and was startled by what I saw.

Three or four opossum were there looking for water. But when they saw me, they suddenly stopped, then quickly one or two of them "died." They rolled onto their backs, put their legs straight up in the air, and hoped I thought they were dead.

Like most animals, an opossum's life is both easy and hard. Mother takes excellent care of the little ones, but she isn't quite equipped for the task. She gives birth to twenty tiny ones, but she can feed only thirteen at a time. A third of them simply won't be able to make it.

Opossums are marsupials, which means the mother has a pouch to protect her young. She teaches them to hunt for food. Opossums also have an extra arm, which serves as a tail. This arm is prehensile (can grasp by wrapping around) and can be used to help climb trees. But there is almost no hair on the tail-arm, and it can suffer frostbite easily.

Most of us have enjoyed pretending. Sometimes we dress up and act like pioneers crossing the plains. Other times we sing silly songs like opera stars.

We often grow up by pretending. That's part of who we are. Many of us have been in church plays and pretended to be Mary or Moses. For a little while, we get out of who we are and become someone else.

It's good. It's healthy.

One man pretends to be rich, yet has nothing; another pretends to be poor, yet has great wealth.

PROVERBS 13:7 (NIV)

Do You Remember?

1. Why do opossums pretend?

2. Where can an opossum hide on its mother?

3. Does an opossum help itself by pretending?

God loves the pretend me and the real me.

178 The Goliath Animal

If you lived in the wilderness, there might be plenty of animals to pick on you. Large animals, fast ones, animals with sharp teeth, creatures that steal your stuff, and rude ones that spit water in your face.

However, there are a few creatures just about everyone leaves alone. One such animal is the white rhino. It is so big and so tough and so fast that practically everything stays away.

My wife, Pat, and I found three rhinos while only half looking for them.

While walking around in Kenya, we found ourselves at the top of a hill where a guard stood to protect humans from the rhinos. His only weapon was a stick. If a rhino had decided to attack us, the guard with his stick would have had to hold back a three-thousand-pound animal.

Pat knelt down a few feet away from one huge sleeping rhino. If the rhino would wake up and charge Pat, it could run at thirty miles an hour. Humans can't run that fast. We had to move quickly and quietly.

Today that picture hangs on one of our walls. Every time we look at it we realize what could have happened if it had awakened and decided to bully us around. I doubt this book would ever have been written.

In a weight-conscious world, we wonder how rhinos got so large. It didn't grow up on peanut butter sandwiches and ice-cream bars. Actually, rhinos are vegetarians. They live on grass, yet they become Goliath-like anyway.

But no matter how much green food they live on, their size becomes what it wants to be. And it stays that way. They are the third largest animal in the world. That makes them forty times larger than a human being.

281

Not many of us would argue with him about his plentiful body. Especially if we look at the sharp horns on top of his broad nose. A rhino could really hurt us.

It's best not to tease people about their size. We might need to be concerned about our own weight, but we certainly don't need to worry about anyone else's.

A champion named Goliath, who was from Gath, came out of the Philistine camp. He was over nine feet tall. . . . His spear shaft was like a weaver's rod, and its iron point weighed six hundred shekels.

1 Samuel 17:4–7 (niv)

Do You Remember?

1. A rhino weighs how much more than a person?

2. How much meat does a white rhino like?

3. Who are better: smaller people or larger people?

God has the gift to love us equally.

179 Play It Safe!

Choose carefully where you go. Make sure you understand the animal you are looking for. After all, even a zoo can be dangerous if we behave foolishly.

There was a place that sounded too interesting to miss. Located in the Bay of Bengal right between India and Bangladesh, there is an area famous for its large cats. And these cats aren't the living room variety. These cats are Bengal tigers.

These cats weigh five hundred pounds, have huge teeth, and look for people to attack. They also can be stealthy. That means they move around quietly. A person usually wouldn't even know there was a tiger behind him.

I wanted to know more about the giant, beautiful beasts, so I talked to a lady from India to see what she knew. My grandchildren gave me a book about Bengal. Then a friend handed me a video about the lives of tigers. And after all this information, I decided I would not go to Bengal to see tigers; it simply looked too dangerous. Adventure is one thing, but danger is quite different. I don't want large-toothed creatures chasing me.

We don't have to be afraid of snakes, but we choose to be careful. Before you touch a snake you need to check with your parents. Before you handle a spider you need to ask a smart adult. And before you pet a tiger . . . well, never mind.

Frankly, I don't care if you call me names like chicken, jelly belly, or even pie face, but if it looks like serious danger to me, I'm out of there. I can always search for butterflies in Central America. Even if the people don't speak English, I still feel safe there.

He who trusts in himself is a fool, but he who walks in wisdom is kept safe.

PROVERBS 28:26 (NIV)

Do You Remember?

1. What does *stealth* mean?

2. What is the difference between adventure and danger?

3. Name a couple of places where we might find wisdom.

God's Word is filled with good direction.

180 They Wear Two Coats

You might never get to vacation in the northern part of Canada, but if you do, be sure and take a camera along. Before you know it, you might be standing face-to-face with three or four musk oxen. They usually scrunch together to protect themselves from harm. Musk oxen are good at it.

Weighing nearly a thousand pounds each, four thousand pounds of ox meat will scare off most creatures. Their height alone should be enough to send people running quickly away. At the shoulders, this type of ox reaches seven and a half feet tall. It is tall enough to frighten off most basketball players.

If you meet a musk ox and keep going toward it, it might simply lower its horns. Should you continue to approach it, it might make the first threatening move. Both male and female oxen carry a set of horns. The female's are smaller, but either one can do some damage.

Because of the extreme weather, adult musk oxen like to grow two layers of fur coats. Personally, I've never met a large, quick animal quite like this one. Despite their remarkable size, they can be rather quick on their feet. Each foot has two toes, allowing it to switch directions and attack if necessary.

If you expect to eat a meal with this ox, be sure and bring along salad dressing. Your main course will be grass in the summer, and during the colder months, you might be glad to receive a twig-and-leaf sandwich.

As the weather gets colder, musk oxen like to move farther north. They are less likely to be attacked in colder territory.

Why call them musk oxen? Every summer the male of the family takes on a horrible odor. This has long been known as a musk smell.

Even though most oxen may not be particularly bright, they do have a good sense of whom they belong to. They know who their enemies are. They understand where they live and when.

Musk oxen can teach us a lesson. If we forget whom we belong to, we could get hurt. Therefore, we remember who cares about us. Strangers are not special to us. We don't follow people we don't know. If people try to lead us away, we go straight home, just as a musk ox will go directly to his relatives.

The ox knows his master, the donkey his owner's manger, but Israel does not know, my people do not understand.

ISAIAH 1:3 (NIV)

Do You Remember?

1. In the winter what does a musk ox eat?

2. Why is it called a musk ox?

3. Who should our master be?

As people, we have only one Master.

181 The Jesus Lizard

A person doesn't know exactly what to expect if he goes to a rainforest. The area could be teeming with all kinds of animals, or you could spend all day there and see next to nothing. That is usually the chance we take with nature. We might run into a herd of elephants one afternoon and a few pesky flies the next.

When my wife and I were told we might get to see a Jesus lizard, I merely shrugged my shoulders. After all, what are the odds? Costa Rica is a terrific place with beautiful scenery and wonderful guides, but how many Jesus lizards can there be?

We were standing by a riverbank, looking into the trees for two-toed sloths, when it happened: Something began to slap the water near us.

Racing across the river came a long-legged green lizard. Its large feet smacked the water with each step it took. Not wasting any time to visit, the lizard disappeared into the foliage along the far bank. It was gone.

I didn't take a picture of the fleet-footed creature, but I don't really need one. To this day, the thin-tailed animal still runs across my mind when I want to see it.

As cute as it is, the Jesus lizard has limited ability. It can't run very far on the surface of the water, but it ran farther than I would have imagined it could. Speed and flat feet keep them going, but once the speed runs out, the feet are not enough to hold them up by themselves.

What it does is not really a miracle. A few basic laws of nature are all that hold it up. When those principles begin to run out, the lizard starts to sink immediately. By then it hopes to be safely on the bank before some hungry animal catches it.

If you ever go looking for a Jesus lizard, you might want to take a camera along. If one does show up, you won't have much time to snap a photo. They aren't likely to stand and pose.

There are many ways to see Jesus. His name is on pencils. His picture is printed on T-shirts. Sometimes you might see an artist's rendering on a cup or a cap. Different people like to see him in different ways.

Jesus said, "You have now seen him; in fact, he is the one speaking with you."

JOHN 9:37 (NIV)

Do You Remember?

1. What are the Jesus lizard's feet like?

2. Would you like to visit a rainforest?

3. Do you ever talk to Jesus even if you don't see Him?

I follow the Jesus who walked on water.

182 Looking for Trouble

T he three people in the car drove down the street aimlessly, calling out mean names as they drove by people. Why did these riders want to irritate people they didn't even know? Did they enjoy upsetting otherwise very nice people who hadn't done anything to them? Actually, it looked like they simply wanted to be mean.

If you and I ate mostly termites like the sloth bear does, we might not always be pleasant either.

A sloth bear isn't terribly quick. It gets its nickname by poking around the forest seeking out termite nests. Occasionally it tosses in a little fruit, maybe a bug now and then, a few flower petals, and just enough meat to perk it up.

Its natural speed is pretty relaxed. If need be, it will climb a nearby tree looking for food left by another creature. It doesn't see life as a fast race unless it needs to.

A perfect day is more like this: If it can find a termite mound, it sits down comfortably by the side. Then it dips a claw into the busy pile of goodies. Slowly it begins sucking creepy-crawlies up into its hungry bear cheeks.

No hurry. Eating is one of its main goals in life.

Like most near-sighted animals, the sloth bear can give in to its quick temper. That's another reason why people have to give the animal plenty of space. The fact that it can't make out your face may cause it to attack now and ask questions later.

The Bible teaches us to stay away from a mother bear robbed of her cubs. We can't be sure how the bear might strike out and hurt us. Her cubs are her first love, and she will try to protect them.

We don't want to hang around people who do foolish things.

Better to meet a bear robbed of her cubs than a fool in his folly.

PROVERBS 17:12 (NIV)

Do You Remember?

1. What do sloth bears mainly eat?

2. What is wrong with its vision?

3. Name something a foolish person might do.

A good God is not a God of trouble.

183 Not Everyone Is Nice

Wouldn't it be wonderful if we could say that everyone is a good person? What if we could tell children that every insect is sweet and friendly? Imagine that bugs could not bite or sting. Suppose sharks liked to kiss or rub noses instead of using their sharp teeth to tear flesh.

Good things happen in nature, and so do bad things. People are the same way. Some will help, hug, and act lovingly. Others will rob, lie, and attack us.

Jesus Christ wanted us to know that. One person will help us, another will behave terribly. We should stay away from that person. If we think we can trust everyone, we will soon learn better.

The same is true of snakes. One snake might get rid of pests from your backyard, but another could kill the good creatures and leave the nasty bugs living beneath your picnic table. It would be helpful to know how to tell a good snake from a bad one.

A viper is a snake we cannot totally trust. One minute it may be resting peacefully in a nest of leaves, enjoying the quiet darkness, and looking calm and innocent. The next minute it may raise its head and cock its neck backward, getting ready to make a vicious strike. In certain areas of the world, this is the most deadly snake in the neighborhood.

Walking along, people are often unaware that they are about to step on a viper pit. The snake will rise up and attack while the person barely knows what is happening. If someone is bitten by this snake, he needs help immediately to save his life.

On the other hand, there are snake charmers who love these slithering creatures. They hold vipers, play music for them, and enjoy showing what friends they might be. Most people prefer to run away at first sight.

Jesus Christ taught us something about people and snakes—both at the same time. He said snakes might turn on us and people may try to hurt us. Therefore we dare not trust everyone because we could meet some especially mean and sneaky people.

But when he saw many of the Pharisees and Sadducees coming to where he was baptizing, he said to them, "You brood of vipers! Who warned you to flee from the coming wrath?"

MATTHEW 3:7 (NIV)

Do You Remember?

1. Do you know anyone who has a snake for a pet?

2. Have you ever seen a viper?

288   3. Do you know someone you should stay away from?

We are better off to have Jesus Christ, the Good Teacher!

184 To the Top of the World

The Lord must have enjoyed mountains because He made so many of them. Tall mountains, wide mountains, some sitting on dry land, and others resting deep in the sea. Some mountains have many birds to live in their many trees. Other places have large animals to roam around the interesting sights.

One of the most fascinating mountains is also the tallest. Mount Everest in beautiful Nepal is certain to grab your attention. Because it measures in at over twenty-nine thousand feet, not many of us are likely to climb to its top.

I knew that if I was going to make it to the peak, I would have to find another way to get there besides hiking. As soon as possible I bought two tickets for an airplane ride for my wife and me. Our plan was to fly over the top in a sixteen-seat aircraft.

We could watch snow blowing off the cliffs and sides. It drifted majestically out across the wide sky. And were we afraid to be that high up in winter conditions? Not at all. We were thrilled and excited, but not the least frightened.

More fun than a roller coaster. Much more interesting than an amusement park ride. And a longer ride than a waterslide. All of those are fun too. But we had done those. Now we wanted to see what God had created that His children could get up close to see.

Among the plentiful wildlife on Everest are the many birds who can hardly wait to meet people of all ages. They might be pleased to sing to their visitors. They might even want you to sing a happy song to them.

289

God is so great and so caring that He knows the name of every bird on this huge area. And He knew them long before there were computers.

I know every bird in the mountains, and the creatures of the field are mine.

PSALM 50:11 (NIV)

1. Where is Mount Everest?

2. How tall is this mountain?

3. Name two ways to go to the top of this mountain.

No mountain is too high that God is not there.

185 Whiskers Used for Flashlights

Prairie dogs (which aren't really dogs at all) live underground and enjoy barking. The bark makes people believe they are puppies. At first sight their front teeth might suggest they belong to the beaver group, but that's not exactly true. They don't have large, flat tails to help them swim. They're too cute to be considered rats, but they are members of the rodent family.

If you take a few minutes to study this three-pound ball of energy with the twitching nose, you might discover it is very much itself. When it sees you coming it will either scurry inside its ground hole or stand up on top of its hole. The ones that stand at ground level are guards ready to watch for trouble and warn the others to stay down.

There was a time when prairie dogs were much more plentiful in western America. Texas alone may have been home to over 400 million of the fleet-footed creatures in one village alone. Many things seem bigger in Texas.

Farmers and ranchers apparently have a great dislike for the fidgety animals. Whenever prairie dogs create homes or apartment complexes, they leave holes in the ground. Later, horses or cows or whatever may step into those holes and break their leg. Unable to repair the hoof or leg, the farmers' animals will die or be destroyed.

No one has invented a flashlight or a miner's cap to help these animals feel their way underground. But they do have a cool set of stiff whiskers.

As they nose their way through the dark tunnels, the whiskers tell them where and when to turn.

Their greatest protection is the barking guard dog. Prairie dogs have a good idea of when a threatening intruder is trying to break in. It then barks or chirps and makes whatever noise it takes to warn the other members. Today many of us have alarm systems on our homes or on our cars to alert us when a thief comes near.

God wants us to have faithful guards or watchmen for protection.

Israel's watchmen are blind, they all lack knowledge; they are all mute dogs, they cannot bark; they lie around and dream, they love to sleep.

ISAIAH 56:10 (NIV)

Do You Remember?

1. Why is a prairie dog called a dog?

2. How do prairie dogs hurt horses?

3. How is God like a guard to us?

Watch over us to keep us safe.

186 The Laughing Hyena

Have you ever met anyone who actually likes being disliked? He wants everyone to think he is a bad dude? Watch out when he comes around. It's the way he walks. The way he fails to smile. Maybe even the way he shows his teeth.

That's the way most of us think of the creepy hyena. It looks quite a bit like a dog, but it's not nearly as cute. It walks stiffly as if it would enjoy getting into a fight. Its neck is rigid and its lip is tight like it is ready for anything. I didn't meet my hyena at the local zoo. It was roaming around an open field in Africa.

291

Hyenas have terrible reputations, and frankly they have earned them. For one thing, they seem to enjoy smelling bad. And if for any reason one wants to be your friend, it will try its best to smell even worse. Its body odor alone is enough to gag almost anyone.

Also, a hyena's jaws are so powerful you might even call them overkill. If a lion finds its supper too hard to eat, it will leave it for the hyena. Hyenas will tear open a meal that the lion had to give up on.

And listen for its laughter. A spotted hyena will laugh to let other hyenas know where to find food. They can be heard three miles away.

When you make up your list of whom to invite to your birthday party, HoHo the Hyena isn't likely to be included. And remember, part of that is definitely HoHo's own fault.

I had never seen a hyena in the wild, but the minute I saw this one, it was as if bells went off for me. "Watch out; stay back; that's disgusting." Maybe if I knew more good things about them or if I saw a hyena help a wounded cat I might feel differently. But for now I'm going to keep my distance, and I'm not inviting any hyena over for the holidays.

Long ago when Christians chose other Christians to be leaders, they had certain standards they used. They didn't want just any goof-off to be a leader. One of their high standards was that the person not have a bad reputation.

They could be fun-loving. They could enjoy the beach. They could enjoy kickball at the park. But they had to have a good reputation. They could not be disliked or mistrusted.

He must also have a good reputation with outsiders.

1 TIMOTHY 3:7 (NIV)

Do You Remember?

1. Where do hyenas live?

2. Why do hyenas stink?

3. Why is a good reputation so important?

292

Far better that God have a good opinion of us.

187 Boy Frogs

I f you are a girl and you want to meet a boy, what would you look for? Would you like a boy who is good at sports or at science, or would you like to meet one who likes to read? Surely something grabs your attention.

When girl frogs are looking for boy frogs, the interests will be entirely different. Frogs don't wear stylish shoes, so that doesn't matter. We have never seen a boy frog listening to an mp3 player, so technology or music wouldn't be high on a female frog's list.

In parts of Virginia and along the Gulf shores of Louisiana, certain male frogs are a hot item. This odd little creature lives in trees and enjoys barking. Read that again.

That's correct. It is a barking tree frog. And girl frogs believe it is absolutely the coolest. Male frogs don't need the latest electronic device to catch her attention. A few deep-throated bellowed barks while seated by the pond might turn her heart to peanut butter.

If she could deny it, the girl frog probably would. But if you watch how excited she gets, there is no way for her to claim she simply doesn't care.

Perhaps the trilling reed frog is more to your taste. You would have to head to east Africa and hang around at night. Once you are there, listen for a high-pitched sound of a birdlike frog who is also looking for an attractive companion.

Take your time. Look around. And keep winking at whichever frog you think you might like.

Aren't you glad people are not frogs? Probably so. We are not waiting for the right bark. Finding the correct person will work out just right for most of us.

293

Each man should have his own wife, and each woman her own husband.

1 Corinthians 7:2 (niv)

1. Where do barking frogs live?

2. Where do we find trilling reed frogs?

3. Is a sense of humor important to you?

It takes the right people for the right relationships.

188 Bird Talk

Early Americans almost decided to speak another language. The settlers had narrowed the choices down to two possibilities: German and English. It's hard to know which language would have been easier for us in the classroom.

If another language sounds hard, try to imagine a different way to talk. Instead of using our voices and our lips, what if today we used our feet or we tapped our stomachs to communicate?

Another form of speaking is possible. Even today we could communicate by wiggling our cheeks or clapping our hands. Imagine if we used our tongues to create sounds instead of words. Some people do that.

Would you like to learn to talk to birds? Turn the back of your hand toward your mouth, and start making sounds on it.

Kiss your hand fairly loudly. Blow air on the back of your hand. Now make a squeaking noise as best you can. These are some of the sounds that some birds could understand. Listen carefully. From a distance you might hear a bird making a similar sound. That particular bird might believe you are trying to talk to it. In return, it could be trying to hold a conversation with you.

If you call a *spssh* sound, maybe you will find a bird or two to talk to. The bird might think you are saying, "Come down," or "Please pick up that stick." It probably won't be a big conversation at first, but it is a start.

Birds can make a similar use of their wings. By rubbing their feathers together they send messages to each other. This kind of communication won't work very well between people and birds; however, maybe we could rub our sleeves together while they brush wing against wing.

Communication means much more than the exchange of words or of voice sounds. Smoke signals, flag waving, and stone tossing are just a few of the possibilities. Bird talk is not likely to become our national language, but it is something to think about.

The author of Ezekiel wrote that he heard wings and it was like the voice of God. He lived close to nature, and the sounds of nature meant a great deal to him.

When the creatures moved, I heard the sound of their wings, like the roar of rushing waters, like the voice of the Almighty, like the tumult of an army. When they stood still, they lowered their wings.

EZEKIEL 1:24 (NIV)

Do You Remember?

1. Can you think of a new way of talking?

2. How can you talk silently?

3. What sound made Ezekiel think of the voice of the Almighty?

God and I can speak to each other.

189 Nature's Cool Choirs

A good choir might wear robes, or they might have on the same clothing they wear to the fish market. It's the people that count. Their talent is important. Their dedication and hard work are important too.

Some of the best choirs are made up of colorful, big-bellied, dark-eyed frogs. They don't wear choir robes and they don't carry guitars, but frogs can be as musical as any group around.

Found in many parts of the world, they do much more than provide a pleasant sound in the evening. Some frogs are poisonous and musical at the same time. Not only can a frog perk up the ears of another frog and maybe make it smile, but it can also make its new friend drop dead. Smart people, and smart frogs, are careful not to get too close to these musical murderers.

If a poisonous frog is going to make friends, it might need a few especially attractive colors. Possibly an extra shade of blue could be helpful, or yellow dots might catch your eye. Green and black apparently are a winning combination. Even orange seems to tempt other frogs to draw close just before they become supper.

The qualifications to become a singing frog appear to be pretty open. Large frogs over five inches wide can be seen singing away. Likewise, tiny two-inch types have learned to munch on small insects while hitting their special notes at the same time.

More than size or color, more than fine tone or deep voice, a good frog choir member simply has to have the "want to." They want to use their voices and they want to eat a good lunch.

Birds seem to sing to the glory of God without realizing it. Frogs have their own methods of producing music.

The two choirs that gave thanks then took their places in the house of God; so did I, together with half the officials.

NEHEMIAH 12:40 (NIV)

Do You Remember?

1. What is your favorite choir?

2. Have you ever heard singing in your backyard?

3. If God created so much music, do you think He must really enjoy it?

Thank God for good voices.

190 A Giraffe Shirt

The next time you go to the zoo or to a wildlife preserve, stop and ask yourself a question: What kind of shirt is the giraffe wearing? Okay, giraffes don't wear shirt—but in a way they do. Look a little bit closer.

Do you wear shirts that have patterns? One has dots on it. Another has squares. A third shirt might have mice or dogs all over it. That's fairly simple.

A giraffe has skin. That skin has a pattern. There are six patterns available for giraffes, but they don't get to choose the pattern the way we do when shopping at a store. They don't say, "I'll take a rose pattern for my skin," or, "How about a lizard pattern?" The design they get depends on where they live. A giraffe from southern Africa gets one design. Giraffes from western Africa are born with another. A Maasai giraffe has still a third.

It gets a bit confusing if one type of giraffe has children with another type. In that case, the pattern on their skin might begin to change shapes. Then it's hard for people who write nature books to keep everything straight.

The same can be true when it comes to colors and people. There are beautiful shades of black people. There are copper-colored people that we have never seen. White people come in very light to pink colors, or they could have a lovely tan. There are too many colors to cover in this short chapter.

In a sense, all of us wear patterns just like the giraffe does. Some of us are kind, and we see kindness in each other. Some of us are selfish or nasty, and others can see that too. The person who takes things or destroys things or tells lies shows what he is really like.

Our life has a pattern just like a shirt or a swimsuit. When people get to know us, they can see what kind of giraffe we truly are.

The Bible teaches us we can change the pattern of our lives. That means that people who enjoy lying can stop lying. That's the truth. Young people who hate other young people can stop hating. Rulers of countries can choose to help people if they want to.

By letting God control our minds we can begin to think like Jesus Christ instead of thinking anything we want.

Do not conform any longer to the pattern of this world, but be transformed by the renewing of your mind.

ROMANS 12:2 (NIV)

Do You Remember?

1. What is your favorite shirt pattern?

2. Where in the world do giraffes live?

3. How can we change our pattern?

Jesus Christ can give us a new way of thinking.

191 Looking for Sweets

In some countries children have to be extra careful near flower gardens. Their biggest worries do not center around bees or butterflies. Some children have to be on the lookout for an animal that looks like a flying squirrel.

Sugar gliders have a strong drive to eat nectar or fruit. An added dash of pollen from a flower or sap from a tree helps balance off a snack. Since they might weigh four pounds, it may take this glider a good amount of sweets to keep it happy.

Sugar gliders don't really fly. Their limbs aren't flapping in order to get them off the ground. Rather, they spread their limbs out as if to form a kite. They then push off from a branch and sail through the air with considerable ease. There are many flying squirrels in nature, but the sugar glider is not one of them. Rather, it's a marsupial.

Sugar gliders enjoy stinking just a little. The scent they give off helps them identify other sailing sugar hunters just like themselves.

As with most nocturnal animals, their eyes are quite large. Sugar gliders aren't likely to be seen in the daylight since they enjoy long naps hidden away in stacks of comfortable leaves on the ground.

If they manage their glide just right, it can last for a considerable distance. Short trips will last 150 feet. Longer glides for the more experienced could take them a startling distance of 375 feet.

The closest thing that passes as a candy machine is a healthy set of fresh blooms. Gliders don't get much chocolate, but they seem to appreciate the good treats they do get.

Most humans enjoy something sweet from time to time. Naturally a few of us eat entirely too much. The Bible tells us that even our soul likes sweets from time to time. If we receive something good, it's like getting a sweet treat; and maybe we didn't even expect it.

A longing fulfilled is sweet to the soul.

PROVERBS 13:19 (NIV)

Hope deferred makes the heart sick, but a longing fulfilled is a tree of life.

PROVERBS 13:12 (NIV)

Do You Remember?

1. What is the difference between gliding and flying?

2. Why do sugar gliders have large eyes?

3. How far can a sugar glider glide?

God made His creatures to enjoy sweets.

192 Pot-Nosed Crocodiles

At some point in your life you may feel embarrassed about the size or shape of your nose. Noses are hard to miss. We can hide our elbows, and our kneecaps stay out of sight most of the winter, but that nose is right out front.

No animal understands that better than the gavial or pot-nosed crocodile. First of all, it has a long, skinny nose lined with many teeth. At the end of that nose, almost on the tip, stands a bulb or pot that cannot be ignored.

The pot only exists on the male gavial, and it is considered very attractive to the female crocodile. She may want to spend time sloshing around in the mud with a handsome set of nostrils.

If she's interested, she better let him know, because the earth is running out of the sharp-looker. There may be only two hundred of the adults still living on the globe. And sixty of these were last seen frolicking in the Narayan River, which flows in Royal Chitwan National Park, Nepal.

No crocodile has fewer numbers than this one. In a few years they may be found mostly in zoos.

Facial and bodily features do not have to be our most interesting parts. Bushy eyebrows or long necks or round eyes are not the things that make us valuable. Kindness, generosity, and a friendly smile are characteristics that most of us prize. Broad shoulders or large hands or even a wide forehead are not really what counts. Likewise, to others, patience or sharing what we have will go a long way.

It's up to us. We have to decide to like our ears or our cheekbones or our skin color. If we dislike our own features, we make life difficult for ourselves.

But the fruit of the Spirit is love, joy, peace, patience, kindness, goodness, faithfulness, gentleness and self-control. Against such things there is no law.

GALATIANS 5:22 (NIV)

Do You Remember?

1. Why is he called pot-nosed?

2. How many of these are left?

3. Have you ever thanked God for the way you look?

God isn't concerned with the outward person.

193 Where Has the Bilby Gone?

Don't go out and look in your backyard. The bilby bandicoot probably never has lived near you. The last reported sighting was in 1931. And even then it would have been in Australia or near there.

Many believe the bilby, which looks like a cross between a mouse and a rabbit, no longer exists. Who knows? You might be the first person to set off across the ocean and actually find one. If you already live in that part of the world, you might get up tomorrow morning and find a bilby hopping around under your breakfast table. But it's doubtful.

Its main occupation seems to be digging. And its favorite time to dig is at night. If you are searching for a bilby in the middle of the afternoon, it is probably off taking a nap.

Bilbies don't wear glasses, but they could use a small pair. While sniffing, scratching, and digging, they are continually bumping into things.

Bilby babies are born in the shortest time that it takes any mammal. In a mere fourteen days it is ready for its mother's pouch. Add on another eleven weeks before it leaves Mother's body and is ready to take on the world. An extra two weeks are spent hanging around the family burrow.

The bilby loves to gobble down insects, and they don't bother to cook mice parts or lizard legs. Eating fruit seeds is a special treat.

Giving birth to one or two young a year, living in a cool underground apartment, and sharing space with other friendly bilbies sounds like a fine life. Maybe some are still alive and prospering. But until we run into one on a dark evening, we may have to accept the fact that they may be gone forever.

Maybe some animals were not meant to stay around forever. Some birds are no longer among us. Some mammals exist today only as fossils. Where have the huge dinosaurs gone? Living beings simply do not remain the same.

If the smaller bilby is never to return, we are glad it used to be here. We will move on now and maybe find a few more new creatures.

Much of life is that way. The Bible tells us of things that have gotten old and have now passed away. New things have come to take their place. That's a good thing. Our God is the God of today and not merely the God of yesterday.

> *By calling this covenant "new," he has made the first one obsolete; and what is obsolete and aging will soon disappear.*
>
> **HEBREWS 8:13 (NIV)**

Do You Remember?

1. The bilby is part of what group?

2. What do bilbies eat?

3. Does God continue to create new animals?

Thanks, God, for being a Creator.

194 A Spider Web for Two

One of the reasons we like to write about nature is because many creatures are caring, kind, helpful, and entertaining. However, that's only half the story. Nature also can be deceiving, cruel, and terribly selfish. Never imagine nature to be only loving and thoughtful. If you do that, you could end up being a crocodile's lunch.

Animals as well as insects can be extremely dangerous. Tiny spiders or huge three-hundred-pound lions could kill a person just as quickly. Respect for nature has to be our number one guideline.

People who play around with spider webs and people who would jump off Mount Everest have one thing in common: They both live foolishly.

Sometime look closely at an old spider web. Now look even closer. Do you see two insects that look alike? Are they motionless? Most likely they are dead and they died together. The first insect thought it saw an easy dinner and stopped to eat. The second insect saw the first one and decided to come near.

The same spider who killed the first insect also hurried along and enjoyed the second one. Two victims dead because they both thought more of a free meal than they thought about losing their lives.

That shouldn't be too surprising. Many of us have failed to consider the consequences before we crossed a street or went through a gate.

Whenever we see two bugs in a spider web, we have to admit that both of them were careless, and it cost them tremendously. The exact same thing could well happen to us.

Be careful of what you trust in. If your friend got hurt going that way, you could get hurt too.

What he trusts in is fragile; what he relies on is a spider's web. He leans on his web, but it gives way; he clings to it, but it does not hold.

JOB 8:14–15 (NIV)

Do You Remember?

1. Would you put your hand in a spider web?

2. What is one dangerous thing you do?

3. Why do you do it?

Our God is a God of safety.

303

195 Escape Artists

Do you have a favorite animal? For most of us, that's a difficult question. Animals, like people, are often special for a number of reasons. Do you enjoy an animal because it is fast or because it is cute? Do you prefer one because it is obedient or because it can pick things up with its beak?

There are several reasons to believe the orangutan should get particular attention. To begin with, it is a fascinating color. If you have seen an orangutan, you know it is orange. It wasn't painted or fed unusual foods. It actually is orange.

If you live near a zoo, it would be worth a trip to see them. Orangutans aren't likely to live in your neighborhood; the friendly creatures live mainly in southeast Asia.

One of the five great apes, it appears to have a pleasant personality. It is even playful with those who know it well. However, one of its problems is that it likes to disappear. If you are visiting with your new ape friend and then turn your back, when you turn around again it may be gone.

The orangutan can sometimes take doors apart, and it has been known to dismantle fences. Don't be surprised if it makes its way across a stream or small river.

Deep down inside it is an escape artist. If you tried to hold it captive, it would enjoy making you look foolish.

Most of us would be better off if we escaped from trouble. There is a time to get out of there. If you see trouble closing in on you, you might need to do a smooth move and disappear.

An evil man is trapped by his sinful talk, but a righteous man escapes trouble.

PROVERBS 12:13 (NIV)

304

1. What color is an orangutan?

2. Describe an orangutan's personality.

3. When is a good time to escape?

God may want us to move on.

196 Sailing Over the Canyon

The vulture is one of the largest birds in the world, weighing almost thirty pounds. It soars above canyons searching for dead animals or recently born flesh. Not an easy job under the best of circumstances, but its outstanding eyesight comes in handy. They don't miss much around the canyon. Not only do they see what other creatures may miss, but their ability to smell small objects at great distances is another plus.

Even at night, a vulture or two may attach themselves to a straight wall and hope to see (or hear) something in motion. If they get bored of waiting, they can cast off from the wall and sail out and glide into space with little or no effort. They can remain in the air and barely move their wings.

Despite the fact that they have so much ability, there are times when a vulture will simply resort to stealing. Suppose a group of lions have worked hard hunting and have caught food for their families. The vulture might circle around the lions, looking for an opportunity to sweep in and carry off a set of spareribs.

Sometimes that's good; sometimes that's bad. If an animal has caught some food but its family won't eat it all, then meat will be left on the ground and become garbage. Who will clean up the garbage? A vulture (also called a scavenger) might hurry in and do its job. It will feed its family and prevent the food from being wasted.

305

Vultures provide a service by picking up leftover garbage. If something did not collect the leftovers, the countryside would be strewn with ugly odds and ends that would breed bugs.

The same would be true if people did bad things and we were never cleansed of it. Today we do two bad things; tomorrow we do four. Next week we do five bad things. They would keep adding up until the world was simply overrun with bad things.

Thankfully God cleans up many of the bad things we do and say. We ask for forgiveness, and then we try not to repeat our wrongs. People are not as bad as we might otherwise become. Neither are you. Neither am I.

Cleanse me with hyssop, and I will be clean; wash me, and I will be whiter than snow.

PSALM 51:7 (NIV)

Do You Remember?

1. What do vultures sometimes steal?

2. How much might a vulture weigh?

3. How would you describe a vulture's eyesight?

Only God can cleanse our insides.

197 First, We Protect Ourselves

Some things would hurt us if they could. But fortunately most of us can do an excellent job of protecting ourselves. That's the way God made us.

Even in a highly dangerous situation, we can usually avoid most animals that could hurt us. If we yell for help or if we throw a stone, most animals run away. But you might be better off staying near an adult just in case your enemy doesn't leave.

The first rule of protection is to protect yourself. By securing your own safety, you can better take care of others.

Because we have hands and voices, feet and strength, speed and good hearing, we are able to chase off most trouble. But we must be willing to use whatever we have. Who cares if we are able to throw a stone if we refuse to throw one?

Try to imagine a striped hog-nosed skunk. This little monster has quite a few ways to scare off a furry attacker. Some skunks have spots to frighten off a predator, but this one has white stripes that run from the head all the way back across its tail and then back again to its flat little skull.

That should be enough to send most of us running. But what if it doesn't? If you are smart, you will take off running when you first see it. Because you are still there, the skunk may turn to its second line of weaponry. He may turn around and spray you with his special musk oil. We are talking about a high-powered smell so strong that it makes you want to run away from yourself.

This stinky creature has several weapons, and most of us do not care to fight with it. One time I put a dead skunk in the trunk of my car because I thought it had lost its stink. But the smell was so bad that I learned to never do that again. A skunk can fight even after it's dead.

All of us should be in the protection business. We need to protect our brothers, our sisters, and ourselves. When we get older, we might need to reach out and protect our parents and grandparents.

We can use our voices, our fast legs, our strong arms, and even our quick hands to help the people we love.

For he guards the course of the just and protects the way of his faithful ones.

PROVERBS 2:8 (NIV)

Do You Remember?

1. How can a skunk attack you?

2. Why does a hog-nosed skunk turn around?

3. What will happen if you put a dead skunk in your car?

May our heavenly Father guard each one of us.

198 A Happy Face

When you choose a favorite animal, try to pick one that has a smiling face. Why have an animal around that looks grouchy all the time? If we hang around a sad face or a mean-looking animal, we just might begin to look that way ourselves.

It might be fun to play with a happy monkey. It could teach us to open up and laugh more. Should we share an area with a howler monkey, we might become a howler. And what about the songbird? He could encourage us to become singers.

Whatever you do, don't spend too much time getting chased by hyenas. If we begin to imitate the irritating laugh, most people will try to stay away from us.

The next time you visit a zoo, take a slow walk around and check out the faces of the residents. Are any of them smiling or laughing? How many do you see that are frowning or even crying? Are any sticking their bottom lip out? You might even find one or two who are mean and will spit in your face.

How can your friends tell if you are in a good mood or a foul one? Do your cheeks rise to indicate a good attitude? Do they drop to warn people to keep their distance? When you're in a bad mood, can you still give a happy face?

We may not be good at imagining the face of God. What does He look like if He knows we are doing something good? Does God ever laugh? Sometimes He seems to change His looks. Does God ever sing?

God's feelings do change! And with that, so do His looks.

"I will frown on you no longer, for I am merciful," declares the Lord, "I will not be angry forever."

Jeremiah 3:12 (NIV)

308

1. Are hyenas really smiling?

2. Name one animal that might spit in your face.

3. Can God change his attitude?

Thanks for adjusting to my unevenness.

199 Songbirds Are Singing

I t's always smart to carry a pair of binoculars with you—maybe in the trunk of your parents' car. Sooner or later you are certain to feel foolish if you failed to bring a second set of eyes along. Suddenly a rapid, colorful, feathery friend will appear in the distance, and you will wish you could see it more closely.

If you happen to travel to the tiny country of Nepal, it may dawn on you that over eight hundred species of birds may be about to encounter you and your family face-to-face. A camera or binoculars would come in handy at the moment you least expected.

In many areas, the possibilities are overwhelming. At one end you could be greeted by an Arctic specimen. Travel to the other extreme of the same country and you'll find a beautiful peacock with gorgeous feathers in the middle of a striking courtship.

Not everyone enjoys cameras, but many people do. You can snap quick shots for the people at home as well as for your own scrapbook. I have a friend who takes excellent wildlife pictures both for himself and to sell. You might want to consider pursuing his hobby. It's fun to see how much satisfaction he derives from creating a collection of prized subjects that he can collect and share with others.

One of the best places to see birds of prey is along the roads and highways in the United States. Red-tailed hawks and owls are good starting places to see how birds search for food. It is illegal to hunt many species of birds, so be friendly and simply take pictures.

If you have a few lively backyard birds, keep a record with your camera and show the pictures at school. Birds captured for food are one thing, but shooting simply for the purpose of killing may not be wise.

All at once he followed her like an ox going to the slaughter,
like a deer stepping into a noose till an arrow pierces his liver,
like a bird darting into a snare, little knowing it will cost him
his life.

PROVERBS 7:22–23 (NIV)

Do You Remember?

1. How many species of birds can be photographed in Nepal?

2. Where is the best place to see birds of prey?

3. Do you have a camera that you use?

Thank you for the gift of songbirds.

200 Snakes in the Forest

While we were students, my wife and I lived in a mobile home. We were packed into a park with many other young couples. It was fun and it provided great shelter, but it was a far cry from a hibernacula. Hibernaculas are dens where some animals spend part of the winter sleeping to keep the cold weather out.

We don't usually think that rattlesnakes enjoy the cold, but actually some of them love having a chilly nose. This is particularly true of the timber rattler. They don't live in the desert; they prefer the north country, complete with woods and a bit of snow.

Fooling many of us, timber rattlers wiggle through spaces we would least expect. Their colors are far more suited for forest than for sand, and they are difficult to hear or see.

More frequently we see their tails rather than their heads. Timber rattlers are usually scurrying away from us into the woods; they seldom go toward hikers or campers.

If you were a timber rattler, you would try to make up your mind in a hurry. When a person shows up, what will you do? Will you coil up ready to defend your brood, or will you take off as fast as you can? Most snakes would rather take off. Many people like to kill snakes, and these slithering creatures aren't as good at protecting themselves as we might think.

But you can relax: Rattlers don't normally look for people as part of their meal. Their favorite lunch consists of a small mouse or a tiny chipmunk.

If you attended a rattlesnake family reunion, you would see as many as thirty different types of rattlers. Should you want to call them by the proper identity, simply call them pit vipers.

Their population is generally kept in check because plenty of animals seriously dislike them. Red-tailed hawks enjoy attacking them. Some coyotes and more than a few red foxes are able to do in a timber rattler.

It's not easy to be a snake. People, animals, birds, and a wide variety of beasts try to injure them. Many people attack or kill a snake with little or no thought to what kind it is.

That's why snakes can't afford to act foolishly.

It makes sense to be careful. Jesus told us to go through life staying alert. There are many situations to watch out for.

I am sending you out like sheep among wolves. Therefore be as shrewd as snakes and as innocent as doves.

MATTHEW 10:16 (NIV)

Do You Remember?

1. Is this the first time you have heard of a timber rattler?

2. Name one favorite meal for a rattler.

3. How many different kinds of rattlers are there?

311

God has a wide imagination.

201 Wool for the Royals

You've probably seen something like it, but you probably haven't seen exactly it. The alpaca and llama are its relatives. Called vicuñas (veye-COON-yas), they live in the high altitudes of Peru.

They're not large animals, so owners cannot expect much hard labor from vicuñas. But when it comes to fine clothing, it would be hard to gather better material than from this creature. Its choice delicate wool was frequently reserved for the clothing of royal families.

Though the wool is a bit pricey, even today we non-royals could purchase a scarf. It probably won't have the emblem of your favorite football or volleyball team, but the material of the gift will be first class.

Ask for vicuña wool by name and see what you find.

Because the long-necked vicuña lives under extreme mountain conditions, it needs to be prepared for all kinds of weather. That's why their bodies have adapted to whatever comes along.

To begin with, the vicuña has a built-in air-conditioning system. In very hot weather it can stand with its thin legs apart, permitting cool breezes to circulate around its lower body. A similar force goes to work in the bitter winter. Air circulating around its legs will help produce a warming effect.

If you are going to live in or around the Andes Mountains, each of these ways to control the climate is vital. Having wool directly on the animal's body is an added benefit.

Somewhat fragile in appearance, vicuñas depend on family connections for protection. Their wool is of such excellent quality that the vicuña lives in considerable danger. Since they only raise one young at a time, parents must show particular caution.

All of us do things that are wrong. Fortunately, God has a way of turning our bad into good. God has abilities we can't even imagine. It is much like Him looking at a pile of rags and turning it into wool. Then picture that fine material turning into first-class cloth. Like vicuña wool.

> *"Come now, let us reason together," says the Lord. "Though your sins are like scarlet, they shall be as white as snow; though they are red as crimson, they shall be like wool."*
>
> **Isaiah 1:18 (NIV)**

Do You Remember?

1. Peru has what range of mountains?

2. Name one relative of the vicuña.

3. Where does the vicuña get its air-conditioning?

Only God can change my faults into wool.

202 Jumping Kangaroos

A small number of animals have pouches on their abdomens to carry their babies—these animals are called marsupials. Wombats, opossums, some moles, and kangaroos are the most well-known marsupials.

Kangaroos live in Australia and New Zealand. Many are as small as kittens, but others can be seven feet tall and weigh over two hundred pounds. Don't let the size of a kangaroo fool you. The great gray variety can hop up to twenty-five miles an hour, and they have been known to jump twenty-six feet. They have no trouble bounding over a six-foot fence and could even clear a ten-foot one!

Not every kangaroo enjoys the ground. Tree kangaroos prefer to jump from branch to branch. They aren't quite two feet long and use their long tails to keep their balance. They can leap thirty feet to the ground without any apparent harm.

One kangaroo you might want to be careful around is the rat kangaroo. They seem to be more like skunks than anything else. If they become

313

excited, rat 'roos can let off a terrible odor. They are actually a cute animal, but their numbers are decreasing in Australia. The rat kangaroo can carry bundles of grass with its curved tail while it moves on all four legs.

Great gray kangaroos are the largest variety, but they start out tiny. Newborn babies are only the size of a quarter. The baby crawls immediately into its mother's pouch. There it can feed comfortably from the mother's body for the next five or six months. During the entire time it might never poke its head out.

Slowly the baby begins to get adventurous. For a couple of weeks, the infant will poke its head out and look the world over. Then one day it takes the big plunge and jumps out.

But the kangaroo doesn't forget the warm protection of its mother. For a few more weeks, the youngster will jump back into the pouch if it gets hungry or afraid.

Mother kangaroos mean a great deal to their young. Young 'roos look up to their mother as the strong and helpful one when they need something.

Most of us really enjoy our mothers. They have done so many kind and loving things for us. We wouldn't do anything to hurt them. That is why so many children are extra careful not to get into trouble. They have a wonderful mother, and they want her to be proud of them.

Happy is the man with a level-headed son; sad the mother of a rebel.

Proverbs 10:1 (TLB)

Do You Remember?

1. What is a marsupial?

2. How big is the largest kangaroo?

3. Name one thing you could do today to make your mother happy.

314   *Thank God for my mother.*

203 The Friendly Dolphin

Would you like to be friends with a dolphin? Perhaps you could join it every morning for a swim or even a quick ballet dance!

Some people have actually done these things and more with wild dolphins. They are not fish, you know. No one knows for sure how smart these mammals are, but a few scientists believe that dolphins are extremely intelligent.

For example, after scuba diving for many years, one woman suddenly discovered that she had a new friend. Each day when she went for a swim a dolphin began to swim alongside her. The lady would swim in patterns and the dolphin would copy each motion. Even graceful, ballet-like turns were copied. One day, however, after six months of close companionship, the dolphin disappeared, never to be seen again.

Where had the dolphin come from? And why did it leave? Dolphins usually travel in groups called schools and are seldom alone. But every so often, over the years, dolphins have left the school and become friendly with people.

One man, who invented an underwater instrument similar to an accordion, took his black box under the sea and played it to the dolphins. The dolphins seemed more than happy with this "music." Three or four of them began to soar through the water to the tune of the song as if they had been trained to do so.

If you want to personally meet some wild but friendly dolphins, travel to Shark Bay, Australia; there a school of dolphins often visits the beach. These dolphins are calm and allow many children to pet them.

Because dolphins are friendly, it is easy for scientists to work with them. Scientists want to know how a dolphin can dive so deep so quickly, and return again without getting sick. That's something man cannot do.

Scientists would also like to study more on how a dolphin's sonar system works. By sending out sound waves, dolphins can find a small metal ball at least a football field away. How do they do that?

Other researchers would like to know more about the dolphin's language. To us it sounds merely like a long string of clicks and other noises, but the dolphin seems to have a definite vocabulary.

James, one of the men who was close to Jesus, may have seen a dolphin. In the Bible James wrote that it was easier to tame a sea creature than for us to tame our own tongues.

Many of us know what James meant. A dolphin can be trained to do amazing things for a fish dinner. But when we try to train our own tongue, it still seems to get totally out of control. We say some really dumb things at times. Later we wish we had kept quiet. Some of the things we say hurt people terribly.

God wants us to let Him control our tongue. He wants us to ask Jesus for help. If we don't, our tongues may go wild and do great damage.

Men have trained, or can train, every kind of animal or bird that lives and every kind of reptile and fish, but no human being can tame the tongue.

James 3:7–8 (TLB)

Do You Remember?

1. What do scientists want to know about dolphins?

2. Which country has a special beach where dolphins allow children to pet them?

3. Have you ever said something that you wish you hadn't? What should you have said then?

Help us use our tongues to say good things.

204 A Good Father

Nature is filled with many excellent mothers and fathers, as well as a few who are not so great. But it would be hard to find a more caring dad than the American sea catfish. He is not only helpful but also very patient.

As soon as Mother catfish lays the eggs, Father catfish takes over. Each egg is laid one at a time and is about one inch around. Father catfish opens his large mouth and carefully tucks each egg inside it. There are at least ten eggs, but some catfish have been found with as many as fifty-five eggs packed inside their jowls.

Carrying eggs in his mouth is no small sacrifice for the father catfish. It may take a month before these eggs hatch. During this time, Dad will not eat one bite of food.

The American sea catfish is called a mouth-breeding fish. Most eggs in the ocean never hatch. For instance, an octopus lays thousands of eggs that are merely eaten by other creatures. Father catfish, however, makes sure his eggs live. Each egg actually hatches inside Dad's mouth. If we could see inside, we might notice a couple dozen eggs plus a few hatched fish swimming around. We can only hope that the father never hiccups and swallows his own baby fish.

Father catfish's mouth works like an incubator. It keeps the eggs protected at just the right temperature until the new fish are ready to hatch.

We would like to have a fantastic father also. Both our mother and father are very important to us, and we want to be able to live with both of them. But sometimes life doesn't go the way we want it to. Once in a while a parent dies while the children are still young. Some parents might get divorced and move away from each other.

But whatever happens in your family, one person never changes: Your Father in heaven is the same today, tomorrow, and forever.

The catfish father does some great things, but naturally he isn't perfect. All fathers make mistakes, even the best of them—that is, all fathers except the God who watches over us. We can talk to Him twenty-four hours a day. He even knows how many hairs we have!

See how very much our heavenly Father loves us, for he allows us to be called his children—think of it—and we really are!

1 JOHN 3:1 (TLB)

Do You Remember?

1. How many eggs can some catfish carry?

2. How long before a catfish egg might hatch?

3. In what ways is God a Father to us?

Thanks for caring, heavenly Father.

205 Farming the Sea

Can you imagine a tractor or a combine working on the ocean floor? This is no longer a dream of science fiction. These and other underwater machines are already at work planting and harvesting sea crops.

Sea farming is a little different from farming in Nebraska. While the underwater farmer does ride a tractor and helps feed the world, he has to wear an oxygen tank and a helmet.

Underwater farming has many purposes. In the Pacific Ocean there are pearl and oyster farmers. They keep a crop of oysters attached to poles to grow pearls. A tiny piece of sand is inserted into each oyster, and they hope it will develop into a pearl.

Much of the seaweed we see floating on the water is actually kelp. This weed is plentiful in the ocean and grows a foot or two a day. Farmers are busy harvesting the crop for industrial use and energy. Also, many people—especially in Japan—eat kelp.

If you don't want to farm in the ocean, maybe you would rather be a fish rancher. Fish ranchers are already in business on the shores of China, Japan, and the Philippines. Instead of taking their chances on catching fish the normal way, they mark off an area and grow their own.

One of the problems with fish ranching is fencing off the livestock. A net fence seems like a good idea, but it always needs repair. Some ranchers have installed pipes that give off bubbles. When these bubbles rise in a steady stream, the fish will not swim through them.

Instead of being a wheat or corn farmer, you might choose to produce fish flour. Fish flour is made by turning dried fish into powder. It's inexpensive, and it leaves no fish taste.

Fish flour is a big help in areas where farming is difficult. Fish is high in protein and can help millions of starving people.

Presently, we receive only 1 percent of our food from the sea. With improved farming, the produce from this source could be greatly increased.

Jesus Christ taught that it is important to feed the hungry. When we help feed the starving, it is just as if we were giving food to Christ himself. Maybe farming the sea is one more way God wants us to use His world wisely.

For I was hungry and you fed me; I was thirsty and you gave me water; I was a stranger and you invited me into your homes.

MATTHEW 25:35 (TLB)

Do You Remember?

1. Name two sea products that are being farmed.

2. How much of our food comes from the sea?

3. How do Christians help feed the hungry? What is something your family could do?

Our world can produce enough food for everyone. Show us, Lord, how to use all of it as you have planned.

206 The Jellyfish Sting

If you ever get a chance to swim in the ocean, look out for umbrella-shaped blobs of jelly before you jump in. And I don't mean the kind of jelly you put on your toast in the morning! Instead, I mean a jellyfish—the kind that my children found when they went swimming in Chesapeake Bay.

The jellyfish is a slimy-looking creature with long, stringy legs called tentacles. Its head is shaped like a mushroom or an umbrella. And the body is so clear that you almost can see through it.

Jellyfish tentacles are covered with stingers. When something touches a stinger, tiny needles dart out and stick through the flesh. These needles shoot poison which can paralyze or kill a fish but merely sting a human being. The jellyfish sting can be painful, but careful swimmers can pick them up by the head and carry them out of the water.

Jellyfish are not fast movers. Often their speed is controlled by the tide and waves. Jellyfish can swim a little by pumping their bodies, but they could never catch a person.

Usually they merely hang out in the water and wait for a tiny fish or microscopic animal to pass by. Then they sting. This sting paralyzes the animal and makes it easier for the jellyfish to eat his prey. A jellyfish doesn't sting everything, however. The pompano fish can make its home under a jellyfish without ever being stung.

After spending three days at Chesapeake Bay, our son came in from swimming with large red marks on his left arm. He had been stung by a jellyfish, but it hurt less than the sting of a bee. We put something on it and he was soon back in the water.

There are some relatives of the jellyfish that can be extremely dangerous to humans. The Portuguese man-of-war is larger and contains more poison. Its sting can make a person very sick.

Sometimes the water is so crowded with jellyfish that it is unsafe for swimming; the swimmers would be stung so often they would become miserable. One sailor sighted a group of jellyfish spread out over 250 miles. He estimated there were over one million jellyfish in this one area.

The jellyfish often gets into trouble because it can't swim better. If a large fish wants to eat it, there is no way for the jellyfish to get away. Jellyfish are merely tossed about in the water.

The same thing can happen to us if we don't have faith in Jesus Christ. One day we might do what is right, but the next day we may do something rotten. One minute we want God to lead us. The next minute we don't care what God says. This type of person is very unstable. Every time a new wave comes, he is pushed along with it wherever it goes. Faith in Jesus Christ, however, holds us steady.

But let him ask in faith, nothing wavering. For he that wavereth is like a wave of the sea driven with the wind and tossed.

JAMES 1:6 (KJV)

Do You Remember?

1. How do jellyfish catch food?

2. How does a jellyfish get around?

3. How can a person change from being like a jellyfish?

Thank you, Jesus, for giving us stability in our lives.

207 The Toughest Glue

What are those little shells you see on the bottom of boats or clinging to the posts at piers? If you grab hold of them while swimming, you can get a nasty scratch on your hands. These tough little shells are called barnacles.

They're more than just a nuisance. When they glue themselves to the bottoms of boats, the small shells can become a real problem. They drag in the water and slow down the boats. Barnacles can also cause rust on some vessels. When my son and I went sailing in Puget Sound, we saw signs that advertised the services of scuba divers: For a few dollars, they would scrape the barnacles off the bottom of your boat.

Not only do barnacles attach themselves to hard surfaces, but they also glue their shells to marine life. Some starfish have tiny "scissors" that they use to clip off barnacles.

Barnacles are living creatures. When they are first born, barnacles are so small they can barely be seen. There are two types of barnacles: the gooseneck and the acorn. Most of these little creatures are eaten by larger sea animals; those who escape being eaten usually float around for a while until they find a place to settle. This is done by pasting their backs onto a surface with a special glue they secrete. Once its tough glue hardens, the barnacle is incredibly hard to remove.

As it sits there, attached to a boat bottom, the barnacle gets ready to eat. Barnacles can do this neatly by opening their secret doors, which slide open like elevator doors. Part of the barnacle hurriedly reaches out and grabs small pieces of food. When the doors are closed, it looks like no one lives there.

Barnacles cannot eat unless they are underwater. However, they also make good eating for fish, birds, and snails. This is why we see so many empty barnacle shells around seawater.

322

Scientists are interested in barnacles for several reasons. First, scientists would like to learn a way to keep them from sticking to boats. Second, they want to know how this glue is made. If we could figure out the glue's consistency, we might be able to glue wood, iron, and even human bones as never before.

As with all of nature, even this glue can't last forever. It is possible for barnacles to be worn off or scraped away. The only things that last forever are in Jesus Christ. For instance, Jesus Christ is our friend and our Savior, and He will never go away.

Even in the times when we are at our worst, Christ sticks close. His love for us is tougher than any glue in the world.

For God has said, "I will never, never fail you nor forsake you."

Hebrews 13:5 (TLB)

Do You Remember?

1. What is a barnacle?

2. How does a barnacle eat?

3. How long will Jesus love you? How long should we love Him?

Thanks, Lord Jesus, for sticking close when the waves get rough.

208 Waves Gone Wild

How high is your house? Scientists have measured ocean waves at sixty feet high. That would be higher than almost any of our homes.

Some sailors insist that waves can be even larger. In 1933, the Navy tanker *Ramapo* was sitting fairly level when a monstrous wave crashed across it. The crew claims it hit the vessel at 112 feet high.

The next time you hear about someone crossing the ocean in a small boat, remember these waves' sizes. It is a tremendously dangerous voyage in a tiny craft.

Not only are waves big, but they are powerful. One series of waves began to attack a British shore and did not quit until it had destroyed a 2,600-ton concrete wall.

During a particularly rough night at Tillamook Rock, the restless sea revealed its enormous power. The waves picked up a 135-pound rock and smashed it against the lighthouse one hundred feet above sea level.

Waves at the beach are fun to use for surfing or just to play in. They are also fascinating to watch. However, we should always respect their strength.

Often the violent waves begin someplace far away and build up as they cross the ocean. In 2004 there was an earthquake in the Indian Ocean. The force of the quake sent waves rolling, triggering the Asian Tsunami (tsu-NAH-mee), which affected a dozen countries and killed more than 225,000 people.

A single wave does not travel across the entire ocean. Instead, one wave pushes another wave, which in turn pushes another, and so on.

Waves are so important to safe travel that they are studied; wave predictions are given just like weather reports. The Navy Oceanographic Office issues wave forecasts twice a day.

People study wave movement in hopes of using waves for energy. As waves steadily beat against the shores, scientists are inventing ways to use their power to produce electricity.

A wave does not have to be only in the ocean to be powerful. Gigantic waves on lakes can tear large ships apart.

Fishermen during the life of Christ knew how dangerous waves could be. A sudden squall could hit Galilee and sink a boat in a few minutes.

Jesus was asleep on a boat when one of these squalls came. The experienced fishermen were immediately afraid. When Jesus woke up He merely told the waves to calm down. The waves instantly obeyed.

If God tells nature to do something, nature will always do it. He wants people to be like the waves and obey Him.

So he spoke to the storm: "Quiet down," he said, and the wind and waves subsided and all was calm!

LUKE 8:24 (TLB)

1. How high can waves become?

2. How can waves be used?

3. Why is it important to God that He be obeyed?

Most of the time we know what is right, Lord. Help us to do it!

209 A Walrus Shopping Center

Are you looking for a household pet? Don't get a walrus!

The biggest problem with keeping a walrus is the fact that it weighs up to two tons. To stay alive, this large sea animal has to eat one hundred pounds of food daily. His favorite food is shellfish. He gobbles down thousands of clams every day. The shells are spit out and the meat is quickly swallowed.

If the walrus's size and food bill do not bother you, think about his tusks. He has two large teeth that point straight down. The walrus uses them as dangerous weapons. If a walrus wants a particular place to sleep or a certain meal, he may be willing to fight for it.

If you buy a walrus, you will need to install a large swimming area. Walruses can dive three hundred feet and stay under for twenty to thirty minutes. Walruses are clumsy on land, but they are excellent swimmers.

Walruses don't like to live alone; actually, they like to live in groups of two or three hundred!

There is no need to worry about clothing. A walrus can live in hot or cold weather. He has three inches of blubber or fat to protect him from the temperature. The walrus also has an amazing blood system. Blood can move quickly around his body to offset heat or cold. After diving, a walrus may be a reddish brown because his blood has moved to the surface of his skin to adjust to the temperature change.

325

Eskimos do not keep walruses as pets, but they do hunt them for practically all of their needs. Catching a walrus is like going to your local shopping center. Walrus meat is used to feed both people and dogs. Walrus muscles are made into ropes. Their ivory tusks are turned into spoons or art carvings. The Eskimo uses every part of the walrus. Even its whiskers are kept for toothpicks.

Living in the frozen northland is difficult. People need to put everything to good use in order to survive. Fortunately God has given the walrus to the Eskimo to meet most of his needs.

All of us have needs too. They go much deeper than food and clothing, though. We need to have our sins forgiven. We need to know what God is like. And we need to know that God loves us. These are real needs. And only God knows how to satisfy these needs. That is why He sent Jesus Christ to live and die for us.

And it is he who will supply all your needs from his riches in glory, because of what Christ Jesus has done for us.

PHILIPPIANS 4:19 (TLB)

Do You Remember?

1. What does a walrus eat?

2. How do Eskimos use walruses?

3. What needs does Jesus Christ meet?

You, Lord Jesus, have given us what we could not give ourselves.

210 What Is a Sea Horse?

When you go swimming, the last thing you expect to see is a horse, but don't be surprised if you see a fish that looks like one. Its tiny head is shaped like a horse and it swims sitting up straight as if galloping.

Sea horses can be found in many parts of the world, but they are most often seen in warm water.

Most fathers in nature have little to do with their babies. A few will, but it is rare when the father cares at all. With the father sea horse, though, it is another story.

The mother lays her eggs in a pouch located on the father's stomach. Then, just like a kangaroo, Father sea horse carries the two hundred eggs around in his pouch until a month and a half later, when they begin to hatch and pop out.

Most sea horses are small. Even when full grown, they usually stretch only to half a foot. Some never become bigger than a couple of inches. If you want to see the big ones, visit the West Coast. There they reach a complete foot in length.

Sea horses enjoy eating. They have no teeth—only a tube-shaped nose. If it is hungry, a sea horse hooks its little tail onto a weed and waits for food. Tiny bits of animal and plant life called plankton drift by, and the sea horse sucks it in. Some plankton are so small you can't see them without a microscope.

Most of us have seen small sea horses in stores or advertised in the paper. They make cute aquarium pets but often don't last long. It is very hard to create the exact water and food conditions they need.

Whatever type of creature we are, sometimes we forget the many things our fathers do for us. God gave us something special when He gave us a dad. Like a sea horse father, your dad plays a terrific part in helping your life. Why don't you give him a thank-you or a hug today?

Honor your father and mother. This is the first of God's Ten Commandments that ends with a promise.

EPHESIANS 6:2 (TLB)

Do You Remember?

1. Where is a sea horse's pouch?

2. How many eggs does a sea horse carry?

3. List some good things your father has done for you.

327

Thank God for fathers.

211 Surprising Icebergs

The sea is full of sudden changes and surprises. One minute its waters may be calm, but in a short time it's possible for a raging storm to appear. When everything is motionless again, maybe half a dozen porpoises will come skipping across the surface.

One of the biggest surprises of the sea, however, is the floating iceberg. If we see an iceberg, we may be fooled by its appearance. It may look relatively small, but there is far more ice under the water than there is on top. Possibly 90 percent of the ice is hidden beneath the surface.

Icebergs are beautiful and interesting, but they are also extremely dangerous. Many people have lost their lives because they were not careful to keep their boats away from them.

The most famous shipwreck caused by an iceberg was the sinking of the *Titanic* in 1912. An iceberg ripped a gigantic hole in the ship, and over fifteen hundred people drowned.

The oceans are filled with icebergs, especially in the North Atlantic. There are many thousands that float around. Some reach five hundred feet above the water and are much larger beneath. Icebergs are such a great problem for ships that there is one agency whose full-time job is to watch icebergs and report their locations. Their work is something like air-traffic controllers at airports.

Some scientists believe icebergs could be used to help the dry areas in the world. They would like to pull a huge iceberg to the shore of a dry country. Water could then be pumped from the iceberg onto the shore. One scientist believes a large iceberg could inexpensively supply all of Los Angeles's water needs for one month.

There is no shortage of icebergs. They continue to break away from large ice areas such as Iceland.

The ocean is full of surprises, and so is the rest of life. Some things like icebergs look great, but when you get too close they can hurt you.

There are some very nice people who tell us we should not follow Jesus Christ. They laugh at us and say we are silly to be Christians. We need to watch out for this kind of teasing. It is as dangerous as an iceberg, and we could end up with our faith sinking fast.

No matter who it is who makes fun of us, it makes far better sense to follow Jesus Christ.

Holding faith, and a good conscience; which some having put away concerning faith have made shipwreck.

1 TIMOTHY 1:19 (KJV)

Do You Remember?

1. Where are most icebergs located?

2. What happened to the *Titanic*?

3. Has anyone ever made fun of your faith? If so, tell about it.

Keep our faith strong, dear Father.

212 The Mean Piranha

Once in a while you meet someone who is quick-tempered and always grouchy. A few fish fit this picture exactly. None is meaner than the eighteen-inch beauty called the piranha.

It lives in South America and is always looking for a fight. A piranha doesn't merely pick on smaller fish. This little terror will attack a human, a horse, or a boat. They travel in schools, and their tough teeth and rapid jaws can tear all the flesh from some unlucky animal in a few minutes.

A piranha looks like a friendly fish. It has pretty colors and is supposed to make good eating. However, if you try to catch one, you will not only need a metal hook but also a metal line.

Their teeth are as sharp as razors and move as quickly as buzz saws. If a visitor to the Amazon is canoeing and accidentally puts his hand in the water, he could lose all the skin. A piranha will bite your stick, pole, or oar and try to take it away from you.

Piranhas are not usually looking for people. Their diet normally consists of small fish. Sometimes they will attack birds on the water or an unsuspecting animal trying to cross the river. There are a few stories of piranhas killing people. But even so, some people in Brazil swim in the same waters where piranhas live.

Most countries would like the piranha to stay in South America. However, pet shops have sold them, and the mean little monsters could get tossed into nearby rivers and lakes. The Florida area would be an excellent place for them to grow, so authorities keep watch. Ten years ago one piranha was found near Miami, but wardens don't expect more.

Piranhas are a strange mixture of beauty and violence. On the outside their colors are beautiful, but on the inside there is a violent temper. When angered, they become especially nasty.

People are too often the same way. We take time to comb our hair and make sure our clothes are neat, but sometimes we are hot-tempered, demanding, and pushy, making us ugly on the inside.

We should be more concerned about our inward attitudes and the way we treat each other than the way we look. Jesus taught us to watch our hearts. It doesn't make any difference how good we look if we are mean inside.

You try to look like saintly men, but underneath those pious robes of yours are hearts besmirched with every sort of hypocrisy and sin.

MATTHEW 23:28 (TLB)

Do You Remember?

1. Where do piranhas live?

2. How big is a piranha?

3. Which is more important: how we look or how we act?

Please change our hearts and minds, Lord Jesus.

213 The Great Diver

It's a beautiful sight to see a flock of large gannets approaching. Have you ever seen one? Maybe you don't even know what a gannet is. It is a sea fowl, a member of the pelican family. Each one is about a yard long and they travel in groups of ten to a hundred. They often search for schools of herring off the North Atlantic coast.

They will spot their prey about a half mile from shore. From a height of seventy-five feet, the gannets begin their dive into the water. Almost like a hailstorm, the entire flock races toward the water.

When the gannet hits the water and breaks through the surface, it causes a terrific splash. On impact, water shoots ten feet into the air. It's a spectacular sight to see a hundred gannets smashing into the sea all at once.

This bird is almost as quick underwater as it is in the air. The gannet swims with its wings half open and feet pumping hard. In a few seconds it catches a herring, eats it, and begins its struggle toward the surface. If its dinner was hard to catch, it may go as far as fifty or more feet deep.

As the gannet comes up through the surface of the water, it flies away immediately. Its wings are so well formed and oiled that the water can't soak into them. Without waiting to dry, they can fly straight out. The great diver soars into the sky and begins looking for another herring school. Before long it hopes to dive again.

If a gannet is to survive, it has to be strong. It must be able to protect itself on land, on sea, and in the air. It leads a rugged life.

Maybe this is why gannets' parents leave the chicks on their own a little earlier than most birds do. A week before a gannet chick can fly, the parents take off. Many times the young gannet will push itself into the water and float for a week. Without anything to eat, it begins to slim down until it is light enough to fly easily. The gannet then takes off, ready to struggle and win as a fantastic diver.

Every creature has to struggle. Whether it is a shark searching for food, a gannet looking for herring, or a young person trying to grow up, all of us face struggles.

When you decide to be a Christian, that struggle continues. People who don't understand might make fun of you. Those who want to live lawlessly might give you a hard time.

Sometimes the struggle isn't so tough, and other times it's terrible. It helps to know the struggle is worth it. It makes more sense to follow Jesus Christ than any other way of life.

Fight the good fight, lay hold on eternal life, whereunto thou art also called, and hast professed a good profession before many witnesses.

1 TIMOTHY 6:12 (KJV)

Do You Remember?

1. What do gannets hunt?

2. Where do gannets hunt?

3. What do you feel is the hardest part about being a Christian? Explain.

We expect to struggle sometimes, Lord. But thank you for your help to overcome.

214 The Gentle Giants

Giant gray whales don't have to be friendly. They are big enough to win a battle with most anyone or anything. If a whale crashes its forty-foot body into a small boat, everyone aboard could be killed. But for some reason this champion of the sea is usually gentle enough to let people pet him.

The gray whale hasn't always been kind. A hundred years ago it had a terrifying reputation. It was a hunted species and constantly in danger.

At that time there were twenty-five thousand gray whales in the ocean, but after fifty years of being hunted, their number was reduced to as few as one hundred. Then laws were passed to protect the large creature. And now there are again thousands of gray whales. Today, though, they are gentle giants.

Off the shores of Southern California, many people sail out to meet the gray whales. Thousands of others watch them from the ocean banks. People in boats have seen these creatures rise out of the water just a few hundred yards away. Air or spray comes spouting out of their backs and shoots fifteen feet into the air.

More than once a gray whale has glided over to a boat and nuzzled close to its side. It will then hold still while the amazed onlookers pet the animal just as if it were a puppy. The whale will usually keep an eye on whoever touches it, but the creature acts just like an old friend.

Many thousands get to see the gray whales every year. Whales migrate from Baja, California, to the Arctic seas and back again each year. The complete trip is over twelve thousand miles. All along the way people line the banks to watch them. There are few better places to observe these travelers than the western coast of Vancouver Island.

The gray whale moves at a speed of almost five miles an hour, so it is slow enough to watch carefully. Each day he covers about ninety miles.

Each winter the whales return to balmy California, where they have their baby calves. Baby gray whales are born with too little blubber to withstand the tough winters of the north.

A few people still claim the gray whale is dangerous and will attack a boat of whalers, but almost all animals will attack those who try to kill them. This is because their lives are controlled by instincts and reactions that God built into them for protection.

God has made us different from the animals, though. He wants us to trust Him for protection, and He also wants us to protect others. We could try to show everyone how tough we are by being rude and nasty or beating on kids who are smaller than us. But instead God wants us to be gentle, kind, and friendly. That's the way Jesus was. So we know that is the way He wants us to be.

333

But when the Holy Spirit controls our lives he will produce this kind of fruit in us: love, joy, peace, patience, kindness, goodness, faithfulness, gentleness and self-control.

GALATIANS 5:22–23 (TLB)

1. Where do gray whales migrate?

2. Why are their calves born in warm water?

3. Do you find it hard to be gentle? Explain.

We thank you, Lord, for the example you have given us for how we should live.

215 Hermit Crabs

Our family was on a trip and it was getting dark. We had stopped at several motels, trying to find a room, but there were no vacancies. The later it got, the more we began to worry. Maybe we wouldn't be able to find a place to stay.

I think that sometimes the hermit crab must feel that way. In order to protect itself, this many-armed little creature must find an empty shell and move in. If it stays outside too long, an enemy will find it and eat crab for dinner.

This househunting presents some terrible problems. For one thing, the hermit crab keeps growing and therefore needs to move to a bigger shell frequently. While he is moving, the crab is in great danger. Besides this, other hermit crabs oftentimes want the same shell he is living in. He might have to put up a terrific fight to keep a roof over his head.

When the hermit finds a house, immediately he gets ready for a possible attack on his new home. The crab's tail has two hooks with which he grabs on to the back of the shell. He then spreads his powerful claws across the opening, ready to tear at anything that dares intrude.

His is a hard life because he knows that his safety can't hold out forever. Sooner or later he will have to move again.

Some pet shops have hermit crabs for sale, but in nature they aren't easy to find. Most of them like to live under more than a hundred feet of water.

When a hermit isn't househunting, it's on a search for food. Not a picky eater, it will feast on living or dead creatures.

Househunting can be fun or it can be frustrating. It's good to know that when we leave this earth, we won't have to search for a place to live. Jesus Christ has gone ahead of us and picked out a tremendous place. When we believe in Jesus as our Savior, we can be sure there is a special home waiting for us in heaven.

There are many homes up there where my Father lives, and I am going to prepare them for your coming.

JOHN 14:2 (TLB)

Do You Remember?

1. What do hermit crabs eat?

2. How do they hang on to the shell?

3. What do you think a home in heaven will be like?

Dear Savior, thank you for preparing a place for us.

216 Yesterday's Monsters

Much of the world has never been explored. There are places and creatures on our planet that no person has ever seen. In the near future we may see some tremendous surprises. Scientists only recently have started to look into the ocean.

In 1976 a Navy vessel was anchored off the shores of Hawaii when something became caught in its lines. They captured the creature and found they had a twelve-foot, fifteen-hundred-pound shark. Scientists agreed that this type of shark had never been seen before. They gave it the nickname "megamouth" because of its large mouth.

They believe megamouth lives at a depth of five hundred to one thousand feet in the Pacific Ocean. Since people do not usually roam that deep, one had never been caught before.

Another unusual fish is the coelacanth (SEE-la-canth). The only way this fish had been seen before was as a fossil. Scientists had thought the coelacanth had not lived for five hundred years. Then one day, a coelacanth fish washed ashore in South Africa. It weighed 127 pounds and was five feet long. A few years later another one washed ashore, and then six more.

Where had the coelacanth been? Does it live someplace where man does not go?

Do you have a good imagination? A larva is a tiny creature just born or hatched. Scientists found an eel larva near the Cape of Good Hope. This newborn larva was over five feet long. How big would that eel have gotten as an adult? It could have reached ninety feet.

Maybe you aren't in a hurry to see a huge sea monster. Think about a small one. When a fur seal was caught off the shores of California, a small fish was found in its stomach. No man has ever seen this fish swimming in the water. Seals can find fish we know nothing about.

Many centuries ago Job described a terrible sea monster. Smoke flowed from this monster's nose. Fire shot out of its mouth. No sword could stop it, and a hook certainly could not catch it.

Did Job really see this amazing monster? There are creatures deep in the sea that no man has yet seen.

God has put an amazing world together. Maybe we will get to explore more of its wonders.

When he sneezes, the sunlight sparkles like lightning across the vapor droplets. His eyes glow like sparks. Fire leaps from his mouth. Smoke flows from his nostrils, like steam from a boiling pot that is fired by dry rushes. Yes, his breath would kindle coals—flames leap from his mouth.

JOB 41:18–21 (TLB)

Do You Remember?

1. What is megamouth?

2. Would you like to explore the deep ocean? Why?

3. Do you think Job really saw this monster?

The world you have made is filled with wonders, God.

217 Poisonous Plants

There are some plants in the sea that are bright and beautiful. Because of their rich colors, we might think it would be fun to pick them. But it wouldn't. Some of them carry deadly poisons and actually eat animals.

One of the most dangerous plants is the urchin, or pincushion. In the water the urchin looks harmless, but if you touch one of its many long needles, you could be in trouble. Deep-sea divers stay away from them because they understand the danger. An urchin needle could break off in a person's flesh and make him terribly sick.

Living in the same neighborhood as the urchin, you might find the colorful sea anemone (uh-NEM-uh-nee). These plants are gorgeous, but if you grab one, you will probably end up with a paralyzed hand.

Anemones don't always wait to be touched, though. If a fish swims nearby, the anemone can shoot out an arm and sting the creature. This way the fish is paralyzed and captured, and the plant can eat it for dinner.

Despite the strong poison of the anemone, there is one fish that isn't afraid of it: the attractive clown anemone fish. This swimmer may have developed a resistance to the anemone sting. While other fish are killed, this creature can be near the anemone without suffering the slightest injury.

Life has some real dangers for people too. We may not be stung by an anemone or stuck by a pincushion, but there are plenty of things that could hurt us.

God understands those things that make us afraid. He wants to be our companion and help us to feel peace. God wants to guide and protect us because we belong to Him. It's great to have someone watching over us.

But all who listen to me shall live in peace and safety, unafraid.

PROVERBS 1:33 (TLB)

Do You Remember?

1. How does an urchin attack?

2. What fish doesn't fear the anemone?

3. All of us have fears. What fear would you like God to help you with?

Thank you for peace, God.

218 Escape Hatch

Submarines have always been dangerous and many men have lost their lives in them. John Day, an early experimenter, tried to prove that he could stay in a submarine for twenty-four hours at a depth of thirty feet. However, in 1774, on his second try, Day drowned.

Modern submarines are not without their problems. In 1963 the nuclear-powered *Thresher* sank two hundred miles off the Boston coast. It plunged 8,400 feet, and all the crew were lost.

In 1968 the submarine *Scorpion* sank near the Azores in the Atlantic. None of its men could be rescued.

If a submarine drops too far into the sea, its metal cannot stand the pressure and will collapse. Engineers are working to build stronger submarines that are able to resist this pressure.

What happens if a submarine drops a few hundred feet and for some reason cannot come up again? How can the crew be rescued? Or can they?

One way to escape from a submarine is to use the escape hatch. Several sailors can stand in this little room and gradually let seawater in. Just before the men are covered with the water, they take a deep breath. As they rise to the surface they slowly let the air out. It is called "blow and go." The sailor will travel a hundred feet or more in a few seconds.

The navy also has special "lungs" or air bags that can be used. They allow the person to breathe as he goes up.

As more people go deeper into the ocean, better rescue devices are necessary. People must be able to escape from tremendous depths.

Scientists have now developed special rescue submarines. These submarines go down thousands of feet. When they find the vessel in trouble, the rescue ship locks itself onto the submarine. After it is locked, the crew can simply climb from one submarine into the other and escape.

Before escape hatches and rescue submarines were invented, life underwater was much more dangerous. I'm sure that each person who went underwater in a submarine was concerned about a way to escape in case of trouble.

God has given all of us the same hope for our lives. Sometimes life can be terribly hard. Often we are tempted to do wrong things. We know we shouldn't do these things, but we feel it's too hard to say no to them.

Don't give in, though. Don't do the sin that tempts you. God will give you a way to keep from doing it. He has promised an escape hatch.

He will show you how to escape temptation's power so that you can bear up patiently against it.

1 Corinthians 10:13 (TLB)

Do You Remember?

1. What happened to the USS *Thresher*?

2. How can one escape from a submarine?

3. What sins have tempted you? How did you escape?

Thank you for escape hatches, heavenly Father.

219 Slow Snails

The next time you go to a restaurant, ask for an order of escargot (ess-car-GO). If they have it, you will soon get a plate full of piping-hot snails. Millions of people enjoy them every year. Those who eat snail insist they have a delicious taste.

There is no shortage of snails. They are found in practically every part of the world, including in salt water and fresh water, and on dry land. Some are shaped in a left-handed position and others swirl to the right.

Snails aren't great parents, but their babies don't seem to mind. The mother will deposit her eggs into a two- to four-inch hole. She will cover the twenty eggs and rub until the spot is smooth. The mother then leaves and never returns.

A month later the eggs hatch. The new snails are entirely on their own and must find food for themselves.

Snails, on one hand, are a friend of man, yet on the other they are enemies. Snails give us food, clean up nature, and furnish medicine. However, snails also ruin crops, pollute water, and make animals and people sick.

The poky snail looks harmless, but clams don't think so. A snail will attach itself to the shell of a clam and slowly begin to drill through. When it reaches the soft clam, the snail slowly sucks it up.

Snails have reputations for being almost as slow as a rock. It is true that they don't seem to get too excited. We don't see snails rushing around.

Many snails refuse to travel if the weather is hot. Land snails often stay still if it's too wet. When they take a nap it may last awhile. They sleep for days, and many hibernate all winter. A few pull back into their shell and sleep for four years. They try hard to avoid too much excitement.

Most of the time we wouldn't want to be snails. However, once in a while it would come in handy. We would be better off if we were as slow as snails at becoming angry.

We all know some people who seem to get angry easily and often. The Bible tells us to keep from getting angry too quickly. It isn't good for anyone if we are a "hothead."

It is better to be slow-tempered than famous; it is better to have self-control than to control an army.

PROVERBS 16:32 (TLB)

Do You Remember?

1. What is escargot?

2. What kind of parents are snails?

3. Are you a hothead or slow to anger? Explain.

Help us control our temper, Holy Spirit.

220 Underwater Carpenters

Few animals have as much imagination as the North American beaver. Although they don't live in the sea, they do live in water. By building wooden dams they back up water, making beautiful ponds and reservoirs.

Beavers are hard workers. With their tough front teeth, sure hands, and webbed hind feet, they make most of what they need.

They begin as carpenters. Using their hatchetlike front teeth, beavers cut down trees as large as three-and-a-half feet around. They eat the bark but drag off the wood to build their excellent lodges.

A beaver lodge serves as a dam, which in many areas helps both animals and people. The pond created by the dam controls floods and holds water until it is needed.

Over the past two hundred years, people have killed off millions of beavers. Some scientists believe there are more floods today because we have fewer beavers to control the waterways.

The doors to a beaver lodge are found beneath the water. Beavers dive under the water and come up inside their snug living room. The lodge has several entrances and exits.

Beavers are not content just to build a home; they are also careful to keep it in good repair. Each fall they patch and remodel it. Sticks are added to any sagging areas and fresh mud is packed into any holes. Because of this careful work, beaver lodges last for many years through tough winters. Some beaver homes are a hundred feet long and have lasted for two hundred years.

As busy as beavers are, they manage to include their family in their work. A beaver selects one mate for life. Mother and Father beaver are careful to train their babies (called kits) for two or three years before letting them go on their own.

To protect his family from danger, the beaver has a special signal. If the father thumps his tail loudly against the ground, it means "dive immediately." The kit who learns his lessons well does not take time to look around or question. The thump sends him heading for the water, and he drops like a rock.

Beavers care about their kits, and the kits that obey their parents often live long enough to start their own beaver lodge.

In this way, beavers are much like people. The children who grow up obeying their parents find life the safest and even the happiest. Rebellious children usually have a harder time.

God knew this and gave us good instructions. Children who obey their parents begin their life in a strong, healthy way.

Children, obey your parents; this is the right thing to do because God has placed them in authority over you.

EPHESIANS 6:1 (TLB)

Do You Remember?

1. When do beavers usually repair their lodge?

2. What are beaver children called?

3. Name something you have learned from your parents.

Thank you, God, for giving us parents.

221 The Alligator Snapper

There is no need to go to the ocean to find a water-loving turtle. In the United States the alligator snapper lives in fresh water. This turtle likes a warm climate, so he normally waddles around in the southern states.

Snappers grow to a large size. The record is probably 236 pounds. On the average, though, they stay closer to thirty-five to fifty pounds. Their length is about sixteen inches.

The alligator has a reputation as a fisherman, but isn't fast or clever.

This snapper has a pinkish piece of skin inside its lower jaw, which wiggles enough to make a tempting sight to unsuspecting fish. As soon as the prey comes close to check it out, the turtle makes a fast snap and has a meal. Then it opens its mouth and waits for another curious visitor.

Alligator snappers aren't completely lazy, however. If the fish bait trick isn't working, snappers will search for food. A few snails or mussels will tide them over until the next fish.

Turtle is sometimes eaten by North Americans, and the snapper is the number-one choice. Five tons are caught annually in the Mississippi Valley. In some restaurants turtle meat is served as a delicacy; many southern folks, in particular, enjoy turtle meat.

It isn't unusual to see small snapping turtles trying to cross the highways of America. Many scientists are baffled by this dangerous trick. Turtles are basically water creatures. What odd urge takes them to highways? Their movement does not seem to be connected to age or even dry seasons. Yet many take up this dry land journey and are killed on the roads.

Whether it's the snapper killed on the highway or the fish that is lured by a funny pink bait into the turtle's mouth, both find out too late that they have made a mistake.

People often fall for Satan's tricks the same way. Satan is clever. Many times he gets us to follow him before we realize it. Satan may be better at trapping people than the snapper is at fishing.

There are two ways to learn Satan's tricks: We need to know the warnings in the Bible, and we need to listen to parents who care about us.

Put on all of God's armor so that you will be able to stand safe against all strategies and tricks of Satan.

Ephesians 6:11 (TLB)

Do You Remember?

1. Where do alligator snappers live?

2. How do they catch fish?

3. How are you tricked into doing evil?

Guard us from life's traps, Holy Spirit.

222 Drinking Water

Water can be dangerous. For centuries men have known this and have selected water that has been filtered through streams or taken from high lakes. Yet only during the past one hundred years have we realized how harmful water can be.

In 1892 Dr. Robert Kick proved the difference between filtered and non-filtered water. He knew that people in Hamburg, Germany, were contracting the dreaded cholera by drinking the city water. The drinking water was carrying terrible bacteria that could not be seen but were killing people.

Today water is carefully treated to protect us from disease. Years ago, and in some places now, water had to be boiled before anyone could drink or cook with it.

In many cities more is done to the water than merely destroying bacteria. Chemicals called coagulants (co-AG-you-lents) are added to take the color out of drinking water. It pulls the color together and makes it settle on the bottom.

The chemicals often leave the water hard and foul-tasting. To get rid of this side effect, something similar to lime soda is added. This softens the water. It is then run rapidly through sand filters to improve the taste and color.

Water isn't hard for most of us to get. If we turn on a faucet, water automatically comes out. We don't usually worry if it contains dangerous bacteria. However, many people in the world still have trouble getting good, safe water. Some people must travel for miles to get it, while others carry water in jars on their heads. These jars can weigh fifty pounds when full.

Jesus cares about our physical needs of food, clothing, and water, but He is even more concerned about giving us peace with God. The person who believes in Jesus Christ has something even more important than water—he has eternal life.

The woman who came to a well in Samaria had to carry the water some distance on her head. When Jesus met her, He talked to her about water because it was on her mind. Then he turned the conversation to something more important. He talked to her about living forever.

If you only knew what a wonderful gift God has for you, and who I am, you would ask me for some living water.

JOHN 4:10 (TLB)

Do You Remember?

1. How is drinking water treated?

2. Who discovered cholera bacteria in water?

3. What does "living water" mean?

Thank you, God, for life that does not end.

223 The Knights of the Sea

The earth's waters are filled with unique characters. Otters are clowns, dolphins are friends, and oysters are jewelers. However, there is no character quite like the hard-shell, armored knight—the lobster.

Most of us don't live near lobsters, so we know little of how they get around. I think it is fair to say there is no odder creature in the sea.

Lobsters seem to do everything either backwards or upside down. The lobster's brain is in its throat. It tastes with its feet and hears with its legs. After a lobster has swallowed, it chews its food with teeth inside its stomach.

If trouble comes close, our friend doesn't run away in normal style. Lobsters will rapidly back away. Even though it looks slow, it can cover ten feet of dry land in one second.

A lobster is like a rhinoceros in that it is nearsighted and hot-tempered. Since it isn't always sure what is going on, it attacks with terror if anything gets close.

When it is young, a lobster isn't afraid to pick a fight with another lobster and then eat it. As it grows older, it seems to give up cannibalism.

Not only is it tough in a fight, but a lobster is great at recovering. If it has a claw or a leg torn off, it can grow the part back. It may take a while, but it can be done even after the lobster has lost a large section of its body.

Often a lobster will have one slender claw and the other will be heavy. It uses the smaller one to lunge out and grab an enemy. Once it catches its victim, it lays the big one on him.

Usually the knight of the sea prefers to hide during the day. At night it climbs out from behind a rock and looks for supper.

A lobster needs all the armor it can get. From its first day, this creature leads a hard life. Only one in ten thousand lobsters will ever grow up. When an elderly twenty-five-pound lobster is caught, the fisherman can see the many marks and scars on its shell. These are evidence of the many battles it has survived.

Some days many of us wish we had a tough set of armor. When you play kickball or football, a good hard suit would come in handy.

But there is an invisible armor that will help us. The Bible tells us that this world can be mean and evil sometimes. All of us feel how cruel life is once in a while. We can protect ourselves by putting on a suit of armor called right living. By doing what is good and right, we keep from being captured by terrible sin.

So quit the evil deeds of darkness and put on the armor of right living, as we who live in the daylight should! Be decent and true in everything you do so that all can approve your behavior. Don't spend your time in wild parties and getting drunk or in adultery and lust or fighting or jealousy.

ROMANS 13:12–13 (TLB)

Do You Remember?

1. How does a lobster escape?

2. Where is a lobster's brain?

3. Why is it hard to do what is right?

Show us how to live right, Lord.

224 Flying Fish

Nature is amazing. A penguin is a bird, but it doesn't fly. An ostrich is a bird, but it's too large to leave the ground. But more strange than this, there are fish that act like birds.

Actually, there are a number of fish that fly. To be more accurate, they sail through the air. The manta ray weighs a ton and a half but glides above the water. Blue marlins and dolphins can leave the sea to do beautiful arches.

The most famous flying fish is a small creature that can be found around the West Indies. If you ever get there, ask the waiter for flying-fish pie. You may enjoy it.

Fish do not fly exactly as birds. Their motions are closer to the flying squirrel. They push themselves out of the water by rapidly wiggling their tails. This propeller gets them airborne and then their sailing fins take over.

Flying fish do not stay in the air for long, but they are fast and can cover a large distance. They have been timed at thirty-five miles an hour. If they stay in the air for thirteen seconds, they can travel six hundred feet, the length of two football fields. This means a flying fish can sail over twice as fast as most children could run that same distance.

347

Few of us have seen a flying fish. In fact, some people used to think they were just a myth. However, flying fish are caught and eaten in great numbers.

Dolphins believe in flying fish. When they land, the dolphin is often there, waiting to eat them.

We shouldn't be surprised. God's world is amazing. There are many fascinating things our Creator has made that we have never even seen. He is the Creator of variety, splendor, and imagination.

When He works in people's lives, God is the same Creator. He might want to do things in your life you have never imagined. His plan for your future may be more spectacular than all the creatures of the sea.

No mere man has ever seen, heard, or even imagined what wonderful things God has ready for those who love the Lord.

1 Corinthians 2:9 (TLB)

Do You Remember?

1. Name a fish that "flies."

2. How fast can a flying fish travel?

3. Name some ways God uses people.

Thank you for a fascinating tomorrow, Father.

225 Run Cars With Water?

Don't forget to water the car." Can you imagine your father saying this? Don't laugh. It isn't as strange as it sounds. Some dedicated scientists believe there's a possibility of running cars on water instead of gas. Since the world is 70 percent water, it would be a lot easier to get this fuel.

For hundreds of years, many people have believed this could be done. The famous science-fiction writer Jules Verne predicted that some of our heat and light would come from water.

It wouldn't be hard to do either. Water consists of two parts hydrogen and one part oxygen. Hydrogen can burn just like other gases. All we would have to do is separate the hydrogen from the water and then burn it. We could pour water into our car and, with the help of a simple machine, the hydrogen would be automatically separated and burned. This sounds easy, and in some ways it is.

Hydrogen power is not new. More than seventy years ago a blimp, the Hindenburg, was filled with hydrogen. It exploded over Lakehurst, New Jersey, in 1937. In our lifetime hydrogen has also been used to power rocket ships and build powerful bombs.

God made man with great intelligence. There are many things we have not yet solved, but there are so many problems we've already conquered.

The biggest problem with using hydrogen to run our car is the danger involved. Hydrogen can be highly explosive. It must be controlled.

Some of our fears of hydrogen are going away. The soap in your bathroom was probably made by using hydrogen. If you use margarine or shortening, it may have been produced with the help of hydrogen. One scientist believes we will soon run our kitchen stoves on water or hydrogen.

Within the next fifty years we might see airplanes, automobiles, trucks, and trains running with water as the fuel. As oil, coal, and natural gas become harder to get, we may need to find other forms of energy.

Life changes quickly. Just a hundred years ago, airplanes and cars were rarely used. No one had a radio then and certainly there were no television sets.

The next one hundred years may be even more exciting. Don't be surprised if someday you tell your son, "Be sure to put a gallon of water in the car."

God created a fantastic world that overflows with good things. He is happy to see us use these resources. Who knows what amazing things might come tomorrow.

The intelligent man is always open to new ideas. In fact, he looks for them.

Proverbs 18:15 (TLB)

Do You Remember?

1. How can a car run on water?

2. What is the main problem with hydrogen?

3. Name some good things God has created.

Thank you, God, for being so generous to us.

226 Pirate Bird

The seas used to be filled with dangerous pirates who attacked and robbed ships. In the early 1700s, many fortunes were taken by crooks armed with swords, pistols, and blaring cannons.

Nature is still filled with its share of pirates. Instead of finding food for themselves, some creatures would rather wait and steal it from someone else.

One famous pirate of the sea is the skua (SCUE-uh). This large sea gull is found around the cold shores of the Arctic. Its close relatives live in different parts of the world.

If the skua wants to, it can work. It fishes and has other ways of collecting food. The problem, though, is that the skua does not want to work. It would rather steal.

This pirate bird keeps its eyes on the smaller sea gulls as they hunt for fish in the sea. When the smaller sea gull dives for a fish and snatches it from the water, the skua moves in like Blackbeard the pirate. The skua chases after the smaller gull and frightens it. In a hurry to get away, the gull will drop its fish. Like a jet plane, the skua drops down and catches the prize in midair.

Many of us have someone in our neighborhood who reminds us of the skua. This person is mean and pushy. Sometimes he takes things from the younger or smaller kids. Instead of waiting his turn, he breaks into line and acts ugly. He acts like a playground pirate.

We may not be able to change people like this. However, we certainly don't have to become like them.

We can still be kind when others are nasty. We can tell the truth when other people lie. We can absolutely refuse to steal even if everyone else steals.

God wants us to do many great things, but He never wants us to become pirates.

If anyone is stealing he must stop it and begin using those hands of his for honest work so he can give to others in need.

EPHESIANS 4:28 (TLB)

Do You Remember?

1. Where does the pirate bird live?

2. How does it steal?

3. Have you ever tried to get even with a school pirate? Should you? Explain how you feel.

Teach us to give instead of taking, Holy Spirit.

227 Ghost Crabs

If you get near the Chesapeake Bay on the East Coast, you will want to spend some time crabbing. Crabs are fascinating creatures that walk sideways, have eyes on the ends of antennae, and have eight legs and one or two large claws. When you handle them, be careful. Crabs are quick and their pinch can be painful.

The Chesapeake Bay is excellent for crabs because it has a good mixture of fresh and salt water. If, because of storms, the water is churned up and the bay gets too much of either, fewer crabs are born.

Crabs are often caught because they become foolish. If you place a chicken neck or wing on a string and drop it into the water, a crab will start nibbling on it. When it begins to eat, you slowly pull the string toward the surface. Usually the crab will be so busy eating it will not notice it is being lifted up.

When the bait and crab are near the top, you slowly put a net under the crab. If you're careful, then you can have fresh crab for dinner.

When we were at the bay, my family caught blue crabs, but there are many different varieties. One of the strangest is the fiddler crab. It has one large claw, and some people think it looks like it is playing a violin.

When a fiddler crab is looking for a mate, it merely waves its huge claw in the air. When the female sees the claw, the male waves harder and faster. He looks like a child screaming on the playground.

While crabs make a good meal, the food they eat doesn't sound nearly as appetizing. They live mainly off dead plants and animals.

The best times to catch crabs in the Chesapeake are during spring and summer. When fall hits, they move out toward the deep center. They evidently want to get away from the cold surface. It is also easier to find oxygen in the deep water during winter.

Not all crabs live in the water. The strange ghost crab makes its home in a hole on the beach.

Ghost crabs are fitted well for living on a sandy, rocky beach. The color of the crab blends in perfectly with the beach. Some days you can see a small shadow hurrying swiftly past your feet. When you look for the crab that made the shadow, there is nothing around.

We often see God the same way we see ghost crabs. Without really seeing Him, we can see what He has done. We look at the sky, the trees, the animals, and the rivers, and we know He is there. It is like seeing His shadow without really seeing Him.

When we see the flag flying, we know the wind is around. When we see the moving shadow, we know there must be a ghost crab. When we see our fantastic world, we know our Creator and God must be there.

Since earliest times men have seen the earth and sky and all God made, and have known of his existence and great eternal power.

ROMANS 1:20 (TLB)

Do You Remember?

1. Where can you catch blue crabs?

2. Why is one kind of crab called a ghost crab?

3. What do you think are two of God's loveliest creations?

The world around us points to a living God. We thank you, Lord, for it.

228 The Underwater Saw

This creature looks more like a science-fiction fish than a real one. However, the sawfish is alive and roaming the wide-open seas.

A sawfish looks like most other large twelve- to eighteen-foot-long sea creatures. The big difference is a huge double-edged saw where other fish have a nose. The saw alone can be as long as a full-grown man.

Its nose doesn't just *look* like a saw, it really *is* one. Each small edge is as sharp as a razor. It cuts through most things in just a few seconds.

Practically every fish has teeth, fins, and a rudderlike tail. That's normal. However, the sawfish is the only one with a carpenter's tool instead of a nose.

The sawfish uses its strange feature in at least two ways. Sometimes it digs into the ground if it is looking for something special. More often the saw is used to prepare dinner. A sawfish will swim into a school of small fish and rapidly begin to saw away. In a minute it has sliced up a large meal and begins to eat.

Fishermen used to claim the sawfish would attack a wooden boat and try to cut a hole in the bottom. It may not be likely, but it is possible.

A few times sawfish have attacked people. When this happens, a person has little chance. Even a baby sawfish can do tremendous injury. Sawfish almost never attack people, so there is little to fear, but marked swimming areas are the safest areas to play in.

One group of people make special use of a sawfish saw. When some people from Thailand catch one, they sacrifice the saw as an offering in their temple.

A sawfish saw is an attempt to please God with a gift, but it isn't the one God most wants. The Bible says there is something God would rather have than a sacrifice. God would rather see us show mercy to each other.

Mercy means helping others. It means we don't hurt people. Mercy means we feed the needy or give shelter when it's necessary. Mercy means we become friends to the kid who is lonely and shy. Mercy means we don't say things to hurt someone's feelings.

Mercy is a word that covers many areas. Always it has to do with the way we treat people.

We can be glad God didn't ask us to go collect sawfish saws. However, He did ask us to care about others. Sometimes that's hard too.

It isn't your sacrifices and your gifts I want—I want you to be merciful.

MATTHEW 9:13 (TLB)

Do You Remember?

1. How long are sawfish saws?

2. How does the sawfish use its saw?

3. What does God ask of us more than gifts and sacrifices?

Teach us to help and not to hurt, dear God.

229 Life in a Seashell

Who wants to spend his life stuck between two shells with nothing to do but watch the ocean run by? That kind of existence seems mighty dull to us land people. However, in the opinion of a simple shell scallop, his life is fast, exciting, and dangerous.

A scallop's life is different from his relatives, the clam and the oyster. To begin with, a scallop can move quickly. This creature has its own jet-propulsion system. When in danger, the scallop swallows water rapidly and then pushes it out again. This motion moves him swiftly away from an enemy. Not only can he get around, but he can also control the direction he travels.

Not every day is an exciting adventure, though. The scallop likes to sit still and eat the tiny food particles or plankton that float by. His life goes on peaceably until the scallop smells a scoundrel. Starfish like to pry open scallop shells and eat them for supper. So when our shelled friend picks up the starfish scent, it scurries away to the bottom of the sea.

When you first see a scallop, you might think it would be difficult to catch because of its terrific collection of small blue eyes. Some scallops have as many as one hundred tiny eyes dotted along the opening in their shells. But despite the large number of eyes, they don't see very well. They merely recognize suspicious-looking shadows and smells that tell them danger is near.

Many of us have seen scallop shells without even knowing it. The shell on the Shell gas station sign is a scallop.

If you are looking for a good-paying job, maybe you could make eyeglasses for scallops. Each scallop will need at least fifty pair. Maybe a few will order a hundred contact lenses! It's hard to imagine someone having so many eyes and yet hardly being able to see.

Worse than this, though, is the fact that sometimes people have good strong eyes yet can't see very well. We often do not notice when someone else needs help. Sometimes we don't see how we hurt our parents, brother, sister, or friend. It is easy to look and yet not see at all.

There are people all around us who need someone to be kind, gentle, and caring. Jesus taught us to open our eyes and see how many ways we can help.

Say not ye, There are yet four months, and then cometh harvest? Behold, I say unto you, lift up your eyes, and look on the fields; for they are white already to harvest.

JOHN 4:35 (KJV)

Do You Remember?

1. How many eyes do some scallops have?

2. What do scallops eat?

3. What needs do you see around you?

Teach us to keep our eyes open, Lord Jesus.

230 What Killed the Dead Sea?

People who can't swim could still enjoy a good day on the lake if they could travel to Israel and wade in the Dead Sea. All they have to do is lie down flat on the water and they won't sink. The water is so dense with minerals that people will not go under.

The Dead Sea is one of the most amazing bodies of water in the world. Normally the ocean contains 3.5 percent minerals, but this lake contains over 25 percent. That is why it is often called the Salt Sea.

This lake is one of the few that has polluted itself. It receives its water from the Jordan River and a number of small streams. These steadily feed the body of water, but there is no outlet. Water can only come in. The only way it can escape is by evaporation.

Since water can't run uphill, there is no channel to release liquid. The lake is situated at 1,292 feet below sea level. This is the lowest level in the entire world.

Fortunately there isn't much rainfall in the area—only two to four inches a year. If there were a large amount, it would cause floods.

The Dead Sea is very large. It is fifty-three miles long and ranges from three to ten miles wide. At its deepest point it is thirteen hundred feet. Because it is located in a hot desert region, evaporation keeps sapping the lake. During the summer months the air temperature reaches 140 degrees. The winter does allow the thermometer to drop below eighty degrees.

As the water escapes into the air, it leaves the minerals behind. They continue to saturate the lake and settle on the bottom. A visitor can see salt lying in the water and pick it up by the handful.

Israel is "mining" the Dead Sea water for its minerals and chemicals. Jordan will soon also have a large mineral processing plant.

In spite of the rapid evaporation, until recently the Dead Sea was growing deeper. But now it is slowly drying up. The nations of Israel and Jordan, which share the Jordan River as a border, have taken much river water for irrigation. Very little water from the Jordan River now flows into the lake.

The people of Israel hope to build a pipeline that will carry water downhill from the Mediterranean Sea to the Dead Sea. The water in the pipeline will not only fill the Dead Sea again, but will also generate electricity for Israel.

The Dead Sea will not always be dead. The Bible tells us fish will someday dance in the water and fishermen will cast their nets. Its damaging salt will be removed and the water will become pure (see Ezekiel 47:7–10).

God is able to make the dead come to life. It's one of His wonderful powers. He even takes dead people and makes them live forever.

Those who believe in Jesus Christ and die are promised a new life. God has the final power over death.

Jesus told her, "I am the one who raises the dead and gives them life again. Anyone who believes in me, even though he dies like everyone else, shall live again."

JOHN 11:25 (TLB)

Do You Remember?

1. Why is the Dead Sea dead?

2. Describe a swim in the Dead Sea.

3. Will you live after death? Why?

Lord Jesus, you have overcome death.

231 The Hammerhead Shark

Sharks aren't as dangerous as most people think. Every year more deaths are caused by beestings or lightning than by these toothy creatures. While we certainly should respect sharks, generally they will swim away from us.

One of the sharks we need to respect is the odd-looking hammerhead. Most sharks have a fairly pointed face, but not this creature. His nose is flat and stretches as much as three feet across. The hammerhead's eyes are at each end of this structure. A close relative of his is called the shovelhead.

Hammerheads love to eat stingrays. Other sharks enjoy stingrays too, but a stingray can generally fight the others. Normally a stingray will try to sting a shark in the eyes, but with the hammerhead it's a different story. Its eyes are set so far from its mouth that the stingray can't defend itself. One hammerhead was found with fifty stings in its back. It had paid a heavy price for its favorite meal.

Sharks' ability to smell is outstanding. If blood is spilled in the water, the scent can be picked up from miles away by a shark. Though unable to see the goal, it can follow the smell to the exact location.

Scientists are now discovering that sharks are almost as good at hearing. A recording of fish struggling was played in the water, and in a few minutes two sharks showed up. They did this without the help of a scent.

The person who is really asking for trouble is the one who spearfishes in the evening in waters that sharks are known to visit. Sharks aim for shallow shores in the evening.

We have little to fear from sharks, though. Most of the time they are happy to stay in their own area, and likewise they want us to stay in ours.

The smart swimmer finds out where the dangerous spots are, and he stays away from them.

Basically, those are the rules of life. We learn early what is dangerous and we try to avoid it. Those who live recklessly often get hurt.

That's part of the reason why God gave us the Bible. He wanted to keep us from getting hurt. God gave us some guidelines. He said not to do this and watch out for that. When we don't listen, we get into trouble.

Pick up the Bible as a book of help. If we listen to its warnings, life goes much better.

I am not writing about these things to make you ashamed, but to warn and counsel you as beloved children.

1 Corinthians 4:14 (tlb)

Do You Remember?

1. What is a hammerhead's favorite meal?

2. Why is spearfishing dangerous in certain places?

3. Tell about a warning from the Bible.

Thank you, God, for the helpful "stop" signs.

232 Seals Go to the Mountains

One of the South Pole's more interesting creatures is the Weddell seal. They are not always the cute little circus performers we are used to seeing; some of these deep-sea divers weigh nine hundred pounds.

Their underwater abilities are the envy of man. The Weddell seal can stop breathing for thirty minutes while searching for food. It dives fifteen hundred feet and can chase down a squid or small fish if it chooses. One Weddell seal was timed during its dive, and it was below the surface for forty-three minutes.

Seals are capable of changing their heartbeats during a dive. Normally their rate is 150 beats per minute, but during a dive they reduce it to a mere 10 per minute. They live off the oxygen already in their bodies. Some species of seal can even sleep underwater.

The Weddell seal weighs a plump sixty pounds at birth, and after only two weeks of nursing on his mother's butterfat milk, junior quickly doubles his weight. However, by the time she has finished feeding her pups, the mother seal loses a total of three hundred pounds and is thoroughly worn out.

A mother Weddell seal becomes completely disoriented at the sight of danger. If an intruder threatens her, she reacts by killing her young pups. However, the mother does care and will remain with her pup for days after it has died.

These seals love ice so intensely that they choose to live under it during the winter. They make holes for air with their teeth. In later life they often have badly worn teeth.

All of these seals lead active lives. But in case it's necessary, they also have a retirement plan that isn't too bad. When Weddell seals become elderly, injured, or sick, they climb to high country. They have been found thirty-five miles from shore and three thousand feet above sea level. This keeps them out of the competitive world but still gives them plenty of cold snow and ice.

When we travel to the farthest tips of the world, the evidence of God's work is startling—the beautiful sunsets, the pure air, and the fascinating life of little-known creatures. Far from being barren ice land, it is rich with the glory of God.

He quiets the raging oceans and all the world's clamor. In the farthest corners of the earth the glorious acts of God shall startle everyone. The dawn and sunset shout for joy!

PSALM 65:7–8 (TLB)

Do You Remember?

1. How long can a Weddell seal stay underwater?

2. Where do they go to "retire" or "heal"?

3. Name some beautiful places you have seen that God has made.

Thank you, God, for a beautiful world.

233 City Under the Sea

What will the ocean be like a hundred years from now? Will there be domed cities like giant shopping malls? Maybe there will be regular bus service running from land to two thousand feet beneath the sea.

Would you be surprised to learn that some scientists already live under the sea? Men have spent weeks in aqua labs. All of their activities and studies take place inside a submerged apartment.

Not only will people work under the sea but so will mobots. Mobots are underwater robots. They can be controlled to help man in his work.

When the time comes to visit the sea, don't be afraid to go. Underwater travel may be safer than on the surface. For one thing, storms will probably have no effect on the sea buses.

Tomorrow's city will be built on the dreams of the famous oceanographer Jacques-Yves Cousteau. He has already built a village on the bottom of the Red Sea, and people have lived in it. As Cousteau has said, "One day soon, men will walk on the ocean floor as they do down the street."

The hope is that people will not be restricted to buildings, submarines, and buses. Some scientists believe people will wear simple headgear with mechanical gills and take pills to prevent them from getting sick from the depths.

Part of the reason why cities do not already exist underwater is that we do not put the same importance on the sea as we have on space. However, it now looks like we could someday live in the sea.

No dream is impossible, especially if God wants it to happen. He has given us amazing abilities, fascinating materials, and tremendous minds. If we dedicate all of these to Him, He may be waiting to use us in ways we never imagined.

Many of the world's great scientists have been Christians. Possibly God plans to use your mind for some of the great wonders under the sea.

I know the greatness of the Lord—that he is greater far than any other god. He does whatever pleases him throughout all of heaven and earth and in the deepest seas.

Psalm 135:6 (TLB)

Do You Remember?

1. What is a mobot?

2. Make up a name for a city under the sea.

3. What amazing thing would you like to see God do?

Thank you for a fascinating world, heavenly Father.

234 Swimming Snakes

Have you ever seen a snake do a headstand? Can you imagine one with its tail sticking straight up? Some underwater snakes do exactly this. They are hunting fish eggs for dinner. The snake buries its head in the sand and leaves its tail high in the water.

Not only does this snake gobble down fish eggs, but it also swallows small stones. The stones don't hurt him.

You don't need to worry about the snake's safety. It's true that it can't see or defend itself in this strange position, but the fish merely pass by. This type of snake is so poisonous everything stays away from it.

Despite its dangerous bite, the sea snake does have a few enemies. The sea eagle not only isn't afraid of this snake, but it also hunts him for supper. This eagle must really have a strong stomach in order to eat so much poison.

The sea snake's other enemy is man. Man often invades the watery world of this creature and hunts it. Sometimes man loses this battle and becomes the victim. Most of the time, though, people are successful. Asians often capture sea snakes for food. Some people love good roasted snake. They also earn money by selling the colorful skin.

Most sea snakes spend their entire lives in the water, but there are a few exceptions. A snake near Japan comes ashore to reproduce. While there, it will roam around the villages and steal fish left out to dry. These snakes must be a scary sight since they sometimes are four and a half feet in length.

Sea snakes are usually small, but a few are enormous. One variety spans twenty-five feet. Not only are they long, but they are also fast. Some can swim backward almost as fast as they swim forward. Their rapid tail gives them excellent speed.

Generally water is safe for swimming. Very few people are ever bitten by sea snakes. In most cases the snake is interested in getting away from people. Most areas do not have poisonous sea snakes.

If you see a snake, the safest thing is to stay away from it until you know what kind it is. Your parents might be able to help you identify it.

Most snake bites do not kill but only make a person sick. The Bible tells us that getting drunk and being bitten by a snake are very much alike. Both can make you dizzy and change your behavior. You may not be able to think straight and you might say stupid things. You also could become terribly sick to your stomach.

We do not want to be bitten by snakes. Neither does it make any sense to get drunk.

Don't let the sparkle and smooth taste of strong wine deceive you. For in the end it bites like a poisonous serpent; it stings like an adder. You will see hallucinations and have delirium tremens, and you will say foolish, silly things that would embarrass you no end when sober.

PROVERBS 23:31–33 (TLB)

Do You Remember?

1. How do snakes hunt fish eggs?

2. What hunts sea snakes?

3. What does your family think about alcoholic beverages?

Keep our minds clear, Holy Spirit.

235 The Leatherback

363

During the days of ancient Rome, the person who caught a sea turtle was well off. He could use practically every part of the reptile.

For example, turtle blood made an excellent whitener for teeth or cure for a toothache. Even earaches could be cleared up with a dose of it.

The largest sea turtle is the leatherback. It isn't unusual for them to be eight feet long and weigh fifteen hundred pounds. If they could be trained, they are large enough to pull an eighteen-foot sailboat.

Despite its huge size, the leatherback has a special diet. It feeds mostly on jellyfish and the Portuguese man-of-war. These morsels are 95 percent water. The leatherback has to eat carloads of them to keep his large factory operating.

There is no other reptile that roams such a large part of the world. They roam the coasts of Norway north of the Arctic Circle as well as the southern shores of New Zealand. The leatherback may visit the shores of Japan or make a casual call on Chile.

Normally they live to be older than humans and reproduce freely. Possibly four times each year the female comes ashore to lay eggs. She deposits 90 to 150 eggs per trip.

It's doubtful these large reptiles merely wander the seas aimlessly. They probably follow patterns and are able to find mates. So far their system has escaped the understanding of man. To learn their swimming patterns might prove to be of considerable value to humanity.

So far the only person who fully understands the navigation of the sea turtle is Jesus Christ. He created and controls them. Even in the dark, mysterious sea He knows where they are.

We never escape the watchful eye of Christ either. We are not a mystery to Him. He knows when we fail and when we win. Jesus knows more about us than we know about ourselves. That's great! This makes it easier for Him to help us.

Christ himself is the Creator who made everything in heaven and earth, the things we can see and the things we can't; the spirit world with its kings and kingdoms, its rulers and authorities; all were made by Christ for his own use and glory. He was before all else began and it is his power that holds everything together.

COLOSSIANS 1:16–17 (TLB)

Do You Remember?

1. What do leatherbacks eat?

2. How many eggs does the female lay?

3. Where can you go to hide from Jesus Christ?

We thank you, our Creator, for holding us together.

236 They Will Fool You

There is little to worry about when you go swimming. Most shores are safe. You will swim the rest of your life and probably never see anything more dangerous than a jellyfish. However, if you travel around the world, always find out about the water before you jump in.

If you swim in the Indian Ocean, you need to know about the zebra fish. Its large black and white stripes will make you want to go toward it. But they have eighteen spines sticking out all over their body, and these spines are deadly poisonous. Just a touch and you could be terribly ill or even paralyzed. Most people would recover, but not everyone.

The lionfish must be one of the loveliest sea creatures in the world. It has bright reddish colors and looks too fluffy to hurt anyone, but despite its beauty, a mere touch and a swimmer would be finished.

Not every deadly fish is colorful and cute. The stonefish is as ugly as mud. Its name describes it well. This little killer looks just like any rock you would find on the bottom of a lake. Unsuspecting walkers are likely to step on this creature in the Pacific Ocean.

Toadfish are gruesome looking. If you see one you will automatically keep your distance.

These are rare fish and not likely to be found anywhere near where you swim. However, it's always important to find out about what lives in the water where you intend to play or fish.

Fish will fool us, but so will people if we aren't careful. There are many religious groups that look like fun to join. They sound good, but that doesn't make them godly. Often these groups are cults; they look harmless but they aren't.

We need to be careful of groups that do not put Jesus Christ first. We need to stay clear of people who insist we give complete obedience to them.

People are fooled because the group looks good. Later they may be terribly sorry they didn't follow Christ instead.

Jesus told them, "Don't let anyone fool you. For many will come claiming to be the Messiah, and will lead many astray."

MATTHEW 24:4–5 (TLB)

Do You Remember?

1. Where is a zebra fish's poison?

2. What should a person do before swimming in a new place?

3. What is one way to know if a group is really Christian?

Help us, Lord, to keep our faith in you alone.

237 Sunken Ships

The seas are filled with tremendous wealth. Much of their treasure comes from natural riches such as fish, kelp, and oil. However, there are also rare treasures from ancient sunken ships: Amazing amounts of gold, silver, mercury, and jewels have been discovered.

One of the most famous finds was from the ancient Spanish ship *San Jose*. The vessel sank near Florida in 1733. Over half a million dollars in gold and silver has been recovered.

The hunt for sunken treasure sounds exciting, but usually it begins in a dusty library. Explorers must first study the records of ships, their destiny, and their cargo. The adventurer needs to know for sure that there are riches worth the risk.

Sometimes the sunken treasure provides great riches; however, more often than not the searchers are fortunate if they don't lose money.

But not everyone who looks for treasure ends up penniless. One man has raised millions of dollars to the surface, including several coins worth $12,000 apiece. A necklace found off a Florida shore sold for $50,000.

Few attempts at recovering old ships are as remarkable as the raising of the *Vasa*. This vessel sank over three hundred years ago and had been forgotten until someone ran across the name. The Swedish government was told about it, and they raised the entire ship. Today it rests in a museum with most of its original possessions still on it.

A couple of teenage boys unexpectedly found some rare treasure while in the Pacific Ocean. The swimmers discovered a large supply of coins and a small bronze cannon. Their finds dated back to 1702.

Recently a sunken ship was found with an unusual treasure on it. The *Tolosa* sank off the shore of the Dominican Republic in 1724. Among the many treasures found was over three million dollars' worth of quicksilver, or mercury.

It must be tremendously exciting to find sunken treasure. Most of us are not going to find gold off the Florida Keys. However, we could find a treasure worth far more. Many things in life are worth more than gold. Mothers, fathers, and friends are each a great treasure.

The Bible speaks of real wealth. It says if we have to choose between riches and a good name, always select a good name.

It's more important that people know you are honest and dependable. If people can trust you, you are already rich.

If you must choose, take a good name rather than great riches;
for to be held in loving esteem is better than silver and gold.

PROVERBS 22:1 (TLB)

Do You Remember?

1. Who raised the *Vasa*?

2. What was on the *Tolosa*?

3. How can you have a good name?

Help us to see what is really valuable, Lord.

238 Private Detectives

Have you ever seen a small head covered in bushy whiskers bob out of the water? If you have, you know how much fun it is to watch sea lions. We spotted them all over the Puget Sound in Washington State. Sea lions are so quick and clever that they hunt salmon with little difficulty.

As man has gotten to know the sea lion, we have learned to enjoy its many abilities. They dive like submarines and are lightning fast. Sea lions can be taught a number of jobs besides playing horns in the circus.

The navy has so much faith in the sea lion's intelligence that they are using them as underwater detectives.

Many missiles are fired over the ocean and then fall into the deep waters. The navy can practice with these weapons again if they can get them back. This is where the crafty sea lion detective comes in.

A large clamp is placed on the sea lion's nose and it dives for the ocean floor. In a few minutes the sea lion hunts down the lost object and bumps his nose against it. The clamp locks onto the weapon. Navy sailors have already tied a heavy cord to the clamp and now have little trouble recovering their treasure.

When the sea lion returns to the ship, it is hugged and fed plenty of good fish. The private detective has brought back its treasure. Sea lions' skills have saved the navy millions of dollars.

Sea lions aren't the greatest brains in nature but neither are they dumb. What really makes them important is that they are teachable. When they are told what to do, they can respond and usually do it correctly.

You and I have far more ability to learn than a sea lion. We may not be able to swim as well, but we certainly think better.

Because humans are so intelligent, God decided to teach us through a book. The Bible is packed with good, wise guidance for our lives. It may not make us swim any better, but it certainly will save us from a great many troubles. The really smart young person lets the Bible speak to him.

Follow my advice, my son; always keep it in mind and stick to it.

PROVERBS 7:1 (TLB)

Do You Remember?

1. How does the Navy use sea lions?

2. How does the clamp work?

3. Name something the Bible has taught you.

Keep our minds open and teachable, Holy Spirit.

239 How Many Arms?

Do you want to think about something spooky? There are millions and millions of arms moving around the ocean. Some of the arms are small, like the ones on starfish. Others are gigantic, like the ones that cover huge squid and octopuses.

How long are squid arms? No one knows for sure. Many squids live deep in the sea and have never been seen by man. The longest squid on record measures sixty feet in length.

369

It isn't just the length of the arms that's amazing; it's also the number. Most octopuses have eight creepy arms. His relative, the squid, has ten. Each arm is covered with suction cups. Every cup grabs with enough force to leave a terrible red mark on your body.

How many of these multiple-armed creatures are swimming around in the ocean? No one can say. We do know that sometimes sailors have been fooled in measuring the ocean. They thought they had found the bottom only to learn that it was a "false bottom" made up of thousands of squid.

Since the giant squid live deep in the ocean, there is little for us to fear. However, once in a great while one of these monsters has come to the top.

On a few occasions an octopus or a squid has wrapped its arms, called tentacles, around a small boat. Usually quick-thinking sailors grab hatchets and begin to cut off the arms. My fisherman friend did this after bringing up a large octopus on his line.

These attacks are rare, and when it happens, it's usually squid; octopuses are generally shy and often will try to get away.

Normally there isn't anything to worry about. People can swim safely in the ocean. The millions or billions of arms won't bother you.

Arms do not have to be bad. Do you remember resting on your parents' arms and thinking about how good it felt? You could depend on them and their love.

When God speaks of His arm, He is talking about the same feeling. In times of stress and in times of happiness, we can relax in the arms of God. Even though we cannot see Him, God wants us to lean on Him.

My righteousness is near; my salvation is gone forth, and mine arms shall judge the people; the isles shall wait upon me, and on mine arm shall they trust.

Isaiah 51:5 (kjv)

Do You Remember?

1. Which creature has ten arms?

2. What is the "false bottom" in the ocean?

3. When does it feel good to lean on God's arms?

Thank you for an arm that reaches out to us, heavenly Father.

240 The Secret of the Submarine

How do submarines work? When they dive under the water, what stops them from sinking to the bottom? How can they come up whenever they want to?

Many people in history have tried to develop a submarine, but not until 1776 did David Bushnell put one to use. His vessel looked like a large ball. It was made of wood and could stay twelve feet under the surface. Called the *Turtle,* this vessel was moved by a hand-cranked propeller.

The *Turtle* attacked a British ship by trying to attach an explosive to the ship's bottom. Bushnell was surprised to find the bottom of the ship covered with copper. The *Turtle* was spotted by the crew and barely escaped.

There was no hope of putting submarines in the sea as long as they had to be moved by a hand-driven propeller. Fuel was also a big problem for submarines. How could they carry enough diesel or gas to travel long distances? Fortunately, this problem has been solved for modern submarines: nuclear subs can circle the earth twice on a lump of uranium about the size of a baseball.

How did inventors solve the submarine's big problem of going up and down? Submarines have a number of ballast tanks built into the bottom or hull. When these tanks hold air, the submarine stays on top. If it wants to dive, water is taken into the ballast tanks. This adds weight and causes the sub to go down. When the sub is to surface, the water is merely pumped out of the tanks.

People have learned to control the tanks. Whether they want to dive twenty feet or forty, they take on just the right amount of water. The crew must carefully check the water/air balance to keep the submarine under control. Otherwise it will sink like a rock or bounce up onto the surface.

Life has its ups and downs like a submarine. When something goes wrong, we often "sink" and feel terrible. Maybe we weren't chosen for something or maybe we failed a test. It's no fun to feel down.

You have let me sink down deep in desperate problems. But you will bring me back to life again, up from the depths of the earth.

PSALM 71:20 (TLB)

Do You Remember?

1. Describe Bushnell's submarine.

2. How does a ballast tank work?

3. What gets you "down"? What brings you "up"?

Thanks, Lord, for giving our lives ballast tanks.

240 Save the Sea Cows!

The manatee is a bulky, friendly creature that likes to munch on soft vegetation. On a good day a manatee can eat one hundred pounds of seaweed. Today there are laws to protect this sea cow, but that wasn't always true. Not long ago manatees were hunted almost out of existence.

Manatees are mammals. They are warm-blooded, have backbones, and give milk to their young. However, despite their size of over twelve feet, they are practically helpless on land. The manatee lives well underwater but has to come up every ten or fifteen minutes to breathe.

In some ways the sea cows seem almost human. They lead very calm lives and especially enjoy getting together. Once in a while you can see them kiss or hold flippers as they swim. Both the mother and father manatee make good parents. The ones that live in captivity are easy to care for and appear happy.

When ancient sailors first saw the manatee, they thought the cows were half-human mermaids. The seamen must have been away from land a long time for their eyes to fool them that much.

The manatee used to have a relative that lived in the cold Bering Sea. They were called Steller's sea cows. This huge cousin weighed over three tons and was thirty feet in length. Whalers hunted the sea cow without caring how many they took.

Today there are no Steller's sea cows left. They have not been seen for 150 years. If laws had not been passed to protect the manatee, they could also have become extinct.

Animals are not as valuable as people, but they certainly are important. Nature would lose its balance if we killed off too many. Animals of both the land and sea help make our life more interesting.

God wants us to use His world and to preserve it. If we over-hunt without caring what happens, we could cause many creatures to become extinct.

Your justice is as solid as God's mountains. Your decisions are as full of wisdom as the oceans are with water. You are concerned for men and animals alike.

PSALM 36:6 (TLB)

Do You Remember?

1. What did the ancient sailors think a manatee was?

2. What happened to the Steller's sea cows?

3. How can we help protect animals from being over-hunted?

If we are to keep animals, we must be wise. Lord, give us wisdom.

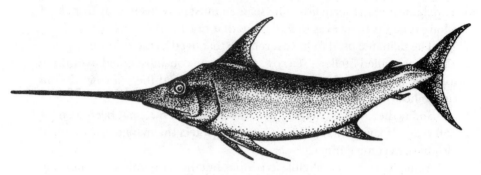

242 Swordfish Attack

Think twice before you go fishing for the powerful swordfish. They are hard to catch and, once hooked, may decide to attack the fisherman. However, if you do manage to bring one in, it will make excellent eating.

Swordfish like to roam around at great depths, and this makes them difficult to find. Some of their favorite foods are jellyfish and squid.

The sword attached to the nose of this fish is not a toy. It is strong enough to pierce hard surfaces—and often has. Most of the time the swordfish uses its spear to slash through schools of fish.

When a swordfish is caught, it might charge the boat. It must be a frightening sight—a four-hundred-, six-hundred-, maybe even one-thousand-pound fish racing through the water and heading directly for the vessel. With its back fin slicing through the surface, the swordfish can drive a dreadful hole in the boat's side.

Not only might the fish attack, but its friends could join in. Sometimes six swordfish have charged a boat at one time.

You'll probably want to cut your line after a swordfish attacks. They have hit boats a dozen times before the fishermen have cut them loose, but it is usually the men who give up, not the fish.

Despite their ability to puncture a vessel, they are still hunted. Hundreds of swordfish are caught off the Florida coast alone.

One of the strangest attacks happened when no one was fishing. The small submarine *Alvin* was near the Carolina coast when, without warning, a swordfish charged. Evidently frightened by the sub's lights, the fish used its sword to pierce the *Alvin*'s seam. The submarine surfaced immediately, glad that the damage was no more serious than a puncture hole.

Fortunately not many people carry swords. However, sometimes people are just as dangerous as any swordfish. Some will enjoy spreading lies about others. The Bible tells us it's just like piercing them with a sword. Sometimes it does as much damage.

We should be careful how we talk about others. It's easy to hurt people with words, and not nearly as easy to heal the injury.

If someone lied about us, we would feel unhappy. God wants us to be sure not to stab others with a sharp sword called lies.

Telling lies about someone is as harmful as hitting him with an axe, or wounding him with a sword, or shooting him with a sharp arrow.

PROVERBS 25:18 (TLB)

Do You Remember?

1. What do swordfish eat?

2. What happened to the *Alvin*?

3. Has someone ever lied about you? Without mentioning their name, tell how you felt.

Help us guard what we say, Holy Spirit.

243 Seashells Are Noisy

Have you ever picked up a seashell and held it to your ear? Do you wonder what causes that sound? Is it the echo of the sea?

Naturally there are some shells you can't pick up. The giant clam can grow to four feet in length and weigh a robust five hundred pounds.

If you live near Australia, there are some shells you won't dare lift. The Toxoglossa is blamed for killing twenty people with its poisonous bite, and it has made many others sick.

In old Africa you would not have thrown away many shells. Some countries use them as a form of money. A shipment of shells can purchase food or a good elephant tusk.

You shouldn't count on seeing every type of seashell in the world. To do that you would have to climb fifteen thousand feet up into the mountains and dive twenty-five thousand feet into the sea. Even then, there are so many thousands of varieties you couldn't hope to see them all.

When you pick up one colorful shell and hold it to your ear, you can hear an amazing sound, like ocean waves. What causes it?

A well-formed seashell is so finely made it can pick up any movement in the air. The little sounds bounce around inside like the echo of the seashores. Sometimes you will be able to hear sounds in the shell that are not loud enough otherwise for your ears.

Nature is filled with fascinating noises. Noise isn't always bad; in its right place noise can be a gift. Used correctly, noise can be used to worship God.

Have you ever been so happy you felt you just had to make noise? Have you ever been so filled with joy that you wanted to shout "Thank God!" Maybe someday you should go ahead and do it. In your living room, in the basement, or in your backyard, look up and shout, "Thank God!" It's one of the best ways we can use noise.

Shout with joy before the Lord, O earth! Obey him gladly; come before him, singing with joy.

PSALM 100:1–2 (TLB)

Do You Remember?

1. How big do clams get?

2. Where are shells found?

3. When was the last time you felt like shouting to God?

There are joyful noises. We use them to praise you, God.

244 The Beaches Come Alive

Every spring an amazing thing happens along the beaches of Southern California. Thousands of small fish called grunions come in with the tide to lay their eggs.

The mother grunion wiggles her tail into the soft sand and sticks her head almost straight up. She deposits thousands of eggs just a couple of inches deep in the sand.

When the female catches the tide out, the eggs are left on their own. The eggs lie quietly in the moist, warm sand and wait for the right moment to hatch.

Two weeks later their time comes. A tide washes ashore and uncovers the eggs. When the eggs pop to the top they begin to hatch. Thousands of newborn grunions begin twisting and turning on the sand. When the tide begins to go out to sea, the baby grunions take a free ride to the open ocean.

Grunions have become a big attraction in California. Many spectators come to watch the unusual event. Some bring buckets and catch what they can with their bare hands.

The grunion is of the silverside family and is supposed to make excellent eating.

We don't know if we will see them, but someday God will raise dead bodies from their graves, similar to the grunions coming out of the sand. The bodies will be taken to heaven and reunited with the real person. When that happens, God will have begun the great resurrection of believers in Jesus Christ.

For the Lord himself will come down from heaven with a mighty shout and with the soul-stirring cry of the archangel and the great trumpet-call of God. And the believers who are dead will be the first to rise to meet the Lord.

1 THESSALONIANS 4:16 (TLB)

1. How deep are grunion eggs placed in the sand?

2. How do baby grunions get to the sea?

3. What noises will be sounded when Jesus returns?

Even though we die, Lord, we look forward to eternal life with you.

245 Are Eels Really Electric?

When I was a child I was afraid to touch an eel. One day I caught one on a line, but no one would grab it. We were all afraid we would be shocked or even electrocuted. We weren't sure if all eels carried electricity, but none of us wanted to find out the hard way.

Now we know, however. There is both good news and bad news. The bad news is that there really are electric eels that can shock us. The good news is that most of these powerful eels live in South America around the Amazon River. There, the electric eel can grow to seven feet long. Their gills are so small they have to come to the surface every fifteen minutes to breathe.

There are many fish that carry an electric shock. However, most of the 250 species give off no more than 50 volts and aren't dangerous to people. The electric eel carries 600 volts, but fortunately it does not shock with its full strength.

Electric eels have other strange features also. For one thing they have detachable tails. If something grabs on to the eel's tail, it merely drops its tail and takes off, leaving the attacker bewildered.

Another odd thing about the eel is the location of most of its organs. Its important body parts are up around its head and neck. This is why eels are often round at the head and slender in the body.

The electric eel doesn't have many enemies. Eels shock fish easily and turn them into a meal, so most fish try to stay away from them.

378

An eel's electricity is just like the kind you have at home. If you could connect an eel to your home, it would turn your lights on. However, after giving its first big shock, it needs to rest its batteries before it can make more electricity.

Wouldn't it be neat if we could slip an electric eel into our flashlight? Then we wouldn't need any batteries. Or how about strapping a big eel inside our car to make it run?

Here is a better idea. Whenever we are facing difficult circumstances or need power to do the right thing, why don't we ask God to help us use His power inside us? God is very strong and wise. And He especially likes to help us.

God is our refuge and strength, a tested help in times of trouble.

PSALM 46:1 (TLB)

Do You Remember?

1. Where do the most powerful electric eels live?

2. What is strange about an electric eel's tail?

3. When would you like to have God help you?

Thanks for your great power, dear God.

246 Strange Stories

Do you ever wonder how some stories got started? The ancient Greeks called the electric ray a narke. Our word *narcotics* comes from this word. The Greeks called it a narke because they believed this ray could cast a spell on people. They thought fishermen should be especially careful of its magic power.

The Greeks also believed a person could remove hair by collecting electric ray brains. And if a woman merely had this fish nearby, it was supposed to make childbirth easier.

Some island people have believed that sharks are actually gods and have worshiped them. Temples and altars have been built to keep these sharks happy.

In Samoa many people believed sharks punished thieves. If someone stole something, they believed that the next time he went to sea he would be eaten.

The John Dory is a fish that has an odd story. Some of these fish live in the Mediterranean Sea. They are unique because they have a large black spot on each side. According to legends, this was a mark left by the apostle Peter when he picked up the fish and found money in its mouth.

One group of Indians believed that the earth began on the back of a turtle. They taught that a gigantic turtle came up out of the sea, and plants began to form and grow on its shell. For years they told their children that the world was riding on a turtle.

Ancient mythology teaches that Venus came from the sea. When she was born she was already an adult and immediately set sail for dry ground on a scallop shell.

It's fun to listen to stories, whether they are true or made up. Both children and adults enjoy listening, learning, and reading. We should know when a story is true and when it is only made up.

One of the best parts of life is hearing the true story about God and His love for us. It's fascinating to hear about His son, Jesus Christ, and all that He has done. It's even more interesting to know that the life, death, and resurrection of Jesus Christ are totally true.

And this is the way to have eternal life—by knowing you, the only true God, and Jesus Christ, the one you sent to earth!

JOHN 17:3 (TLB)

Do You Remember?

1. How did the Greeks try to remove hair?

2. One group of Indians believe that the earth began where?

3. How much of the story of Jesus Christ is true?

We thank you, Lord, that the true story about Jesus has been given in the Bible.

247 The Singing Penguins

Do you have trouble telling one penguin from another? Evidently the emperor penguins have the same problem. So in order to solve this problem, they sing. Singing helps them to find and recognize each other.

But these penguins have even worse problems: They can't tell the girl penguins from the boy penguins. When they meet, they politely bow to each other and then start to sing. The female has a gentle tone while the male sings loud and long.

Emperor penguins live in the coldest place in the world. The temperature in the Antarctic often drops to 80 degrees below zero. Yet the cold doesn't seem to bother them at all. The emperor picks the dead of winter to lay eggs and hatch chicks.

When hundreds of emperor penguins come together into a huge choir, what a noise they make! All of them are singing and looking for a mate. The entire group together is called a turtle.

The mother lays her eggs in May, which is the cold fall in Antarctica. Instead of a warm, soft nest, the egg is placed on the cold, open ice.

When the father sees the egg he breaks into a solo. Mother pushes the egg over to the father. He sits on it and sings some more choruses.

How does all this happy singing affect the babies? It doesn't take long to find out. If you place your ear close to the egg shell, you can hear the unborn chick singing. It won't be long before it joins the enormous choir.

Emperor penguins aren't the greatest parents in nature. Many chicks become lost and die. The only way a chick can find its parents is to sing a few bars. It hopes to soon hear a familiar song and know its parents are near.

We aren't emperor penguins, but many of us enjoy singing. Songs are important in nature, but they are also important to people. We have many reasons to sing, but none better than to sing praises to God.

It doesn't take a great voice to sing to God. He wants to hear what we feel. When our hearts are filled with love and thanksgiving, singing comes easier.

Sing to the Lord, for he has done wonderful things. Make known his praise around the world.

ISAIAH 12:5 (TLB)

Do You Remember?

1. In connection with penguins, what is a turtle?

2. When do emperor chicks begin singing?

3. What is your favorite church song?

We thank you, God, for giving us a reason to sing.

248 Puffed-Up Toads

If there are toads living near you, be thankful. This little relative of the frog is your friend. Every day it works hard to keep the insect population down.

Toads are such good insect eaters that some farmers have bought them and placed them near their crops. In South America they help protect the sugarcane fields.

Most toads stay out of the water whenever they can, but they need to live near a pond. They lay their eggs in watery areas. If you have a couple of toads, you may soon have thousands. A female toad sometimes lays twenty thousand eggs in one year. Toad eggs later open to become the long-tailed tadpoles we see so often.

The toad population is kept down by its many enemies. Birds, skunks, and even dogs and other animals love a good toad snack. However, the greenish creature is not completely defenseless. Toads have small glands behind their eyes that shoot a sickening liquid. Not only will this make most attackers retreat, but in cases where the creatures are small, it can kill.

If everything works correctly, nature stays in good balance. Toads eat insects and skunks eat toads. Hopefully this stops the population of any creature from becoming too great. If either of these fails to do its job, parts of the world end up with too many insects or too many toads. God created them to feed off each other.

The male toad has a fascinating way to let the female toad know he's around. He sits by the side of a pond and croaks. His sound is different from any other creature.

At the same time, the toad puffs up its throat to a huge size. When he does this, his throat sends out a pale light to make him a little easier to locate.

The male toad sits there filled with pride as he puffs his throat. In effect he is saying, "Look at me, girls. Have you ever seen such a good-looking toad?"

Maybe the apostle Paul had toads in his backyard. Several times he told people not to get puffed up. He was talking to people who like to brag. Oftentimes we like to claim we are better than we really are. It's like puffing up and saying, "Look at me. I'm terrific."

There is nothing wrong with knowing you are a good ballplayer. You can thank God for that. Neither is there anything wrong with knowing you can read well. You can thank God for that too.

The problem, however, is that we often like to brag, and we forget to thank God. That's being puffed up. The well-balanced person knows he or she can do things, and thanks God for those abilities.

What are you so puffed up about? What do you have that God hasn't given you? And if all you have is from God, why act as though you are so great, and as though you have accomplished something on your own?

1 CORINTHIANS 4:7 (TLB)

Do You Remember?

1. How do toads defend themselves?

2. Where do toads lay eggs?

3. What does "puffed up" mean when people do it?

Praise God for all He has given us!

249 The Team Shark

I t isn't always pleasant to think about, but most sea creatures live by eating other sea creatures. This is the way God made them. It's a perfectly normal part of nature.

One of the most interesting hunters in the ocean is a shark named the thresher. These sharks are harmless to man, but they eat great amounts of fish.

A thresher's tail is its outstanding feature. It is often as long as the rest of the shark's body. It gets its name from its unusually long tail and the way it uses it. When a thresher sees a school of fish, it surrounds them with its long tail. The fish become frightened and pull into a tight circle. This makes it easy for the shark to get a large dinner in one big gulp.

Man doesn't know much else about the thresher. Few of them have ever been caught, though once in a while one might get tangled in a fishing net. Possibly most of these sharks live far out to sea and at depths where man has seldom been.

Normally the thresher does well fishing alone. However, some fishermen believe it is also a team shark. Once in a while two of them will cooperate in herding fish together. When their prey are collected, both sharks share the meal.

Maybe thresher sharks are much like people. There are times when we get along well alone, but there are some times when we need the help of others.

There are usually plenty of things to do in our rooms or while playing in the backyard. However, it isn't good to be alone all the time. That extra person or team can be a great help when we need someone around.

That's why Christian friends are important. We need others who can be a good influence on us. We also need to be a good influence on our friends.

Jesus understood that adults need other adults and children need children. Life goes so much better if we can gather a few kind, Christian friends around us.

After this the Lord appointed seventy-two others and sent them two by two ahead of him to every town and place where he was about to go.

LUKE 10:1 (NIV)

Do You Remember?

1. How does a thresher get its name?

2. How do two threshers work together?

3. Why do we need Christian friends?

Thanks, Lord Jesus, for friends we can count on.

250 Why the Ocean Groans

When God made the oceans, they were beautiful places. They are still lovely, but if man isn't careful, our seas will become polluted and ugly.

Some lakes and rivers that used to be plentiful with fish are now "dead seas." The government has had to prohibit fishing in a few areas because of too many harmful chemicals in the water.

A scientist was asked to test the water in a certain river. He collected the samples and left them. When he came back the water was gone; in an hour and a half the acids had eaten the bottom out of the bucket. This is unusual, but it shows how bad things can get.

Many things pollute our waters. Sewage, industrial pollution run-off, and agriculture can all be harmful. One of the biggest problems is oil spills. In one year a gigantic oil spill in the English Channel resulted in the death of twenty-five thousand seabirds. There was a large oil spill off the southern coast of California. Ten years later some varieties of marine life had not yet returned to the area.

It is estimated that four thousand oil tankers are sailing the open seas. There are three thousand drilling platforms around the United States.

In the past we thought our waters could handle anything. We have dumped waste, chemicals, and garbage into them. One ocean explorer says he has seen pollution all over the world.

Hopefully we are smart enough to turn this around. Many industries are changing their methods of dumping waste. Oil companies are taking added precautions. Some lakes and rivers that were "dead" now have fish again.

We have abused God's gift of water. We have made it ugly and unsafe. By being careful and considerate we still have time to correct our mistakes and keep water as a helpful resource.

Human beings do some highly intelligent things. We are also capable of destroying nature. God has left the choice up to us.

For all creation is waiting patiently and hopefully for that future day when God will resurrect his children. For on that day thorns and thistles, sin, death, and decay—the things that overcame the world against its will at God's command—will all disappear, and the world around us will share in the glorious freedom from sin which God's children enjoy.

ROMANS 8:19–21 (TLB)

Do You Remember?

1. What causes ocean pollution?

2. How can we help stop it?

3. How else can we protect God's world?

Thank you for a beautiful world, heavenly Father. Help us to know how to protect it.

Index

WILLIAM L. COLEMAN is the author of more than one hundred books on a variety of topics. Combining his experience as a pastor, researcher, writer, and traveler, he is noted for his effective communication in the area of family relationships and practical spirituality. He has three adult children and five grandchildren, and he lives with his wife in Aurora, Nebraska.